POWER CRUISING

Cruising on a plane.

POWER CRUISING

The Complete Guide to Selecting, Outfitting, and Maintaining Your Power Boat

By Claiborne S. Young

PELICAN PUBLISHING COMPANY
GRETNA 1999

First edition, January 1990
Second edition, May 1999

Photographs by the author
Artwork by Carrie Duvall

Library of Congress Cataloging-in-Publication Data

Young, Claiborne S. (Claiborne Sellars), 1951-
Power cruising / by Claiborne S. Young ; [photographs by the author ; artwork by Carrie Duvall. — 2nd ed.
p. cm.
Includes index.
ISBN 1-56554-635-0 (pbk. : alk. paper)
1. Motorboats-Purchasing. 2. Motorboats-Equipment and supplies. 3. Boats and boating. I. Title.
VM341.Y67 1999
623.8'231'0296—dc21 98-54167
CIP

Manufactured in Canada

Published by Pelican Publishing Company, Inc.
1000 Burmaster Street, Gretna, Louisiana 70053

POWER CRUISING

is dedicated to all the new captains and mates
who are just entering the happy ranks of boat owners.
May your time on the water be as happy as our own!

Contents

Preface

I OFTEN SKIP "prefaces" myself when beginning a book. However, please take a few moments to read this one. Only then will you know what this book is, and perhaps more importantly, what it is not about.

I have sought to present enough information for the first-time owner of a larger power craft to make intelligent decisions about buying, outfitting, maintaining, and cruising in his or her new "pride and joy." Sometimes the necessary topics are discussed in depth while in other instances, the reader is referred to additional sources of instruction. New boat owners or those simply contemplating their entry in this happy rank and file *will* find most everything they need to begin what can be one of the happiest undertakings of their lives.

This work was *not* undertaken with the seasoned boater in mind. Fellow cruisers who have seen many a wave, as has this writer, will undoubtedly find any number of topics treated with less depth than they might prefer. Furthermore, this work does not pretend to encompass everything you will ever need to know about owning a boat.

Power Cruising is dedicated to the proposition that a boat need not be a hole in the water into which one pours money, and the happiest two days in a boat owner's life are *not* necessarily when the boat is bought and the day on which it is sold. Together we will explore the many "tricks of the trade" that will help you enjoy your boat in a manner that does not strip your wallet to its last recesses and brings more than a few smiles to your face.

Let our cruise begin!

Acknowledgments

FIRST AND FOREMOST, I want to thank my "first-rate first mate," Karen Ann, without whose loving help and skill as a talented photographer this guide would not have been possible. A very special thanks also goes to my proofreader and good friend, Andy Lightbourne. Without his aid, assistance, and genuine love for the water and boats, this project would have been ever so much more difficult.

Grateful acknowledgment is also paid to Spooners Creek Yacht Harbor of Morehead City, North Carolina, for allowing their facility to be the frequent subject of this guide's pictures.

I would also like to acknowledge the assistance given by Chuck and Corinne Kanter, authors of *The Galley K.I.S.S. Cookbook*, for all their help in formulating the galley advice section of this book. Similarly, Mr. Milt Baker of Bluewater Books and Charts in Fort Lauderdale, Florida, was most generous with his time and advice about electronic aids to navigation.

A very special thanks also goes to my good friend and talented artist, Carrie Duvall, for the wonderful sketches presented herein.

Finally, I wish to thank Dr. Milburn Calhoun, Kathleen Calhoun, Nina Kooij, Christine Descant, and the entire staff of Pelican Publishing Company, who have done so much to encourage me and make this book a reality. I'm a lucky author to have such a fine and caring publisher!

POWER CRUISING

A well-outfitted, planing-hull powercraft.

Introduction

It was Easter weekend, 1978, and the "first-rate, first mate" and I were merrily underway on our first cruise of the new boating season. Our plan had been to depart from Morehead City, North Carolina, early in the morning and cruise in our twenty-two-foot I/O-powered research boat to the tiny village of Bath. The round trip journey encompassed a passage of some 120 nautical miles. We should have arrived at Bath by midday, toured the state's oldest town's historic district for an hour or two and whisked back to Morehead in time for dinner. Perhaps it really is true that the best laid plans of mice and men often go astray. Certainly, in this instance, nature conspired to thwart our plans and change our lives.

Our cruise began under sunny skies with mild breezes. The NOAA weather forecast called for a beautiful day, though there was a mention of "breezy" conditions during the afternoon. With the thrill of the season's first sojourn before us, the prospect of a little wind did nothing to daunt our adventurous spirits. A quick passage up the ICW (Intracoastal Waterway) from Morehead to the often choppy Neuse River revealed a water surface that looked like nothing so much as a mill pond. We skirted past the village of Oriental, unofficial sailcraft capital of the state, and quickly cut into the so-called Hobucken Cut connecting the Neuse and Pamlico rivers.

We had just cruised into the mid-width of Pamlico River when we spotted a ruffle on the water's surface quickly approaching from the west. Within fifteen minutes the wind had risen from a gentle breeze to a screaming forty-knot banshee of a gale. Several sailcraft nearby were caught with too much canvas aloft and suffered knockdowns. One did not have auxiliary (engine) power and called for help on the VHF. Being good mariners who always endeavor to help a fellow boater in need, we quickly hurried over to the craft in question and tossed a tow line to the bedraggled captain who stood dripping on the bow.

That was some ten-mile trip up the Pamlico with the waves breaking over our bow and the brackish spray hitting us full in the face. With our tow behind us, it was impossible to maintain enough speed to keep the bow riding out of the water. Even if the sailcraft had not slowed our progress, the severe chop probably would have beaten us to death if we had attempted to travel at planing speed.

Finally, the first mate sighted Bath Creek and in a few moments our grateful craft slipped into calm waters. Unfortunately, this comforting harbor did not solve our difficulties. In those days, Bath lacked any lodging facilities. What were we to do? The forecast called for a forty-five-degree low during the night, and the prospect of sleeping in our open cuddy cabin was considerably less than appealing. With the time lost hauling the sailboat into harbor, the afternoon was now well advanced. If we attempted to return to Morehead, it would be dark before making landfall, even with ideal cruising conditions. With the gale blowing, our arrival time was seriously in doubt, yet the prospect of spending a cold, damp night on the boat held no greater charm. Our options were, as the saying goes, somewhat limited.

In the end, we made what in retrospect was a foolish decision. It was with more than a few misgivings that we thrashed our way back out into the Pamlico and headed south for the ICW intersection. Once again, the salty spray flew over our bow, soaking us from head to foot. By the time our craft finally nosed into the northerly headwaters of the Hobucken Cut, neither of us had a dry piece of clothing on our bodies.

Near the mid-point of the passage between the Neuse and Pamlico rivers, the tiny village of Hobucken briefly guards the waterway's banks. We stopped at a small fuel dock to take on some gas. With the wind screaming past, the attendant looked at us in wonder as we announced our intention to continue on to Morehead.

Well, we might not be the best decision makers in the world, but it took only one glance at the huge swells on Neuse River to convince us that our journey was over. A quick cruise back to Hobucken returned us to the fuel dock we had just left behind.

We found a small country store just behind the pier (long since closed) operated by a kindly older gentlemen who had recently moved to Hobucken upon retirement. Our plan, hastily sketched out while skimming back to Hobucken, was to hire someone to drive us back to Morehead.

There we could get a much-needed night's sleep and return the next day with our car and boat trailer. Unfortunately, while quite sympathetic, the store's proprietor had other plans for the evening, but he did promise to make some calls and try to scare us up a ride.

As long as I live, I will never forget sitting in that old store, wet, dog tired, and cold with a splitting headache. Finally, after some two hours, our new friend was able to convince a local teenager to undertake the journey. We squeezed into the back seat of a tiny compact car and imitated sardines during the ninety-minute trip back to Morehead.

At some point during this uncomfortable journey the "first-rate, first mate" and I reached an unspoken agreement that it was high time to purchase a larger power craft that could take rough water without drowning its occupants and provide comfortable shelter for several days (at least). The next morning we began perusing larger power vessels and the rest, as they say, is history.

Perhaps, with the benefit of hindsight, that weekend was the best thing that ever happened to us. As a direct result, we have had some of our most memorable experiences together and, eventually, I found my niche as a boating writer. Make no mistake about it, owning a larger power (or sail) boat that allows you to simply pitch out the hook or moor to a friendly marina and spend the night in comfort and security is one of the greatest experiences imaginable!

Nevertheless, in the ten years that have passed since acquiring our first larger power boat (and several sailboats as well), I calculate that we have made just about every mistake possible in owning, outfitting, and maintaining a pleasure craft. What few mistakes (and the number is minuscule) we may have avoided, I have witnessed fellow boaters commit. The burned hand truly teaches best. Consequently, I feel particularly qualified to help my fellow captains avoid the numerous pitfalls that have visited their consequences upon our boating life and often-emptied pocketbook. If I can help you, the reader, avoid even some of these errors and make boat ownership a bit more fun, then my task will have been joyously accomplished.

Planing-hull powercraft with full flybridge enclosure.

CHAPTER 1

Purchasing Your First Larger Power Craft

SO, YOU'VE MADE the big decision. It's time to purchase your first larger power boat that you can cruise on and live aboard for days at a time in relative comfort and security. Make no mistake, the tasks ahead of you can be some of the most enjoyable and rewarding of your life, but they are also formidable. Obviously, your first job is to select the right boat for you, one that will fit your cruising needs as well as your budget. Being a successful boat buyer calls for careful planning and consideration. If there is one way to ensure failure, it's to rush in headlong and buy the first craft that strikes your fancy. Consider for a moment the following experiences.

One would-be cruising couple in our marina decided to buy their first larger boat after achieving success in their chosen professions. Their plan was to take a year or two off from the dollar treadmill and cruise leisurely south into the Florida Keys and Bahamas. They combed the regional boatyards and yacht brokerages for the perfect vessel. Finally, our soon-to-be-disappointed cruisers purchased the largest boat they could possibly afford, a fifty-foot, 1972 model Chris Craft. As would be true for almost anyone under the same circumstances, they were bursting with pride when they brought their new craft home to the marina. Disillusionment was not far away, however. The experienced vessel in question needed more than a few repairs, and lots of additional equipment for long-range cruising. After only a few weeks, the new retirees discovered they did not have enough money to properly repair or maintain their new home, much less outfit it for a long cruise. As the months rolled by, the Chris Craft sat in its slip slowly becoming shabbier and the captain and his first mate ever more despondent. The end was not far away. The boat was finally sold for less than the original purchase price. Our would-be cruisers reentered the corporate world and bid a less-than-fond goodbye to boating forever.

This sad tale is repeated with slight variations year after year in marinas from North Carolina to Alaska. The whole situation could be dramatically different with a more intelligent purchasing decision. Our own experience in buying our first larger power boat shows that we only avoided a similar mistake by good fortune.

The morning after the "Easter Weekend fiasco" we lost no time in heading for the large yacht brokerage just up the road from our motel. As we drove in, a thirty-five-foot power cruiser perched atop a cradle at the entranceway immediately caught our eye. Manufactured by one of the most respected names in the marine industry, the boat commanded instant attention. After finding a salesperson, we climbed aboard and were immediately captivated. Balmy visions of swinging on the hook at an isolated anchorage and cooking a good meal far from any vestige of civilization danced in our heads. It was truly wonderful to contemplate the prospect of having a vessel large enough to live aboard for days at a time. Thoughts of leaving the motel and launching ramp scene behind were all too enticing.

Then, it was time for reality. After inquiring as to the vessel's price, we were shocked to learn that the boat sold for $96,000 (and that was a 1980 price)! We glumly sat down and tried to calculate how we could possibly make the loan payments on such a prodigious amount of money. Fortune smiled on us that day. Fate had decreed that we would find a commodity all too rare in the yacht brokerage game—an honest, helpful salesperson. Her name was Wendy and when I reflect on how her able assistance changed our lives, we owe her more than a debt of gratitude. As the "first-rate, first mate" and I continued our laborious calculations in the cockpit, Wendy sized up the situation and led us by the nose to another vessel docked on the water.

We were more than a little reluctant to leave our "first find" behind, but with a mixture of logic and cajolery, we were persuaded to inspect a thirty-one-foot craft that actually had more living space than the larger vessel. We were immediately struck by the airy interior, which promised many a comfortable evening tucked snugly at the slip or swinging peacefully at anchor. When we inquired about the price, Wendy informed us with a smug smile that the boat sold for $35,000. It seemed too good to be true. Where was the catch? Would this boat sink after the shoreline had sunk below the horizon?

Eleven years and hundreds of engine hours later, we were still cruising and researching happily aboard the thirty-one-foot, *Kaycy* and it hadn't sunk yet. Thanks to Wendy, we found the near-perfect boat for us, and, as they say, the rest is history. How different might our lives have been if a greedy salesperson had exploited our visions of cruising bliss while still enraptured aboard the more expensive boat?

These stories are not meant to intimidate you. They should merely serve as reminders that the purchase of your first larger power boat is not a matter to be taken lightly. Take heart! In the following pages we will explore together some of the most important considerations for finding the boat that is right for you. Remember though, don't be too serious about it all. As cruising author W. S. Kals once said, "The most important thing in boating is to have fun!" That should be true of buying your first larger power craft as well. So, take your time, keep a clear head, read the rest of this chapter carefully, and prepare for many years of wonderful cruising, without once going broke.

FIRST CONSIDERATIONS

Many of you who are considering the purchase of your first larger power craft will already own a smaller outboard or I/O craft. Your experiences with a boat in the 15- to 22-foot range can be both helpful and harmful when making your purchase decision.

Many owners of runabouts make the mistake of selecting a boat that is not really large enough to live aboard comfortably for several days. After the 16-footer sitting in your driveway, a 28-foot cabin cruiser can seem mammoth. But, ask yourself, will it be large enough for you to live on comfortably for a weekend or even longer? Can another couple stay with you and not feel like fellow sardines? Quite simply, be very careful to buy a boat that is big enough for your cruising needs, both now and for at least a few years down the watery road. Purchasing a boat that is too small, and then trading up, is an exercise in frustration and dollar disposal. Keeping your budget in mind at all times, make every effort to purchase a boat that you can live with for several years to come.

Speaking of budgets, the first story in this chapter points out a consideration often overlooked by many first-time buyers of larger power cruisers. When trying to decide how much boat you can afford, buyers have more to consider than just the purchase price. Along with death and taxes, you can be assured there will be maintenance, repair, and monthly dockage costs, not to mention such niceties as fuel to feed your hungry engines. Owners of smaller power boats usually underestimate these hidden costs in a dramatic fashion. When figuring your boating budget, be *sure* to include as many of these secondary costs into your financial calculations as possible.

Armed with these thoughts, it's now time to consider just how to go about buying that new vessel. Again, remember, take your time, keep a clear head about you, and have fun with it!

BECOMING AN INFORMED BUYER

The first thing you should do to prepare for your purchase is to become an informed buyer. Strive to learn as much as you can about a wide variety of boat models and types. One of the best sources for this sort of information is boating magazines. You will find many of these slick, marine-oriented publications at your local newsstand. Marine magazines are divided into two distinctive camps, those for power boaters and others oriented toward sailcraft. Obviously you should choose those that are pointed towards *power boats*. Take plenty of time to peruse the pages a bit before laying out the cash for your new vessel. No one ever bought the wrong boat from being too informed.

If you are lucky, you may even be able to find a review or "boat test" of the model or models that you may be considering. Sometimes, you can write the magazine's editorial offices and request reviews that have appeared in back issues. Usually, this service is advertised in a "Readers Service" section near the back of the volume. I have found these articles to be most informative, and you should make every effort to obtain copies of the reports that apply to the boats you have under consideration. Sometimes, however, a boat is so new, or, conversely, has been on the market for so long that you simply cannot find such a review. Keep the faith; there are other means to acquire the information you need.

Boat shows are great vehicles for information about a wide range of boat types and models. Visit as many of these happy events as your schedule and the offerings in your particular neck of the woods allow.

If you enjoy boats (and you must to have read this far), shows are great fun and a super place to meet fellow would-be cruisers. Plan to spend several hours at a show. Go aboard as many boats as you can. Soon, you will begin to compile a good catalog of just what is available in your size and price range and, just as importantly, what is not. Talk to the dealers and listen to their conflicting claims. Just remember not to take anything you hear as gospel truth without verification on your own part.

You should also visit as many yacht dealerships and brokerages in your region as time allows. While not as convenient as boat shows, you can still board a variety of craft, listen to the dealers, and become generally informed about what is and is not available. Remember, the more vessels you inspect, the greater your knowledge of the boating market will become, and a knowledgeable buyer is usually a happy buyer.

One ready source of information that is often overlooked by first-time buyers is commercial marinas. This data-gathering source demands a bit more diplomacy on your part than is needed in more formal surroundings, but the reward is liable to be some of the most accurate information you will ever obtain. Try to talk to the marina manager, dockmaster, mechanic, or, best of all, fellow boat owners. Ask them if they are familiar with any of the models you may be considering. Usually, most marina personnel are happy to take the time to give you their opinion unless other matters are pressing. These people have nothing to gain by recommending one model over another, and since they work on boats every day, they have often heard something good or bad about a particular craft. It was just this sort of information that once saved us from what would have been a tragic mistake.

After writing cruising guides for several years, we toyed with the idea of purchasing a larger, slower, but more fuel efficient research cruiser. At the Beaufort, North Carolina, boat show, it seemed that our dream craft had just sailed into port. We found a trawler-type yacht that had a great price tag and seemed to be of quality construction. For most of the afternoon we crawled over the vessel from stem to stern, including a close inspection of the bilge and engine room on my belly. Nothing seemed to be lacking, and it was with a feeling of discovery that we journeyed back to the marina, Fortunately, the dockmaster, Bruce, happened to be working near our slip when we arrived and it was only natural to mention our great find. After scratching his head for a minute, he went to the office, checked his records, and informed us that several new owners of the craft in question had recently docked overnight at the marina. Without exception, all the crews had complained that their new boats were so light they floated and bobbed like corks on the water. So much for our new discovery. We were saved by the bell, whose name happened to be Bruce on this occasion.

However you choose to get your information, above all, take the time and effort to make a thoughtful and informed buying decision. Maybe you will find a helpful salesperson like we did, or maybe you won't be so lucky. Your own knowledge is the only real insurance you have against an aggressive, uninformed salesperson. *No one has ever made the wrong boat-buying decision by knowing too much!*

NEW OR USED?

One of the first considerations you will face when buying your first larger power boat is whether to buy a new or experienced (used) craft. It may be, however, that this question should not be the first you should answer. I suggest keeping an open mind as you shop the various models, hull types, and sizes. It may be that you will find just the boat you want and can save a good piece of change by purchasing a used version of the prospective craft. On the other hand, you may decide on the security of a new boat. There are certainly pros and cons for either choice.

New boats generally come with some sort of warranty protection, which is often lacking in used vessels. Dealers will usually stand behind a new boat with much greater dependability than its used counterpart. Certainly, a new yacht will usually give more years of service than a used one. If you plan to keep your new purchase for many years without moving up or trading, this could be a prime consideration. Another serious concern, particularly if you are on a tight budget, is the credit differences between new and used boats. Finance companies will almost always allow longer and more liberal terms for a new boat. Financing can be quite difficult for boats that have plied the waters for ten years or more.

However, new boats are usually far more expensive than experienced craft. Most new boat buyers will discover the need to purchase a goodly quantity of basic boating equipment that might be included in the purchase price of a used vessel. Unless you can write a check for almost any boat without worrying about the rubber content of the document, these are very real considerations.

Used boats have their own set of problems and concerns. When buying a used craft, *you* must decide on her condition. As already mentioned, warranties are either nonexistent or very minimal at best. No matter how fine a boat it was when she left the factory, if it hasn't been well cared for, believe me, you don't want her. As a first-time boat buyer, this is not the time to engage in a major renovation project on a vessel that needs expensive, far-reaching repairs. Rescuing a "diamond in the rough" is a gargantuan task that should be left to the *experienced* captain.

Consequently, those buyers who decide to go the "used" route must inspect their prospective craft as thoroughly as possible. If you miss a major fault, such as a cracked engine block or a frozen generator, two weeks later you could be looking at repairs running into thousands of dollars. Don't worry overmuch. In the following section we will explore what inspections must be undertaken to help ensure that you buy only a well-maintained, used craft. If you have already decided that a new boat is in your future, you may want to skip this section, but, on the other hand, you may find it informative for future boating activities.

INSPECTING THE USED CRAFT

After examining boats for many years, experienced captains will tell you that they get a "feel" for how a boat has been treated. While some of this mystical expertise can only be acquired after years of experience, the following advice should give you a good leg up on that "old-salt" knowledge.

You will not find any lack of used boats to examine in coastal areas. Most marinas are at least marginally in the brokerage business. You may also find brokers who specialize in used craft. I suggest trying them all. You never know where your perfect boat might be docked. When buying used craft, I have never found any great advantage of one type of dealer (marina or broker) versus the other. When purchasing a new boat, warranty and financing considerations make the dealer selection more critical. However, with used vessels, as already noted, warranties are usually nonexistent or minimal at best.

Exterior Examination

First, take a good, long look at the boat's exterior. Look for something as simple as whether the boat is clean. Is the gel-coat (fiberglass finish) shiny and waxed or is it weathered and chalky? Is the exterior teak (if any) a well-oiled warm brown, or is it dirty and gray? Look at the stainless-steel bow railing and deck hardware. Has it been polished or is it rusty and pitted? Check the vinyl fabric on any exterior seats. Has it been cleaned, dressed, and well cared for, or is it stiff, dirty, and cracked?

This external condition of a boat is sometimes referred to as "cosmetics." While cosmetics certainly do not tell the whole story of a boat's condition, the well-cared-for boat will usually have its exterior appearance in A-1 condition.

Occasionally, a boat's cosmetic condition can be a misleading clue to the vessel's condition. Sometimes, dissatisfied owners have been known to let a boat just sit in its slip month after month. While the vessel may be basically sound, it looks like a wreck. Beware, though; my experience suggests that most boats with poor cosmetics are harbingers of other problems below.

Unfortunately, it is all too easy for the unscrupulous yacht broker to have a couple of dockhands spend several days with polish, wax, and teak oil on a used boat that has serious internal problems. Cosmetics, therefore, cannot be depended upon as the sole criterion for determining what kind of care your prospective craft has received in its past life. You must look below the surface for the rest of the story.

The Bilge

After inspecting the exterior, have the dealer open the engine room hatch. This is your opportunity to thoroughly inspect the engine, generator, and all other equipment on which the boat depends for reliable operation. Is there evidence of oil leaks, or is the bilge floor reasonably clean? Unfortunately, minor oil leaks are a fact of life for 90 percent of all marine engines, but a bilge that shows extensive evidence of oil leakage is another story. If you spot large-scale oil spills in the bilge, you probably need took no further. Chances are the boat has real problems.

Does the engine have extensive rust? In a saltwater environment, some rust is to be expected, but an engine that is encrusted in rust, particularly around its joints with the manifold, can indicate a power plant with problems.

Take a close look at any visible electric wiring. Are the insulations cracked or discolored? In a well-cared-for vessel, you might find a little grease on some wires, but otherwise the wiring should appear new. Repairs of this variety can be *very expensive,* so take the time to make a thorough inspection.

Inspect the battery. Are the terminals rusty and corroded, or do they show evidence of being scrubbed? If they are not in good condition, this is a good sign that the craft has not received the proper care.

Now, with a piece of cloth or paper towel in hand, pull out the oil dipstick. Take a close took at the oil on the end of the metal rod. Is it dark and dirty, or fresh and clean? Sniff the oil. Does it have a "burned" smell? If so, then you may be looking at an engine with internal problems, or at least one that has not received the proper care. Ask the owner how often he changes the oil. If he does not change it at least once a season, it could eventually mean expensive, internal engine repairs. Remember, any engine depends on clean, well-circulating oil to lubricate all its internal moving parts. Oil that is allowed to stay in an engine season after season will become clogged with carbon and other combustion byproducts, resulting in rapidly accelerated wear. It does not take too much imagination to understand how expensive it can be to disassemble an engine in order to replace its internal parts.

If your prospective boat is equipped with gasoline engines, look at the flame arrestors (air filters in automobile language) on top of the carburetor. If they are dirty with black deposits, this could be a tip that the former owner has not taken proper care of his craft. As any good captain of gasoline-powered craft knows, flame arrestors should be cleaned regularly for both fuel economy and safety.

If so equipped, check the engines' raw water filters. These units are large filters that are found between the raw water intakes and the water pump. Ask the owner or broker to point them out. Many of these devices have a glass housing, allowing for easy inspection of the sea water strainer. Obviously, these units should be kept clean for proper cooling water flow. If your inspection reveals dirty filters, it certainly raises yet another question as to the boat's previous maintenance.

Those with mechanical experience might request permission to pull a spark plug and check its power tip for wear. A worn plug that is past its replacement time could be a good sign that the engine has had less than the best of care.

Now, have the owner or broker start the engine(s) and generator. This is not quite as simple a test as it might seem. Boats often sit for days (sometimes weeks) at a time without being started. Therefore, the engines or generator may not start as readily as your car. However, if you hear the starter grinding away time after time without any sign of life, the engine(s) most likely need(s) repair. Any boat owner that lets his power plants deteriorate to this level can most certainly not be depended upon for past care.

While none of these problems described above, taken individually, are a reason to discount an otherwise well-cared-for craft, the careful buyer can sometimes spot a definite pattern of ill use if several of these conditions are observed. If a systematic pattern of poor engine maintenance emerges from your inspection, you are strongly advised to look elsewhere for his used purchase.

Even if the engine compartment passes all the above tests, you cannot be sure that the engine(s) or generator is really functioning properly. There are many, many power plant problems that can only be spotted by a professional. For this reason, if a boat passes the just-described tests to your satisfaction, I strongly recommend that you next employ a qualified marine mechanic or surveyor to make a thorough inspection of all the boat's mechanical equipment. Often, he or she can spot expensive repairs that might escape even the seasoned boat buyer's best inspection.

A good mechanic will conduct compression tests on all cylinders, check the engine's timing and carburetor jets, and give the entire power plant a good "once over." The expense of hiring such a qualified professional can be more than offset by the money you may save in expensive engine repairs. If the boat's power plant passes all the mechanic's tests, you can continue negotiations and further inspections with confidence that all is mechanically well in the bilge.

Finally, before leaving the bilge, look for one of the most obvious, but often overlooked problems of a used craft—*leaks*. Older boats that have not been properly maintained can leak around the propeller shafts and thru-hulls. Even worse, a boat in really poor condition might be leaking through a crack in the hull. Look for excess water. If you spot what seems to be more than can be accounted for by recent rains, no effort should be spared to track down the water's source. A leaking stuffing box around a propeller shaft, or a thru-hull with a weeping valve can be fixed when the boat is hauled. Of course, you will need to figure in this expense with any other necessary repairs. A crack in the hull is more serious and could require expensive service work.

Judging the Interior

Now, take the time for a thorough inspection of the boat's interior. Look for obvious flaws that need repair. If any are present, discuss the expense of the necessary work with the owner or broker. Examine all the interior lockers and cabinets. Are they neat and tidy, or are they incubators for a crop of mildew? Check the galley. Make sure the stove and refrigerator (if any) are operating properly. Now, take a good long took at the head (bathroom in landlubberese).

Flush the toilet and make sure it is working without a hitch. Repairs to this necessary piece of equipment can, surprisingly, be some of the most difficult and expensive maintenance on a boat. The different types of marine toilets or MSDs (marine sanitation devices) and their particular advantages will be discussed later in this chapter.

Take It Out!

Finally, there is *absolutely no substitute* for taking the boat out on the water. Of course, the owner or broker will accompany you on such a sojourn, and this is only as it should be. While underway, you can gain a quick but thorough insight into just how well the boat's mechanical and electronic equipment is operating. If an engine fails to start or a transmission does not engage properly, then you know, without a doubt, the boat needs what will undoubtedly be expensive repairs. Insist that each piece of electronic equipment be turned on. Make note of any units that fail. Take the helm yourself, under the owner's or broker's supervision, of course. After you get your head out of the clouds from the exhilaration of being at the wheel of a larger boat for the first time, make a critical assessment of how the boat handles. If it's not what you expect, there could be problems ahead. Don't let the broker convince you that any handling difficulties are simply due to your inexperience with larger craft. Different boats handle very differently, and if you aren't comfortable with the way a prospective craft takes the water, it's not the one for you.

Haul-out?

In 1980, I probably would not have recommended that buyers considering a used, fiberglass hulled craft spend the extra money to have their possible purchase hauled out of the water. If no leaks were obvious and the marine growth around the waterline wasn't ridiculously heavy, then all would have been well. However, that situation has changed—sometimes dramatically.

"Boat Pox" or "hull blisters" have, for whatever reason, become more and more of a problem for fiberglass boats of all types and prices since 1980. When this condition occurs, water becomes trapped between the outer and inner layers of fiberglass. This usually results in "blisters" or bubbles that protrude from the bottom of the hull. If allowed to go untreated, the boat can eventually become waterlogged, resulting in considerable loss of speed, fuel efficiency, and seaworthiness. Sometimes, in a bad case, the blisters are so large as to be obvious, while a minor incidence can be harder to spot. Repairs are expensive and finding a yard that can fix the problem the first time can be a real headache.

So, whether to haul-out or not to haul-out, that's the question. If you do, you might go to the expense and still miss a case of boat pox that is just beginning. A marine surveyor, as discussed below, would certainly be better qualified to spot any blistering problem, no matter how small. On the other hand, the expense of a haul-out (not to mention a surveyor) is not something to be taken lightly. Usually, the hauling services alone will run into several hundred dollars. So, it's your decision, and there is no one right choice in every case. However, as a rule of thumb, if the boat in question is over two to three years old, I would recommend hauling out, and possibly a hull inspection (at least) by a qualified marine surveyor.

Conclusions and Marine Surveyors

Finally, after all these tests and inspections are concluded, I suggest you ask yourself whether the boat "feels right." This is a hard question to define, but as you look at more and more used craft, your sense of a vessel's "rightness" will become more acutely developed. Even in the early stages of your nautical awareness, be sure to take the time to sit down and think over all you have seen, the problems as well as the things you like. Put together, does this craft feel comfortable to you? Does it seem to have been well cared for? Has the former owner taken pride in his craft, or is he just anxious (possibly too anxious), to get his money out of the boat? If you can honestly say that the vessel in question feels right, then it's time to talk price and financing. If it doesn't, then you had best move on.

Now, suppose you have looked over your prospective used craft as closely as you can, and have decided that it looks good and "feels" good. There is still one more step that you should probably consider. In fact, if you finance your purchase of a used vessel, your bank or finance company will probably require this procedure. As an inexperienced purchaser of larger power craft (otherwise why would you be reading this book), even your best inspection, following all the rules outlined above, *could* miss some vital flaw. Possibly not, of course, but those buyers who want to be sure of their purchase before writing out the check should consider employing a marine surveyor to examine their proposed purchase.

A marine surveyor is quite simply a professional who, through training or experience, theoretically knows what to look for to determine whether a boat is really in good condition or whether some hidden problems are waiting to trap the unsuspecting buyer. If you are lucky enough to employ a good surveyor who knows his stuff, and he or she gives the boat a stamp of approval after a meticulous inspection, then you can be about as sure of the vessel's condition as anything in the inexact boating game. Additionally, if the surveyor should spot problems, he or she should be able to give you an idea of the needed repair cost.

Unfortunately, there is one great problem associated with marine surveyors. While there are two national boat surveyor organizations, there are still no standardized licensing procedures by public or private authorities to separate qualified marine surveyors from those who don't know the bow from the stern. In theory, anyone could come into a port town, hang up a marine surveyor sign, and be off to the races. To avoid this problem, inquire about surveyors of good reputation at several area marinas. Don't take the word of a single marina or brokerage with which you are dealing. It is just barely possible that an unscrupulous broker and surveyor could have a "working relationship," and you could be the loser in such a deal.

Of course, a surveyor, like any professional in this day and time, is going to charge a goodly fee based on the length of time necessary to thoroughly inspect the vessel in question. Hourly rates vary widely from region to region and surveyor to surveyor, but it is probably safe to conclude that the expense involved will not be trivial. Normally, a qualified surveyor will require that the boat be hauled out of the water, and you will have to bear this expense as well.

A Last Word of Advice

While the best bargains in power boating are certainly available in the used market, it's also true that more first-time owners of larger power boats are disappointed by used craft than their brethren who opt for new boats. Never forget, major marine repairs are notoriously expensive and can make for a rotten start to owning your first larger craft. So, take your time; in fact take plenty of time. When you find the boat that passes all the tests (probably including a professional survey), handles well, and, most importantly, feels right, then go ahead. Remember, even if some repairs are necessary down the road, you will have paid considerably less in the first place than you would for a comparable new craft. So, go forward with confidence, knowing all the while that every boat will require maintenance and occasional repair.

HULL DESIGN

Most small craft power boaters are not aware of the intricate role that hull design plays in larger boats. With small boats, it's generally a "V" or tri-hull and little else is usually said about the particular hull style. However, with larger boats, the hull design can radically affect your vessel's speed, cruising range, fuel economy, seaworthiness, and living space. Due to these very serious considerations, buyers of either new or used power cruisers *must* take their prospective craft's hull design into consideration.

Three basic choices of hull types are available in modern power cruisers, with interesting variations between differing brands. The basic varieties are planing, full-displacement, and semi-displacement hulls. All have their own individual merits and drawbacks.

Planing Hulls

For many years, the most popular power boat hull in the USA has clearly been the *planing* variety. With the increase in gasoline and diesel fuel prices that began in the 1980s, this popularity has decreased somewhat, but you will still see far more of this hull design on the water than any other. Former owners of smaller power craft will be more familiar with the planing hull than the other available designs.

Put simply, this type of hull will "plane" or ride on top of the water after a certain speed is achieved. This minimizes water friction and allows for relatively fast cruising speeds. However, considerable power (and fuel) is required to keep the boat on its plane.

A planing hull is by far the fastest of the three designs. Typical cruising speeds range from 17 to 25 knots. This quick pace can be very valuable to those for whom time is short. Professional charter captains invariably use planing-hull boats to get their clients out to the fishing hole as quickly as possible. Boaters who enjoy cruising under power but have limited time for their watery pursuits, invariably choose this design, Often, in a single weekend, such craft can make a lengthy cruise and still return to the docks in time for everyone to head for the office Monday morning.

As almost always seems to be the case, there is a price for all this speed, and it can be considerable. Planing-hulled vessels require a

Classic wooden planing-hull powercraft.

very prodigious amount of fuel to cruise under power. Typical consumption is one mile to the gallon or often considerably less with boats in the 40-foot range. On a cruise of 200 miles, you will need to purchase a minimum of 200 gallons of fuel. Be sure to fit such fueling expenses into your budget when considering a boat with this type of hull!

A planing boat's poor fuel economy can drastically curtail its cruising range. Obviously, if you consume a gallon of fuel per mile, and there are 200 gallons of fuel on board, you can only cruise 200 miles before it's time to find a marina with a fueling dock. By contrast, some full-displacement, trawler-type boats can travel almost a thousand miles between fuel stops.

The planing hull is fairly seaworthy. Unless seas build to dangerous levels, this type of craft gives a pretty good ride in both head-on and following seas. Sometimes planing hulls with flatter bottoms can jar the fillings out of your teeth in a rough head-on sea, but the yawing from side to side so characteristic of full-displacement hulls is mercifully absent. If waves should build above six feet, however, there is some danger of broaching (capsizing from the side) or pitchpoling (having the stern flipped over by a following wave). However, for the vast majority of pleasure boating activities, the planing hull is acceptably safe.

Planing hulls are also characterized by a shallow draft. Typically 3½ feet of water is enough to keep you from finding the bottom. This "shoal draft" can be a considerable advantage when cruising in coastal waters where shallow water is all too frequent a companion.

Full-sized cockpits are a normal feature for planing-hull boats. While some look on a large cockpit as a waste of cabin space, it is ideal for fishing, and taking one's ease in good weather while swinging tranquilly on the hook.

Since the early 1980s some manufacturers have introduced planing-hulled vessels with rear cabins. This design has been more typical of trawler hulls in times past. Now, cruisers who need maximum speed and plenty of living space can find both in this thoughtful compromise design. Of course, the large cockpit described above is missing in this sort of configuration. There is usually a small "sun deck" above the rear cabin but it is not an ideal fishing platform.

If your budget dictates that you must purchase a craft in the 28- to 30-foot range, the planing hull is liable to be your only practical choice. Purchasers of larger boats, however, should weigh the speed and relative seaworthiness of a planing design against the fuel efficiency and cruising range of the other available choices.

Trawlers and Full-Displacement Hulls

Full-displacement hulled boats or "trawlers," as they are usually called, are the most seaworthy, fuel-efficient power boats on the water. They are also the slowest. This type of hull has been used for many years by commercial fishermen and shrimpers. Boaters who visit the southeastern coast of the United States will undoubtedly observe a host of so-called shrimp trawlers with their high peaked bows and

Trawler with full-displacement hull.

large boom nets. It is not by accident that waterborne professionals have made full-displacement hulls the design of choice. These salty captains and crew need a fuel-efficient design that they can depend upon in the nastiest weather. Years and years of experience testify to the fact that trawler-type hulls fill the bill.

Until the 1970s, trawlers were usually built from wood in small, but knowledgeable boatyards located along the Southeastern and Gulf states' coastlines. Since the steep rise in diesel fuel and gasoline prices following the 1973 Arab oil embargo, more and more companies have begun building trawler hulls from fiberglass and adapting them to pleasure craft use. Some of the best of these pleasure-trawler designs are built in the Far East, particularly Taiwan. The U.S. also has several manufacturers of this reliable vessel. However, if you know where to look, you can still find wooden shrimp trawlers being painstakingly constructed by hand in the backyards of coastal natives in remote areas. This is part and parcel of the coastal tradition and I, for one, hope it never dies.

Unlike planing hulls, full-displacement boats ride "in" the water rather than on the surface. Thus, they do not require the power to keep them "on top," but the friction from the surrounding water is considerable. What all this means in cruising terms is that pleasure trawlers often get five, six, or even seven miles of waterborne travel to a gallon of fuel, but the typical cruising speed is only 9 to 12 knots. Obviously, it's going to take a long time to reach a particular destination, but, unless you are heading for points offshore, you will probably not have to fuel up until reaching your intended port of call.

Full-displacement hulls are also very seaworthy. Capsizing, of any variety, should never be a problem in any weather short of a gale. However, you should also be aware that rough seas produce a very different motion than that of a planing hull. Since this type of boat rides "in" the water, you are subject to considerable "yawing" or "wallowing" from side to side and sometimes pitching from bow to stern. While, as already noted, this motion is usually not dangerous, it can sometimes turn even the cruising veteran green with "mal de mer" (or sea sickness, if you will).

One special concern with pleasure trawlers is lateral drift or leeway. Traveling at their slower speeds, an unnoticed side-setting current or wind can sometimes ease a trawler out of a narrow channel, just when the captain thinks he is pointing just where he should be to avoid the shallows. This problem can be remedied by watching the track over your stern as well as your course ahead to quickly note any slippage.

Trawler hulls invariably carry the deepest draft of all power boats. Some even have a weighted keel, reminiscent of sailcraft. This weighted ballast helps control the uncomfortable motion discussed above. One thing you don't want is a "lightweight" trawler, unless you have a stronger stomach than this writer. On the other hand, too much weight can slow you unnecessarily. Most pleasure trawlers available today strike a pretty good balance between weighted ballast and cruising speed. You will also discover that most full-displacement hulls, due to their very nature, have more strength of construction than their planing counterparts.

The deep draft of a trawler can be a genuine cause for concern when operating in shallower coastal waters. Many full-displacement boats draw well over four feet. However, there is a bonus. If you run aground with a planing hull, the exposed propellers (props for short), shafts, struts, and rudders are subject to considerable damage. However, in many trawler designs, the prop, and sometimes even the rudder, are protected by the hull's deep keel. Thus, if you find the bottom with a trawler, and are subsequently pulled off, often times you can go on your way without any underwater hardware repairs. This is not an inconsiderable advantage, particularly when you remember that the only boaters who never run aground are liars or those who *never* leave the dock!

Trawlers are usually built with only minimal cockpits, and maximum cabin space. Rear heads (bathroom) and bunks are the norm in pleasure trawler design. Many manufacturers are now installing queen-sized beds in the rear cabins of trawlers over forty feet in length. This is great news for cruisers but less than ideal for fishermen. I have found the interiors of pleasure trawlers to be the ideal "live-aboard" environment. Usually, every inch of room is utilized to provide the maximum storage and living space. Look for yourself, but don't be surprised to discover that the cabin arrangements of a full-displacement boat are unbeatable.

In the final analysis, trawlers are ideal for those who are not in a hurry and have considerable time to spend on the water. As an example, converted sailboaters often take to a trawler in later years. Full-displacement boats are also very good live-aboard vessels. If you plan to spend a lot of time dockside in your marina, rather than underway to a particular cruising location, a trawler would be an excellent choice. Obviously, however, if you are a captain who needs to get there and back over a weekend, or one who is primarily interested in fishing, this design is clearly not your cup of tea.

Semi-Displacement Hulls

In 1978 the pleasure boating world was turned upside down by the introduction of the "Mainship 34." This quality craft could cruise at typical speeds of 14 knots and still boast fuel economy of 3 to 5 miles to a gallon. The Mainship was the first of the new "semi-displacement" hulls.

Semi-displacement designs operate exactly as their name implies. A portion of the hull (usually the stern) remains in the water while the bow rides on the surface. This action decreases water friction to allow for higher speeds without requiring the power necessary to keep the entire hull on top of the water. It is an ingenious design and one that has now been with us for many years.

Obviously, semi-displacement designs borrow something from both full-displacement and planing hulls. This hull is faster than a trawler and considerably more fuel efficient than a planing boat. Also, as you would expect, it draws more than a planing hull but less than a full-displacement boat. Some would even argue that it's the best of both worlds, or at least a very good compromise.

The seaworthy qualities of semi-displacement hulls also seem to be split between the two other designs. The ride in a rough seaway is certainly better than a trawler, even if not quite so good as a planing hull. In really heavy weather, this design is less subject to broaching than a planing hull, but not as stable as a full-displacement boat. One characteristic that seems unique to semi-displacement hulls is a problem associated with heavy following seas. Reports indicate that boaters caught in such a situation may have trouble keeping their craft in a straight line when going from the crest of a following wave to the trough below. Again, if you stay in port when particularly bad weather threatens, this should not be too great of a concern.

Cabin and topside layouts have varied greatly with semi-displacement boats. The original Mainship 34 had a small cockpit, but later a Mainship 34 II was introduced with a bigger cockpit and a smaller cabin.

To summarize, semi-displacement hulls seem to be an excellent compromise. They have some of the fortunate characteristics of both planing and full-displacement hulls, while mitigating the deficiencies of the two older designs. If you can find the interior layout that fits your needs among this design's somewhat limited selection, it could be that you have found your ideal boat.

POWER PLANT

The heart of any power cruiser is its power plant. Sailors can afford to be somewhat contemptuous of their auxiliary engine. After all, they can always raise the sails. Power boaters do not have that luxury. When the engine fails, your only recourse is to call for a tow. If one isn't nearby, it could be a very long day!

So, the selection of the proper engine is a very critical choice for any first-time purchaser of a larger power craft. There are literally hundreds of models and brands to choose from. We cannot hope to give even a perfunctory overview of this huge selection here. However, it is heartening to note that practically all of these many choices will provide reliable power for years to come.

Gasoline vs. Diesel

There are two basic types of power plants available in modern power craft, gasoline and diesel engines. To choose one or the other is to make a very basic decision that will affect your cruising future for as long as you own the boat in question. Unfortunately, there is not a clear choice that is right for every cruiser. Both engine designs have advantages and disadvantages, and you must decide which best fits your needs.

Gasoline engines are usually found in most power craft from 28 to 33 feet in length, though there are exceptions. You will also find some gasoline motors in larger power boats. This power plant has the advantages of being initially cheaper and considerably lighter than its diesel counterpart. However, against these advantages, this design's diminished reliability and lack of fuel efficiency must be considered.

As many of you already know, gasoline engines ignite the gasoline vapor in each cylinder by a spark plug. This means that owners of gasoline motors must contend with an increasingly sophisticated ignition system that produces the current to spark the plug. Ignition problems are *not* a rare occurrence aboard gasoline-powered craft, and it's often difficult or impossible for the boat owner to locate and correct the difficulty himself. Then, there is the yearly spark plug maintenance, along with the less frequent replacement of distributor caps, rotor buttons, and spark plug wires.

Even in this day and age of mandated, sealed marine ignition systems, captains of gasoline-powered craft must contend with the dreaded possibility of gasoline vapor explosion. This catastrophic event occurs when heavier-than-air gasoline vapors collect in the bilge. An errant spark can cause a violent explosion and fire, possibly setting off the main gas tank. A boat can burn to the waterline in seconds!

Fortunately, such explosions are rare in this day and time. Coast Guard regulations now require manufacturers of gasoline engines to seal the distributor cap and alternator. Flame arrestors are also required on all carburetors to minimize the possibility of a backfire flame setting off any vapors that might be present. All modern gasoline boats are also equipped with large bilge vents and bilge blowers, which, hopefully, evacuate any gasoline vapors before they have a chance to explode. Still, even with all these precautions, an occasional explosion is sometimes reported in the boating press.

Gasoline engines are also less fuel efficient than diesel motors. Quite simply, gasoline has less energy potential, ounce for ounce, than diesel fuel. Consequently owners of boats with diesel engines can usually expect some advantage in fuel economy, assuming all other factors, including hull design, remain constant.

As a cruiser who once piloted a gasoline-powered craft, I think this type of power plant is quite safe *if* adequate precautions are *always* observed during startup and fueling. Before attempting to crank the engine, *be sure* to run your bilge blower for several minutes. This wise procedure should help to evacuate any dangerous fumes from the bilge. After fueling, you should operate the blower for a minimum of five minutes before attempting to start the motor. Don't allow some itchy fuel dock attendant to hurry you on your way. The safety of captain and crew is certainly worth the few extra minutes.

If asked my own opinion, I would not advise a first-time larger power boat purchaser to abandon a prospective craft *just* because it has a gasoline engine. However, even after saying all this, it's only fair to observe that, increasingly so and rightly so, a gasoline power plant is *not* the engine of choice in the marine industry.

Diesel engines have a fundamental difference from their gasoline counterparts. Diesel fuel is less refined than gasoline, does not produce explosive vapor, and has a higher energy potential than gasoline. Secondly, diesel engines ignite the fuel-air mixture in each cylinder, not by a spark, but rather by heat and pressure. This means that the engine does *not* require a sophisticated ignition system, but its case or block must be heavier and stronger to withstand the increased heat and pressure. This combination produces a much heavier power plant, horsepower for horsepower, than a comparable gasoline motor. However, in the opinion of most boating professionals, the lack of an ignition system to fail or maintain, plus the absence of explosive vapors, more than compensates for these shortcomings.

Modern diesel engines use a fuel injection system rather than a carburetor to deliver a fuel-air mixture to each cylinder. In recent years, some gasoline engines have also begun to use such a system. However, it's only fair to note that in comparison to carburated gasoline engines, the diesel fuel injection system is clearly the more reliable and easily maintained of the two.

Buyers must also consider the increased cost of a diesel power plant. The heavier engine block construction, coupled with the sophisticated fuel injection system, require a larger initial investment than would a gasoline engine. However, many old-time captains (and some newer ones as well) would argue that the decreased maintenance and increased reliability of a diesel motor make for a less expensive power plant in the long run.

Finally, when considering a diesel engine, you should be aware of the possibility for fuel contamination. Diesel fuel is much more subject to degradation, water collection, and bacterial growth than gasoline. A bad load of diesel fuel can wipe out an engine in no time at all. A gummed-up injector pump resulting from contaminated diesel fuel can be a costly object lesson in preventive maintenance. To avoid this sad happening, diesel engines are usually equipped with large fuel filters/water separators. These units must be serviced regularly and replacement filter elements can be expensive. Fuel additives are also a very good idea to stabilize the diesel fuel and inhibit the growth of harmful bacteria.

So, what's the bottom line? Of course, the decision is yours. If you buy a used craft, the type of power plant is certainly *only one* of the criterion that you will consider. However, if I was buying a new boat, and could possibly fit it into my budget, this writer, for one, would most certainly opt for a diesel engine. On the other hand, if I could not afford the extra cost, I would certainly choose to purchase a gasoline-powered craft rather than no boat at all.

Twin vs. Single

A second major power plant decision facing the purchaser of his first larger power boat is whether to opt for single or twin engines. It should come as no surprise that single engine boats are considerably cheaper. You will also be faced with exactly one-half the maintenance and repair costs of twin engine craft. Additionally, there is usually more bilge access space available with a single power plant, allowing easy service access to the engine.

However, twin engines give a very real margin of safety that should not be taken lightly in coastal cruising. Consider the following story. One February the "first-rate, first mate" and I were cruising in the Florida Keys. Our craft had been completely checked by a qualified mechanic just before leaving port. After a glorious week of cruising in the gin-clear waters of lower Florida, we had begun our journey home when, after powering down while cruising through a "No-Wake" area, the starboard engine refused to turn more than 2,000 RPMs. A quick inspection through the bilge hatch quickly revealed the trouble. The seal on the starboard water-circulating pump had failed, and when the engine ran fast enough, it threw the leaking seawater high enough to be sucked into the carburetor. We shut down the starboard engine but were able to make Key Largo with the port motor. Early next morning, we had a new pump and were on our way to Miami. Less than two hours up the waterway, we began to smell something burning. A quick check of the instrument panel did not reveal anything amiss, so it was back for another look at the bilge. This time I didn't see anything immediately wrong, although the smell was stronger than ever. Fortunately, I looked over the stern and saw we were not getting any cooling water flow out of the portside outboard exhaust port. This time we switched the port engine off and were able to make port with the other. A thirty-minute cleanout of the outboard, port exhaust riser cleared up the problem.

Now consider, if we had a single engine craft, it would have been necessary to call for not one, but two commercial tows. With the U.S. Coast Guard now providing only emergency towing service, this would have been an expensive proposition indeed. It's not difficult for the reader to understand why I'm personally biased towards twin-engined power craft.

Another advantage of twin power plants is increased maneuverability. Those used to outboard or I/Os are usually more than a little intimidated when docking a larger power boat. Don't worry. Practice makes perfect, and we've all bumped a few docks from time to time. Twin engines can alleviate this problem to a great extent.

By putting, for instance, the starboard engine in forward with the port at neutral, a twin engine boat will turn more rapidly to port than would be possible with the rudder alone. If you really need to turn on the proverbial dime, put the starboard engine in forward and the port in reverse. If the engines are matched, you can turn the boat in a circle whose diameter is only equal to the boat's length. In high winds or strong currents, the increased, close order maneuverability of a twin engine boat is a very serious consideration.

Additionally, single engine boats with rudders have very limited maneuverability when powering astern (backing up). In many marinas, it's desirable to dock stern first. This can be quite a chore without twin engines, particularly in high winds. Conversely, with twin power plants, a reversal of the above-described procedure allows even the inexperienced captain to wheel his stern first one way, and then the other.

Of course, there has to be a down side. Twin engine boats are much less fuel efficient, and you will have twice the maintenance and repairs. For all these disadvantages, many modern pleasure boaters (particularly those with planing-hulled vessels) generally choose a twin engine craft.

Size

Those first-time power boaters who choose to purchase a new craft will most likely be faced with various engine options of differing horsepower. Generally speaking, the larger horsepower engines are less fuel efficient, even if faster. With planing hulls, unless speed is a primary consideration, you might consider asking your dealer which engine is the most fuel efficient, and make your selection accordingly. Planing boats need all the help with fuel efficiency they can get. With full-displacement boats, it might be best to opt for a power plant with a little more horsepower. Those few extra knots of speed could mean the difference in making port before a storm.

Don't be too confused by this issue. The vast majority of boat manufacturers have selected *all* the various engine options for their craft with an eye towards suitability. It would be hard to go too wrong, whichever option you choose. Quite simply, if fuel economy is uppermost in your mind, ask which is the most fuel efficient. If you want speed, pick the unit with the most horsepower.

While it strays a bit from our subject of size, this also might be a good time to ask your dealer if he knows of any difference in reliability and ease of maintenance between the various engine options. If he does suggest one over the other, you should give a lot of weight to this recommendation.

CONSTRUCTION

The construction of your prospective craft is perhaps second only to power plant considerations. Whether you are contemplating a new or used vessel, the material from which it is constructed and the way in which it is laid out will affect your life aboard as long as you own the boat.

No one expects the first-time purchaser of a larger power craft to be a marine architect. Indeed, even experienced power captains are often at the mercy of boat manufacturers and designers. Fortunately, it makes good business sense to design the best boat for the money. There is more than a little competition in modern pleasure boating, and this healthy rivalry goes far toward ensuring that practically all the craft you consider will be of competent design. After saying that, however, you must still decide which design and which construction materials fit your particular needs.

Wood vs. Fiberglass

Today, the vast majority of power boats are built from one of two basic materials. You can opt for a boat made from traditional wood or one constructed of modern fiberglass. The tradition of wooden boat building runs deep in almost all coastal areas of North America. Anyone associated with boating for more than a few years cannot help but feel some of the romance and pride in the old-world craftsmanship associated with those few builders who still ply their art in the medium

Classic wooden motoryacht.

of wood. Indeed, there are a few advantages to wooden boats that should not be dismissed out of hand.

It is much simpler to make alterations to wooden boats than their fiberglass counterparts. Wood is a very adaptable building material, while fiberglass, once it is molded, may as well be set in concrete. Even so, most of us would need the services of a qualified marine carpenter to undertake alterations in a wooden boat.

Set against the romance and adaptability of wooden boats is a maintenance schedule that could daunt the hardiest cruiser. A few years ago, there was a classic Egg Harbor 43 docked near our own boat. It was obvious that the owner took pride in his craft. The captain always carried out all necessary maintenance every fall and spring. As an added precaution, he kept his classic craft in a covered slip to mitigate the destructive effects of sun and rain. Then, one day he noticed a series of cracks on the partition separating the main cabin from the cockpit. He summoned the marina carpenter and they soon discovered extensive dry rot. Four months and many thousands of dollars later the damage had been repaired. It had been necessary to replace large portions of the cockpit partition, the sides of the cockpit, and cabin walls. Who is to know when the secret villain of rot might strike again?

In warm, southern waters, wooden boats are subject to attack by saltwater worms. These insidious pests can invade the bottom of a seemingly healthy boat and, in extreme cases, the craft can even sink. To avoid this hazard, it is necessary to haul-out and bottom paint a wooden boat at least twice as often as would be required for a fiberglass vessel.

Wooden boats often shrink and expand during the transition from warm to cold weather. This can cause cracking of seams and joints, necessitating a considerable caulking job in the spring.

Add to all these tasks the annual sanding, painting, and searching for rot, and you begin to understand why owning and maintaining a wooden boat is a labor of love that few modern cruisers can afford both in terms of time and money. For these reasons, and many more, most boat buyers will choose to purchase a fiberglass vessel. From this point forward, we will assume that you have opted for one of these trusty, albeit somewhat artificial craft. The purchase, care, and outfitting of wooden boats is a subject all to itself, which is addressed in various other publications. If you should choose to ignore my advice and purchase a classic, wooden boat, I can only wish you the best of luck.

Fiberglass Finishes

Fiberglass is a strong, reliable building material, but its finish does require maintenance. The particular finishing material selected for your prospective craft will determine just how much time and effort you will have to expend to keep your "pride and joy" shining like new.

Most fiberglass boats are finished with a smooth epoxy compound known as gel-coat. This finish must be compounded (or polished) and waxed *at least* once a year to maintain a glossy appearance. Even with this preventive maintenance, after five or more years it may be necessary to recoat or repaint both the hull and superstructure (topside fiberglass) to maintain an attractive finish.

The quality of gel-coat can vary greatly. Whether you are considering a new or used boat, inspect the finish very carefully. Look for cracks or thin spots in the gel-coat. If you spot many of these imperfections, you should probably look elsewhere. There are few more expensive and/or frustrating tasks to boat ownership than trying to obtain good gel-coat repairs.

Some fiberglass boats, particularly of the more expensive ilk, are now finished with an epoxy-cyanide compound known as Imron. Imron is extremely expensive and must be renewed very five to eight years, *but,* unlike plain gel-coat, this finish is mostly immune to weathering and oxidation. Consequently, that "like new" finish seems to go on and on, at least until it begins to flake and recoating becomes necessary.

Sometimes in the spring, after two or three days of laborious polishing and waxing on our boat's plain gel-coat, I used to step back and inspect our work with pride. It was more than a little disconcerting, however, to look just down the pier at a Hatteras fifty-six-foot, long-range cruiser (Imron finished) and see that it still looked better than our own craft, even though no one had touched it for six months. It's at times like these that you wish for an Imron finish. When it comes time to recoat, you would be glad to have only plain gel-coat.

There are several other exotic fiberglass finishes including Awlgrip and two-part polyurethane. Awlgrip is extremely durable (even more so than Imron), but it is difficult or impossible to touch up a small ding. Polyurethane finishes are a bit newer to the boating game and can sometimes be applied by *experienced* boaters (as opposed to a professional yard). Usually, both these finishes and their imitators are used on older boats to refinish the gel-coat. To my knowledge, there are no new power boats shipped from the factory with these finishing materials. Of course, if you are considering a used craft with one of these finishes, particularly Awlgrip, you can proceed with confidence.

Strength

Fortunately, most stock power boats on the market today are built with adequate hull strength. There have been rare exceptions, but the Coast Guard can usually be depended upon to remove such undependable models from the market within a fairly short period of time.

You, as a new boat buyer, cannot really hope to judge for yourself whether a boat is of strong or weak construction. Many captains who have been around power boats for years do not really have a clue about which boats have the best constructions, except possibly by reputation. Therein lies your best bet to make a determination as to the quality of your prospective craft. Try to obtain a test report about the particular boat in question. The strength of construction is usually dealt with in a more than adequate fashion in such articles. Additionally, use all the information resources mentioned earlier in this chapter to research the prospective vessel. While this is an area that you need not be too concerned about, a little research can give you a telling insight into your boat's true craftsmanship quality.

The Bilge

One item of a boat's construction that is often overlooked by the first-time buyer is the working and access space in the bilge. You will *never* find an experienced captain taking this matter lightly, however. You need only own one of those best-forgotten craft that need a midget to change spark plugs or that requires removal of the generator to change the hot water heater, and bilge access space will never again be at the bottom of your priority list.

Have the dealer open all the available bilge hatches. Is there good access to the engines and their accessories, or will you have to crawl along the hull simply to reach an outboard manifold or spark plug? Don't stop with the engines. Look at the generator, batteries, fresh-water pump, and air conditioning (if any). Can all this gear be easily accessed, or would it require one of the aforementioned midgets for service work?

Be warned! Bilge space is not a matter that can be confidently left to the boat manufacturer. Several years ago, one of the United States' finest power boat builders featured a forty-three foot cruiser that had a bilge so crammed full of equipment that many mechanics simply refused to work on the boat. If professionals had such problems, imagine how the owners fared.

INTERIORS

Don't overlook a careful inspection of your prospective craft's interior. The internal layout will largely determine how comfortable the craft will be to live on for extended periods. Cruising stories to the contrary, most boaters will spend a goodly portion of their time on the water living aboard their boats while docked at a marina. A thoughtful, roomy, well-laid-out interior is one of the best means of assuring a happy life aboard. If you purchase a boat that makes ineffectual use of interior space, your floating lifestyle will suffer in direct proportion to the thoughtfulness, or lack thereof, of the interior design.

Main Cabin

First, take a good, long look at the main cabin (sometimes referred to as the salon). Ask yourself where you and your mate can sit for an evening of relaxation. Is there a good spot for a small television and/or a music system? How about another couple? Can the cabin accommodate four comfortably? Try to visualize where everyone would sit. Is this a comfortable arrangement or is it somewhat akin to a subway during the rush hour?

Galley

Next, inspect the galley. The first priority here is work space. Naturally, you can't expect as much physical room in most marine galleys as you would find in a home kitchen. Vessels above 50 feet in length might boast otherwise, but the first-time purchaser of a craft from 28 to 45 feet will most likely find that cooking aboard is a challenging new experience. Counter space is at a premium! There is never enough of it, and the more the better.

Now take a look at the galley storage space. Are there sufficient cabinets to store your plates, pots and pans, and dry foodstuffs, without having to crowd everything together in a disorderly fashion? Again, you must expect to accommodate some reduced space in a boat (as opposed to the average home), but there must be sufficient storage space to organize your cooking gear and food or you will spend half your time in the galley trying to find the potato peeler or the butcher knife.

The key piece of equipment in any galley is obviously the stove and/or oven. With boats under 34 feet in length, an oven is sometimes not available. In this case, you might want to consider a marine microwave oven as discussed in Chapter 4.

Alcohol is the traditional galley stove fuel of choice for power boats. It is clean and safe but notoriously inefficient in the production of heat. On the plus side, alcohol fires can be put out with water and there is practically no danger of explosion. Older stoves of this variety require pressurization of the fuel tank before lighting. This is accomplished by a plunger pump. The process must be repeated periodically while you are cooking to maintain pressure.

Alcohol stoves of this ilk can be a real pain to light. To burn properly, a pressurized alcohol burner must first be heated. This is accomplished by placing a small amount of alcohol around the burner and then igniting the liquid. Once the fuel has almost burned down, the burner can be turned on and theoretically the alcohol mixture will vaporize, giving the hot blue flame so familiar to most power boaters. Unfortunately, it is all too easy to get too much alcohol in the cup, resulting in a pyrotechnic display that can be alarming and occasionally dangerous.

Newer alcohol stoves use a wick absorption system that does not require a pressure pump. These units are much easier and safer to operate than the older pressurized models, but they are still very inefficient producers of heat, compared with an electric or CNG stove.

Today, more and more power boats are being equipped with electric or alcohol/electric stoves. This latter variety is really the best of both worlds. When dockside power is available or the generator is operating, you can cook with the convenience of an electric range. When at anchor, the alcohol alternative frees you from the generator.

"All-electric" galleys are fine at dockside and as long as that temperamental piece of equipment known as the generator chooses to cooperate. If you should anchor out and the generator refuses to start, it's cold sandwiches for supper.

LPG (liquified petroleum gas or propane) and CNG (compressed natural gas) are two other possible galley fuels, though these two varieties are more common on sailcraft than power boats. Propane is easy to use and efficient, but there is some danger of explosion. This gas is heavier than air, and should there be a leak in the system, propane will collect in the bilge or on the galley floor. An errant spark could set off a catastrophic explosion.

While propane conflagrations are not too frequent, the possibility of explosion has led many boaters over the last decade to choose CNG as a galley fuel. CNG is used just like propane, but this gas is *lighter* than air. If a leak should occur, the vapors will simply disperse in the air, greatly reducing the chances of explosion.

Larger power boats are equipped with a refrigerator in the galley. This is a great advantage over most sailcraft in the same size range, which usually come with only an icebox. The best variety of marine refrigerator runs off shorepower (120 volts AC) at dockside and automatically switches over to 12-volt, battery operation when underway. Some boats, usually in the 40-plus-foot range, have a strictly 120-volt fridge. Obviously, these designers expect you to run the generator while underway, just to keep the beer cool. This is not my idea of the optimal cooling procedure. Not only will you be using extra fuel, but the generator (usually notable for its touchy temperament) will quickly rack up a prodigious quantity of engine hours.

Open the refrigerator and look at the available storage space. Is it adequate for a weekend's worth of food and cold drinks? How about a week-long trip? When you open the refrigerator do you have to vacate the entire galley just to swing the door open?

Storage

The boat has not been built that has too much storage space. In fact, some long-time boaters have been known to claim that the boat has not been built that has even *sufficient* storage. So, take these old salts' philosophy to heart: buy a boat with as much storage space as you can find.

Check out all the lockers and cabinets. Ask yourself where you can stow such diverse items as clothes (both flat and hanging), charts, mechanical tools, and navigational equipment such as binoculars, hand-bearing compass, etc. Nothing can close in on you faster than a cluttered boat! If you can't find readily accessible storage space, including at least one hanging locker, for all your essential equipment and personal items, then *another* boat should be in your future.

Sleeping Quarters

Many (in fact, most) boats in the 28- to 38-foot-range have a berth in the shape of a "V" in the forward cabin. This "V-berth" is the main sleeping compartment in boats lacking a rear cabin. As such, it demands your careful inspection.

Take a moment to actually lie on the mattress and check its comfort. It's awfully easy in the excitement of buying your first larger boat to tell yourself that a too hard, or too soft mattress in the V-berth is something you will get used to. Awakening to a backache many a morning could change your mind.

The well-equipped craft will come with a so-called V-berth filler. This rather essential piece of equipment is simply a board and fitted mattress that fits snugly in the center of the "V," thereby giving you a sleeping surface without a hole in the center. Unless you are a very quiet sleeper or enjoy waking up on the floor, a V-berth filler is a piece of equipment that you won't want to do without.

Pleasure craft equipped with a rear cabin often feature a traditional shaped bed. Larger boats sometimes feature a queen-sized mattress. Again, you should take the time to actually lie on the bed and examine it for comfort. Size is no substitute for a poorly designed (too soft or hard) mattress.

Many boats come with a sleeper couch in addition to a V-berth. These units are usually similar to those found in homes. There are, however, several special considerations for boat buyers to keep in mind when inspecting these couches. First, make sure the sofa opens and closes *easily*. It is more than a little frustrating to discover that your sleeper couch is jammed after a long day of cruising. Inspect the couch's floor fastening. If the unit is not attached securely to the cabin floor, it will *move* about in a rough seaway, possibly injuring other equipment or parts of the cabin. Finally, insist on opening the

Typical V-berth (without filler).

couch and lying on its surface. These sleep sofas are notorious for having lumpy mattresses. If your prospective craft can lay claim to one of these instruments of torture, you might want to think twice before laying out the cash.

Dining Arrangements

Over the past several years, one of the most debated features of interior power boat design has been the question of permanent dinettes versus a fluid arrangement involving a high-low table. You must choose your boat's culinary arrangement based on your desire for an easy-to-use dining area as contrasted with the need for additional space.

Permanent dinettes usually consist of two fixed benches with a table between the seats. The table is often hinged to the cabin wall so that it can be swung up out of the way when not in use. This plan has several advantages. When it comes time to set out dinner, it is a very simple matter to swing the table into position and then call all hands to chow. After a long day of cruising, when you are so tired it seems as if it's an effort to bat an eye, this enhancement should not be taken lightly. Also, many permanent dinettes can be quickly converted to overnight bunks, thereby enhancing the sleeping capacity of your vessel.

On the other hand, fixed dinette plans are a notorious squanderer of precious interior space. In vessels under 36 feet, the lost space can be an especially acute problem. Consequently, many manufacturers have now opted for a high-low dining table. This unit doubles as a low-level

Fixed dinette.

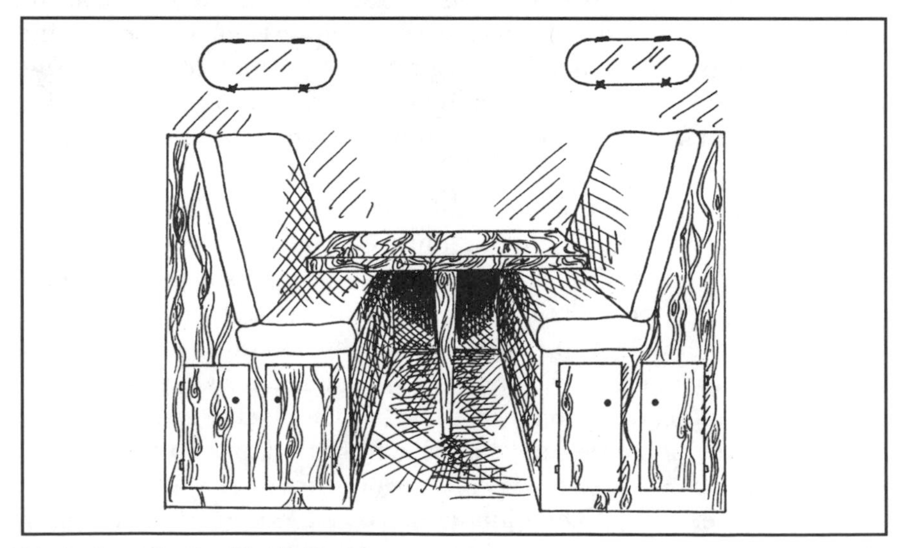

Typical permanent (fixed) dinette.

coffee table in the main cabin between meals. When it's time to sample the galley's latest offerings, some member of the crew must raise the table, make sure all the catches are secure, and then arrange chairs from the cabin around the eating area. As already mentioned, this can be a thorn in your side after a long day, but the space-saving qualities of this arrangement may make the inconvenience worthwhile.

Cruisers who use a high-low table should make *sure* that all the table's braces and stops are secure before placing any food on the surface. On one occasion, my ace research assistant, Bud Williams, was obviously relishing the smell of frying bacon, hot coffee, and cheese omelets as the aromas wafted from the galley. It was his job to set up the high-low table. Unfortunately, in his haste to enjoy his breakfast, he failed to check the drop-leaf supports. It was not long before Bud was contemplating his wonderful breakfast as it sat atop the cabin carpet.

As a boater who once put up with a high-low table for better than ten years, there have been times when I have certainly envied those cruisers with a permanent dinette. But then, I looked over our cabin and wondered how I could possibly give up the space necessary for a fixed dinette plan. You must make the decision for yourself. Just keep in mind the advantages and disadvantages of both plans, and choose which best fits your cruising and live-aboard plans.

The Head

Most first-time buyers of larger power boats are initially shocked at the size of a boat's head (bathroom for you landlubbers). Incidentally the term "head" is used interchangeably to refer to a marine toilet, or the entire onboard bathroom. Quite simply, a marine head (bathroom) is considerably smaller than most any bathroom found in a shoreside house. This tight arrangement is necessary to conserve cabin space. However, some designers have been known to take their space conservation a bit too far. As you inspect the head of your prospective vessel, take the time to decide whether there is really enough room to perform all necessary activities, or do you have to be first cousins with a midget in order to fit the allotted space.

One of the most pleasurable experiences that I had after we first bought the *Kaycy* was taking a hot shower while at anchor, far from the most remote vestige of civilization. Our former boat had a head arrangement often referred to as a unitized shower. Quite simply, when it comes time to wash off the day's salt and sweat, the whole head becomes the shower. There is a drain in the head floor and a shower curtain to protect the door and sometimes the toilet paper.

Typical marine "head" with separate stall shower.

This is a very practical, space-saving concept, but it has one large drawback. After every shower, someone must take the time and effort to wipe out the entire head. This can be quite a chore after a long day of fighting the waves. Wet towels can also begin to accumulate during a long trip. My first mate and I have a standing arrangement that whoever wipes out the head is exempt from that night's bed-making chores.

A separate stall shower is certainly to be preferred. Unfortunately, this design is often not available on boats under thirty-four feet. If you have any choice, however, pick an enclosed shower. The added convenience will enhance your cruising experience immeasurably.

The marine head (toilet) is a mechanism that requires careful consideration. It is now quite illegal to dump unprocessed human waste overboard. Fines for breaking this dumping law can run as high as $10,000! Consequently, most power boats come from the factory with a standard manual flush/holding tank system. With this design, sea water is manually pumped into the toilet bowl by a plunger pump, and the waste is dumped directly into a holding tank. The tank must be periodically pumped out from a facility equipped to handle this sort of waste disposal.

There are several distinct disadvantages to the holding tank design. First, pump-out stations can sometimes be hard to find, though more and more marinas do offer this service. Secondly, there is almost always some objectionable odor with this sort of system. Many boaters eventually opt out of a holding tank via an onboard waste treatment system.

Since the government imposed stiff fines for overboard dumping of untreated waste, several companies have begun manufacturing on onboard waste treatment plants. Probably the best known system is "Lectra-San," manufactured by the Mansfield Corporation. While all of these units are somewhat costly, when coupled with an electric flush motor, they do allow you to *legally* dump thoroughly treated waste into the surrounding waters, except in official zero discharge zones. Boaters fortunate enough to have such a system aboard seldom need to look for a waste pump-out station. Also, there is usually less of an odor problem from an onboard waste treatment plant.

No matter what sort of marine toilet you find on your prospective craft, insist that the owner or broker demonstrate its operation. *Be sure* everything is in good working order. There are few more expensive repairs in the boating game than service work on marine toilets. In many ports, it's almost impossible to find a technician who is willing to perform such repairs.

Don't forget about storage in the head. You will need at least one cabinet to stow personal grooming items. Wet towels often collect on a boat. Numerous towel racks in the head can help alleviate this situation.

Shorepower Systems

Practically every power boat over twenty-eight feet in length comes standard with a 120-volt shorepower system. This feature inevitably includes a dockside cable connector and switch panel. Shorepower is almost essential for comfortable life aboard. With AC power you can watch your favorite football game, fire up the hot water tank, and even vacuum the carpet. If the craft you are considering does not have this necessary facility, better look elsewhere.

Shorepower systems come in 20-, 30-, and 50-amp varieties. The 50-amp setup is normally reserved for larger power craft (over 45 feet) while a single 30-amp shorepower cable is usually found on craft without air conditioning from 28 to 45 feet. Twenty-amp systems are the least desirable as they do not provide enough current for many onboard duties.

Each one of these shorepower systems (or levels) uses a unique shoreside plug. You must either find a marina that can match your particular plug configuration or keep a supply of adapters aboard (a very good idea indeed).

Be sure to inspect the breaker panel. It should be easily accessible and well marked. Crawling into the bilge to flip the air conditioning or heater breaker in the middle of the night is not my idea of boating fun.

Take a good look at the electrical receptacles in the main cabin, galley, head, and sleeping quarters. Each of these compartments should have at least one outlet (preferably more). If none are available, it could point to an interior design that lacks forethought.

Other Considerations

During warm (not hot), dry weather, there are few cruising delights to compare with letting the fragrant, salty airs circulate throughout your cabin. Unfortunately, without hatch and window screens, mosquitoes, black flies, and other winged pests are likely to pay you a visit. If you purchase a used boat, you will almost certainly find these near-essential screens already in place. Even new boats often come standard with screens while others offer this equipment as an option. Make no mistake about it. You will want good quality, close-mesh nylon screens for all your windows and hatches. If your boat does not come equipped with them, figure the costs of adding the screens in your buying budget.

Nylon is the material of choice for boating screens. Salt air will destroy aluminum mesh in short order. Be sure to select screens of good quality nylon for long life.

Boaters who live aboard their craft at a marina for any length of time become all too familiar with "dock walkers." This group of non-boaters can't seem to believe that anyone would actually live on a boat, even for a weekend. I have known them to walk up to our boat and peer unashamedly through windows and hatches. This can be a bit disconcerting when you are in the middle of a shower. The cure for "dock walkers" is window curtains and hatch covers.

You will find that nearly all boats are now equipped with these practical accessories, but the quality of the curtain and cover fabrics vary widely. Mildew-resistant materials can be a big plus. Even with these resistant fabrics, you will need to visit the cleaners every other season or so. Those boaters whose craft is not equipped with mildew-resistant fabric make their local dry cleaners very happy.

Final Interior Thoughts

After you have performed all the inspections recommended above, take a few moments to stand alone in the boat's main cabin.

Try to visualize where you, your mate, and possibly several friends can sit for an evening of relaxation. Where can you put a television so that it is readily visible to everyone in the cabin? Now, think about an average day on the water. Is there room to prepare breakfast in the galley while someone else is taking a shower and a third member of the crew is stowing the bed linens? Try to visualize a number of onboard living situations. Look around the boat's interior and ask yourself if the craft can handle these situations. If it can't, what are the alternatives? A few extra moments spent inspecting your prospective boat's interior can go far toward ensuring a happy life aboard.

EXTERIOR LAYOUT

Don't overlook a careful inspection of your prospective craft's exterior layout. Look for line cleats, anchor chocks, bow and stern rails. At a minimum, all boats should have sturdy cleats on both corners of the stern, on both sides of the boat, and a particularly sturdy binding post with two line chocks on the bow. Does this deck hardware appear to be strong enough to do the job or does it look as if it should be found on a runabout? Does the deck hardware seem to be located where it should be for easy access to the lines when docking or anchoring? Is the hardware's stainless steel smooth and shiny, or does it have a pitted surface? Poor quality stainless could indicate short cuts in other aspects of the boat's construction.

Now, inspect the deck passageways from the stern to the bow and back again. Is there ready passage with plenty of room for larger individuals from one end of the boat to the other? Are there enough hand holds to steady yourself when going forward in rough weather or must you perform a balancing act to keep from hitting the drink?

Look around to see how much teak or mahogany woodwork you can find on the boat's exterior. Looks great, doesn't it? Well, just remember that it is a never-ending chore to keep it looking that way. While I certainly prefer "some" of this traditional material on my boat to save it from a "plastic" appearance, too much teak or mahogany can make you a slave to steel wool and a paint brush.

Take it from someone who been has forced to go forward in rough weather many a time. A well-thought-out exterior plan is invaluable on any boat. Your boat's layout will affect docking, anchoring, or even such mundane activities as sunning. A careful inspection now can save many a headache in the future.

STANDARD EQUIPMENT

If you should choose to buy a used craft, you will, of course, have to accept the equipment you find aboard. As already mentioned, however, you will likely find more accessories on a used boat than would be available on most any new craft.

On the other hand, if a new boat is your choice, you should take a careful look at the standard equipment that is shipped from the factory at no additional cost. It is strictly my own opinion that the more standard equipment a manufacturer includes, the more that particular firm is concerned with giving you good value for your money.

Standard equipment does vary widely from one boat builder to another. Some such as Silverton and Mainship include just about everything you need to power away into the sunset. Others make such basic items as cabin carpeting an additional cost accessory. Check the following list against the standard equipment included on any new craft you might be considering. If a majority of this equipment is available only as an extra cost item, you might want to keep your hand on your wallet and took elsewhere. A well-equipped factory boat should include:

1. Pressurized hot and cold water—a hot water tank can be a real pill to install later

2. At least one anchor, anchor rope (or "rode"), anchor chock, and deck pipe—a deck pipe allows neat storage of the anchor rode in a rope locker below deck (see Chapter 3 for a complete discussion of anchor types)

3. A galley refrigerator, preferably a combination 120- to 12-volt unit

4. A shower in the head—on smaller boats under 34 feet you may have to settle for a unitized shower

5. Galley stove and oven—again, on boats under 34 feet a built-in oven may not be available

6. Complete shorepower system including dockside hookup cable and interior breaker panel

7. At least a manual flushing head (toilet) with a holding tank system

8. Breakers and/or fuses for 12-volt power

9. Complete interior carpeting

10. At least one bilge pump with an *automatic water level switch*

11. Enough fire extinguishers to meet USCG regulations

The really well-equipped craft will also include:

1. V-berth cushions
2. Full instrumentation on the flybridge—if your craft is so equipped
3. Four life preservers and throw ring
4. One main cabin chair
5. A salon sleeper couch
6. Cabin window curtains, screens, and hatch covers
7. A complete set of dockside mooring lines

Many boats come equipped with both upper (flybridge) and lower (main cabin) helm stations (steering wheel and engine controls). While this was the standard for many years, several manufacturers have now begun to question the necessity of this arrangement. Lower helm stations are intended for use during inclement weather, but the limited visual perspective from this position can be unnerving, to say the least. In eleven years of cruising on the *Kaycy* we used our lower station exactly twice.

With this minimal use in mind, some boat builders now offer a lower helm station as an option or omit it entirely. If it is a matter of choice, you must decide between the reduced cost of having a flybridge station only or the added safety and convenience of both. You can save a considerable sum of money by omitting the lower station. However, the first time a driving thunderstorm is your companion while piloting from the flybridge, you might just wonder if it was the wrong decision. This is an instance where there is no one right choice. You must make the decision for yourself, based on your cruising plans for the future. Fair-weather cruisers who usually make short cruising hops can probably get by with a single station. Those who plan to cruise over longer distances may want to seriously consider the second helm position.

How to Get a VHF Radio and Depth Sounder

Here's a tip sure to save you money. While most used craft buyers will find a VHF radio and depth sounder aboard, these two basic pieces of nautical equipment are not often included as standard equipment on new boats. However, it has been my experience that most dealers are so anxious to close the deal on a new boat, you can usually talk them into including a VHF (and antennae) and depth sounder in the deal. Be sure your arrangement

Flybridge helm stations.

includes *installation* of these units. As a first-time boat buyer, this is not the time to learn about the intricacies of VHF and depth sounder installation.

OPTIONS AND ACCESSORIES

New and used boats must be considered separately in any discussion of options and accessories. Obviously, the more electronics and accessories found aboard a used craft, the better. Just be sure to insist on seeing each piece of equipment in action before closing the deal. Repairs to marine accessories, particularly electronics, can cost more than a few shekels. (Please see Chapter 4, "Practical Accessories," for a complete review of the equipment you might look to find on a prospective used craft or want to install on a new one.)

Surprisingly enough, it is often less expensive to install accessories on your new craft *after* you tuck your new purchase safely in a marina slip. First, quality equipment can be obtained at substantial savings through the many fine marine discounters that now offer prompt

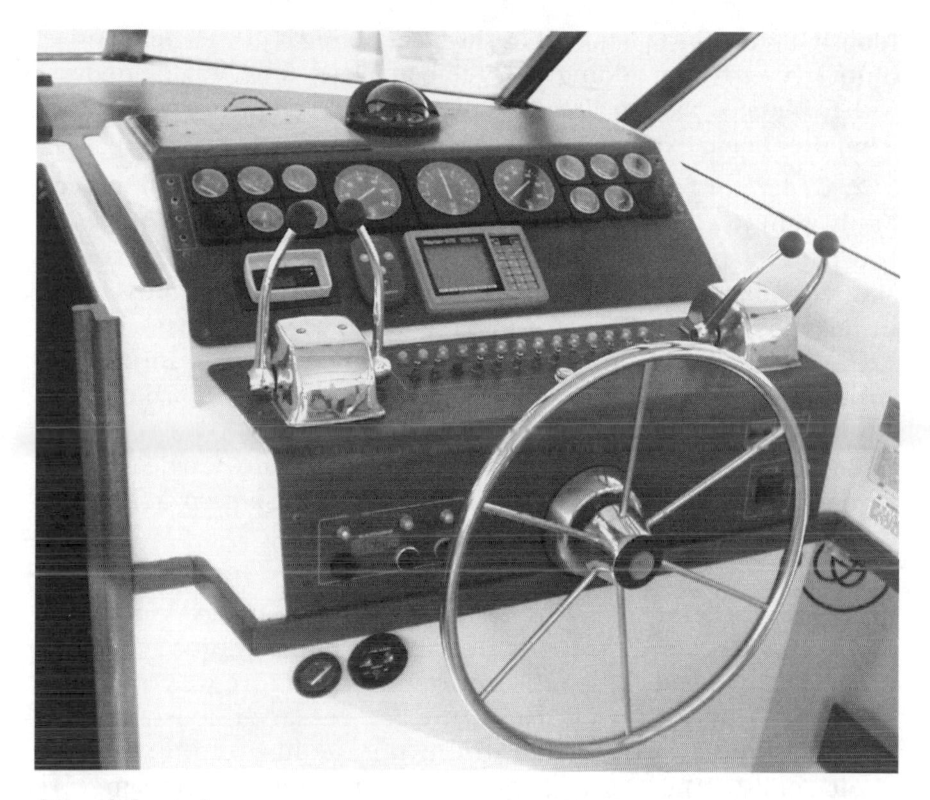

Lower helm station.

delivery to boaters all across the USA. Then, you may be able to install the unit yourself, saving even more money. Even if this is not practical, the discounted price of the equipment will usually more than offset the cost of professional installation.

However, should you decide to purchase a new craft *that must be ordered from the factory,* there are certain accessories that might be better installed during construction. The equipment listed below can be easily included at the time of manufacture, while adding such accessories at a later time could be costly and time consuming. If these special instances, you can save money by specifying this equipment when ordering your new boat:

1. Freshwater Cooling. This is a great idea for long engine life. At first you may be hesitant to spend the $500 to $1,000 per engine for this accessory, but, trust me, when you see the saltwater cooled boat in the next slip having its rusted-out engines and/or manifolds replaced to the tune of $10,000, you'll be glad you weren't penny wise and pound foolish. Factory installation of freshwater cooling is just as inexpensive, if not more so, than adding the system at a later time. Taking delivery with freshwater cooling already in place will prevent your engine block from ever being exposed to internal saltwater.

2. Generator for AC Power. Boaters who anchor off often will certainly want to consider having a generator for 120-volt AC power. If you plan to spend most of your time docked at marinas, this is an accessory that you might want to forgo. While it is quite possible to install a generator at a later time, it is usually less expensive for the manufacturer to mount this heavy piece of equipment during construction. Check the factory-installed price against a local dealer's equipment and installation estimate.

Be sure to specify a sound insulation box if you do decide to order a generator. Boats that lack this device seldom use their generators due to the excessive operating noise.

I will never forget our first trip to the *Kaycy* after the marina installed a generator aboard *without* an insulation box. We arrived about 10:00 P.M. and promptly cranked up our new piece of equipment. I think we woke up the entire marina before we could shut it down. On another occasion, my ace research assistant, Bud Williams, and I were anchored out on a cold evening. It was a choice of listening to the generator racket all night or freezing. We froze.

3. Marine Air Conditioning. Don't kid yourself! If you cruise in waters south of Norfolk, Virginia, you *will* want an air conditioning system aboard. The best variety for marine use is a water-cooled model with a reverse cycle (à la a shoreside heat pump) that can double as an onboard furnace during cold weather. (See Chapter 4 for a complete discussion of marine air conditioning.)

While it is done every day, installation of a marine air conditioning system after factory construction is a tedious and time-consuming job that can often challenge your installer's creativity. In this instance, it is almost always less expensive to specify factory installation.

4. Galley Stove Upgrade. If you decide the standard factory galley stove is inadequate for your purposes, it is considerably less complicated and usually less expensive to allow the factory to install a better unit. The stove and/or oven are usually set directly into a galley cabinet. It does not require too much imagination to envision the problems of installing a larger or smaller unit into the cabinet. I suggest consulting your manufacturer's option list and specifying a stove and oven that you can live with comfortably for years to come.

DEALERS

Many boat buyers in their haste and enthusiasm to purchase their first larger power craft tend to overlook the importance of finding a good dealer. If you are buying a used boat, you might be dealing directly with the owner, but even most used craft purchases are conducted through a broker. An honest, reliable dealer is one of your best sources of information about prospective boats. Unfortunately, not every buyer will be lucky enough to find a "Wendy" when they go boat shopping. So, you must proceed with caution and shop not only for the right boat, but the right dealer as well.

Additionally, if you have problems, complaints, or warranty repairs after the sale, your dealer or broker is the one who must handle these matters. So, take the extra time and effort to find a good, reputable dealer with servicing capabilities. First-time large-boat ownership will be a happier experience for the extra effort.

First, look for a dealer or broker who is *in,* not just playing at, the service business. Even if you decide to have your boat serviced elsewhere, particularly with a new boat, you may have warranty repairs that must be performed by your dealer. To check on your dealer's servicing capability, find out how many service technicians he employs. If there is just one, the lone mechanic may be there just for appearances and to help the potential buyer feel secure. On the other hand, a very small, but otherwise reputable dealership may have only one repair person by dint of the operation's size.

Take a walk around the boatyard and try to determine how much space and resources (tools, boat lifts, etc.) the dealer gives to service work. This is a classic case of "the more the better."

Try to strike up a conversation with one of the service personnel. Find out how long they have been servicing boats and whether they seem to have a real feel for their trade. If the service person is new to the game and he or she is the only such technician employed by the dealership, it could mean trouble ahead.

After inspecting several craft, carefully check your potential dealer's claims against the knowledge you have hopefully gleaned from boating magazines, marine shows, and other means. If the dealer seems honest and is genuinely interested in helping to mate you with a craft that fits your needs, you can feel confident that you have found a reliable firm. However, if he seems to jump from boat to boat, trying to anticipate which of his craft you are more likely to buy, and only then begins to extol the virtues of a particular boat, there might be a problem.

Finally, boat dealers are often your best source for federal documentation and marine financing. While few marine dealers actually handle their own financing, most have a relationship with a marine finance company and/or local bank. This working arrangement can help speed up the often complicated business of obtaining the right financial arrangements. Both documentation and financing will be considered in detail at the end of this chapter.

WARRANTY

With used craft there is usually very little offered in the way of warranty protection, even by legitimate brokers. As one popular television program put it, it's a classic case of "buyer beware." Consequently, as already discussed, it's very important to make the most detailed survey of a prospective used vessel before the checkbook comes out.

New boats, on the other hand, usually do come with a warranty. This protection can vary widely from one brand to the next. An important part of buying any new boat is to review the differing warranties of the various vessels you are considering. Some of the questions you should ask are:

1. *How long is the warranty period?* The longer the better.

2. *What is covered in the warranty and what is not?* The more the better. The engines, transmission, and drive systems, at least, should be fully warrantied.

3. *Does routine service work have to be performed at the dealership from which you purchased the boat in order to maintain the warranty?* I would hate to think that I had to take my boat back to the dealership for a simple oil change just to keep the warranty valid.

4. *Can the dealership authorize warranty repairs, or must a factory representative be present?* If you must wait for a factory rep every time you need warranty service, it could mean long delays while your boat is out of commission.

Don't just take your dealer's word about the warranty provisions. Take a few extra moments to sit down and read the "fine print," Somewhere between all the whereas's and wherefores, you might find a provision that could change your mind.

FINANCING

Unless you are one of those lucky people who can simply sign a check for their first larger power boat, you must concern yourself with financing your purchase. Marine financing is one of the least considered parts of buying a boat, even for experienced cruisers. This lack of forethought can lead to future problems as witnessed by our own experience.

When purchasing our pride and joy, the *Kaycy*, our finances were at a low ebb, and we needed the lowest possible monthly payments. Our dealer was able to put us in touch with a finance company that offered fifteen-year terms. We jumped at the chance and did not really bother to read the loan agreement too closely.

Only later did we discover that our agreement committed us to a so-called "rule of 78" loan. This variety of financing is just fine *if and only if* you maintain the loan contract for its entire period and never attempt to pay the balance off early. When things improved and we tried to pay off the loan, it was only then that we discovered there would be a *hefty* penalty for early close-out of the contract.

While today, fortunately, "rule of 78" loans are little more than a bad memory, our experience does serve to point out how important it is to take your time when obtaining marine financing. As we have been discussing in practically every aspect of this chapter, the rule of thumb is not to let the enthusiasm for your first larger boat blind you to calm, rational, and timely considerations. Financing is just as subject to this rule as the selection of the proper hull type or power plant.

If you have selected a sturdy used craft as your first larger vessel, then you might as well know the bad news up front. Banks and private finance companies alike refuse to extend as long a loan term on used boats as their new brethren. With boats that have plied the waters for ten years or better, it can be difficult to obtain *any* type of financing. Before getting your hopes up too much, check with a loan institution to see whether the craft you selected can be financed. If the answer is yes, then inquire about the longest possible term for the loan. The answer to these two questions should go far in determining whether you can afford the vessel in question.

As previously discussed, one of the best sources for marine financing advice is your dealer or broker. Most reputable dealers have a working arrangement with at least one marine finance company and/or local bank. With such an arrangement, the dealer or broker can advise you about the best rates and terms available. Normally, a dealer does not receive any compensation for recommending one finance company or bank over another, so it is really in his best interest to point out the best deal. However, be sure to check at least one other competing bank or finance company before making any commitment. This procedure will insure that you are receiving competitive terms.

One of your first decisions will be whether to finance through a bank or a lending company that specializes in marine financing. Both options have advantages and drawbacks. Banks generally give you a lower rate of interest. Sometimes this sort of lending institution does not require federal documentation of your new boat. This can result in a real savings of time and money. However, banks generally give shorter terms (usually seven years at the most) than marine finance companies and, in my experience, seem to be more conservative in their loan decisions. In a borderline situation, you may discover that a private company will extend credit where a bank will refuse the loan.

Private marine finance companies are just the opposite of banks. They give longer terms, up to fifteen and sometimes twenty years, and seem to be less restrictive with their credit. However, their rates of interest are usually slightly higher and they invariably require federal documentation of the boat being financed. Look at your financial needs and choose accordingly.

Another option is to finance your craft through one of the large boating membership organizations that seem to be gaining increasing popularity in the USA. You must pay a small annual fee to join such a group, but many boaters will find this miniscule expense to be more than justified. These organizations have huge memberships, and this collective buying power allows them to offer very attractive rates and terms. The largest organization of this type at the present time is Boat Owners Association of the United States (Boat/US for short) located in Alexandria, Virginia.

In times past, your next consideration would have concerned what type of loan you should acquire. With the advent and eventual domination of simple interest loans, that question is now largely moot. For those of you who don't know, simple interest means that you only pay the interest on the principal balance of the loan for the time it is actually borrowed. In other words, if you pay the loan off early, there is no penalty. This is definitely a superior mousetrap in the financing game, and far better that the "rule of 78" trap in which we landed. All banks and most private finance companies now offer this type of loan exclusively.

Another issue in marine financing that you may need to consider is the fixed versus the floating or variable rate loan. As you might expect, fixed-rate loans have the same interest over the entire life of the contract. Floating loans change their interest rate, and consequently their monthly payments, at the end of a six- or twelve-month period, based on one of several national interest rate indexes.

Why, you might ask, would anyone choose a variable rate loan over the fixed variety? Why insert all that uncertainty in a boat loan? After all, if interest rates should rise dramatically, your monthly loan payments would also rise significantly above the levels you expected to pay. The answer, quite simply, is that some people are willing to take a gamble. The *initial* interest rate of a variable-rate loan is always less than the rate of a fixed loan at the time you initiate the financing agreement. If interest rates stay the same or drop, then you will save a good chunk of change. If rates rise, however, the outlook is considerably less rosy.

It is very difficult for me to advise the reader as to which course to take. I suggest looking at the difference between the interest rate for a fixed versus a variable loan. If the difference is small, take the fixed plan every time. Should the gap be large enough to drastically affect your monthly payments at the time of purchase, you may want to at least consider a variable-rate loan, particularly if the difference means that you can afford the boat you want. Always remember, though, what could happen if rates rise sharply.

Finally, no matter what type of financial institution or what variety of loan you choose, any firm financing your boat is going to require a certain income level on your part. Lending institutions consider an adequate monthly paycheck to be one of the best sources of security for their money. The lender will also take other aspects of your financial portfolio into account such as whether you rent or own your landside home, how long you've been employed, plus a whole bevy of other figures that we lowly, nonbanking mortals cannot hope to understand. To avoid disappointment, go over the income guidelines with your dealer *before* submitting a loan application.

As already alluded to in the account above, most marine finance companies and many banks require that a boat be *federally documented* before it can be financed. This documentation procedure allows your financial institution to register a lien against the boat, much like a deed of trust held by a savings and loan for a home loan. Should you default on your loan payments, the finance company can foreclose and seize the vessel. It is easy to understand why financiers want this extra protection for their loan money.

So, what is federal documentation? In theory, it's only a procedure to register your vessel with the United States Coast Guard. That description, however, is deceptively simple. In years past, it used to require a set of forms six inches high to federally document a pleasure craft. A personal visit by a team of Coast Guard officers was also required. The process could, and often did, take months to successfully accomplish. Thankfully, since 1990 the procedure has been somewhat simplified. It is still not a task for the first-time buyer of a larger power boat to undertake himself. Even though it will probably cost $100 to $200, you should engage either your dealer or finance company to handle all the paperwork for you. All you will have to do then is sign your name on the dotted line several dozen times.

When boat buyers opt for a local bank or their dealer is not in a position to help with documentation, there is still another means to simplify federal documentation. Should you find yourself in such a position, national boating organizations such as Boat/US, discussed earlier, can come to your aid.

FINAL THOUGHTS

Well, you've found her—*the* boat for you! It's large enough to meet your cruising needs. You are satisfied as to hull design, power plant, standard equipment, construction, and interior layout. Furthermore, you have taken the time to choose a reliable dealer or honest former owner and are happy with the factory warranty (if any). You have secured the financing arrangements that are right for your monetary circumstances from a company that can give you documentation support. Now that this formidable task is behind you, get ready for some of the greatest experiences of your life. Over the remainder of this account, we will examine together how to outfit, accessorize, maintain, and finally go "a-cruising" in your new pride and joy.

Good luck!

CHAPTER 2

What to Do While Awaiting Delivery

IF YOU HAVE CHOSEN a used craft or even a new boat that your dealer already has in stock, then, of course, it won't be necessary to wait for the delivery of your new floating home. On the other hand, if you must wait (and it can seem like forever) for the factory to build and then ship your new craft, the necessary nautical tasks outlined in this chapter can certainly make the time pass more quickly. In either case, there are certain responsibilities and chores associated with owning a larger boat that should be accomplished before any others. This chapter will review those pleasurable duties. Take care of these essentials *first,* and you can move smoothly into the enjoyment of your first larger power vessel.

CHOOSING THE RIGHT MARINA

Discovering a reliable, well-maintained, full-service marina that fits into your budget is one of the most important initial responsibilities facing the new boat owner. Unless you are one of those lucky captains who has his own dock at a shoreside condo or beach home, the choice of where to berth your boat is almost sure to affect your boating pleasure (or lack of it) for years to come. There is no substitute for a good home-base marina where you can expect quick and efficient service as well as good shelter from bad weather and security from theft and intrusion. Marinas lacking these qualities can only lead to trouble.

"Once inside the stream, we were immediately greeted by the sight of several sunken boats..."

Fortunately, most modern marinas are well managed, efficient operations that captains and crew can use with confidence. There are exceptions, however. I well remember that while performing research for my North Carolina cruising guide we came across one marina on New River that was memorable, to say the least. First, we spent some thirty minutes hunting for the entrance, even though we had a chart that showed its location. Finally, after comparing notes with a local native, we were directed to a small creek, barely visible along the shoreline. Fortunately, on this particular day our research was being performed in a sixteen-foot, outboard-powered runabout. On the way in, our prop stirred the sand repeatedly. One could only wonder how a larger vessel could ever traverse the so-called channel without running aground.

Once inside the stream, we were immediately greeted by the sight of several sunken boats in the few slips along the shoreline. One particularly large pleasure craft was half sunk just in front of what we took to be the fuel dock. It was obvious that all the piers still standing were in very precarious condition. Indeed, it looked as if a good wind would blow them down. Thinking that the marina was surely closed for business, we had begun to head back out to the river when a voice hailed us from the "fuel dock." After motoring gingerly over to the pier, we inquired if this was indeed the marina for which we were searching. The reply was affirmative. I then inquired if they took transient boats for overnight dockage. With cheery confidence, the attendant informed me that transients stayed there "all the time." Now, perhaps there is a mean streak in me, but I just couldn't let it go at that. Looking around at all the fallen piers and sunken boats, I asked the attendant where they managed to dock transient craft. His immortal reply was, "Oh, around."

Such forgettable operations as the one described above are mercifully rare, but you must still take care to select a marina that fits your particular needs. Try to visit all the marinas in the general area you are considering as a home port. The same rule applies here as is true when buying a boat. Take your time and make a careful, informed decision. The more facilities you visit, the more knowledgeable you will be and the better your chance of making the right choice.

Shelter

If the marina you choose does not provide adequate shelter from foul weather, your vessel will always be at risk. There are few more worrisome times for a boat owner than those times after watching the evening news at home, miles away from your boat, and hearing about

A well-sheltered dockage basin.

the approach of a coastal gale. Even if your craft is not actually damaged, the worry and anxiety can be unnerving to say the least. Knowing your craft is snugly tied in a protected harbor can make the difference between a restful or sleepless night.

Take a good, long look at the shelter afforded to the marina docks. If the piers are exposed to a long stretch of water, even from one side, a severe storm could result in damage to your craft. The longer the open stretch of water, the worse the conditions might become.

This condition of open water and wind is often referred to as "wind fetch." Quite simply, the longer the distance that wind blows over the water unobstructed, the higher the waves and chop will become. If the water is open for a mile or more on any side of your prospective marina's piers, stiff breezes will have enough "fetch" to raise a threatening chop. Conversely, if the marina is located in a sheltered area, where there is no more than a few hundred yards of open water (at the most) on any side of the docks, the wind, short of a hurricane or full gale, will not have enough fetch to stir the waters into a menacing froth.

Ideally, you should look for a marina in a protected bay or cove, or one that has its own artificial breakwater. Breakwaters, as their name implies, are manmade walls, usually of concrete, which enclose a harbor and obstruct wind and waves. You can think of them as an artificial shoreline that partially negates a condition of long wind fetch.

If possible, talk to some of the marina's longtime residents and casually ask how their boats have fared in rough weather. There is no surer tip-off to a harbor's safety than the memories of those who have been there through many a storm!

Docks and Slips

The docks or slips to which your craft will be tied at a marina are critically important. They should be strong and secure. Pilings ought to be placed where all dock lines can be conveniently secured. If you observe what appears to be shaky, substandard docks at a prospective marina, you can just about bet the old homeplace that the facility is not properly maintained.

A second consideration when deciding upon a marina is the type of dockage afforded by the facility. Basically there are two choices, fixed piers or floating docks. Fixed piers, as their name implies, are constructed of wooden or concrete pilings driven into the ground below the water. The dock surface, constructed of planks or sometimes concrete (and occasionally metal), is then

Open slips at fixed wooden docks.

Open, floating dock slips.

attached to the pilings. When the tide rises or falls, vessels moored at fixed piers rise or fall with the changing water level. Docking lines must be loose enough to accommodate low water while still snug enough to keep the boat secure at high tide. This arrangement is perfectly acceptable *if* the tidal range on your home waters does not exceed four feet. In regions that exceed this range, it is difficult to maintain the proper length of dockage line in all stages of the tidal rise and fall.

Mooring in regions with excessive tidal range is best accomplished by floating docks. This sort of berth begins, as does fixed piers, with wooden or concrete pilings being driven into the bottom strata. Then, wooden or concrete dock surfaces that contain large amounts of floating material (such as styrofoam) are attached to the pilings by movable hooks. When the tide rises or falls, the docks move up and down with the change in water level. You can tie your boat snugly to this type of dock. Since the docks themselves rise or fall with the tide, it is not necessary to leave much play in the dockage lines.

We have had several different craft moored in fixed slips along the North Carolina coast for many years. Once we acquired the knack of judging the amount of slack to be left in our lines, the change in water level has never been a problem for us. However, the average tidal range in our marina is only three feet. Along the South Carolina coast, boaters are faced with a six- to eight-foot change in the water levels. If I were mooring my new boat in the "Low Country," I would not consider anything but floating docks.

Covered Slips

Some marinas have a number of slips that are covered by a waterproof roof. You might seriously want to consider such a dockage arrangement if your marina is so equipped. The reduced maintenance brought about by removing your boat from direct sunlight and rain is significant. In the long run, the useful life of your boat will be considerably enhanced by docking in one of these protected moorings. The extra protection for the gel-coat alone will cut your fiberglass polishing and waxing time in half. This reduced fiberglass maintenance is enough by itself to persuade many boaters to opt for a covered slip.

The bad news is that covered slips come at a premium price. In many marinas, the dockage fee can be double that of an open pier. You must decide whether your budget can stand the prodigious

Covered slips.

dockage fees, and then balance the increased cost against the long-term savings in maintenance and boat longevity.

Power and Water Connections

Any marina worth its salt will have 120-volt power connections and city water taps conveniently available to every slip and dock. If you do not find these essentials in place, look elsewhere.

As discussed earlier, your boat might be equipped with any number of differing amperage onboard electrical systems. Twenty-, 30-, and 50-amp electrical services all use shoreside plugs that are unique to their particular power rating. Fifty-amp services even have two different types of plugs (range type and twist lock), complicating the situation further. Of course, conversion plugs are available that allow, for example, a 30-amp system to be plugged into a 20-amp shoreside service. However, while such an arrangement is fine for an overnight stay while cruising, your home berth should have a power service that is rated at least as highly as your onboard system. For example, if your craft has a 30-amp system aboard, you should find a slip that allows you to plug into a 30-amp service, or, by using an adapter, a 50-amp connection. Hooking a 30-amp onboard system to a shoreside 20-amp service, on a long-term basis, is not a good idea.

Be sure your prospective marina has the power connections your boat requires convenient to the slip you are considering. Dockside power is one of the most basic needs in your home berth. It's nothing to muck about with. If the marina you are considering cannot supply you with the amperage and type of shoreside connections you need, move on.

Dockage Rates

Monthly dockage rates vary *widely* in different parts of the country. It would be impossible in the scope of this work to even give some idea of a norm. For instance, one well-known marina in Fort Lauderdale, Florida, now charges a cool $2,000 per month for the privilege of mooring at their docks, while in my own marina on the North Carolina coast, you can get an open slip for about $175 or a covered slip for a little more than $300. Just down the waterway from us, there are some marinas with fewer amenities that offer dockage for about $125 a month.

Your only real insurance against excessive dockage fees is comparative shopping. Be sure to visit *several* marinas, even if you have already picked out the one you like. Compare the varying monthly dockage fees and balance these figures against the services and extras afforded by each marina. Plug these numbers into you boating budget and you can make an intelligent decision about what marina you can and should afford.

Service Work

Another very important consideration in choosing a marina is the facility's ability to perform fast, reliable, and reasonably priced service to your boat and its engines. As a new boat owner, it can be a real burden to seek out reliable service organizations yourself. As sure as your boat floats, you *will* need periodic repairs on your vessel. Imagine how much more convenient it would be if you had only to turn to the trusted personnel at your marina with any service problems.

Make pointed inquiries about whether the marina in question can handle hull, mechanical, and electrical maintenance and repairs. If any of these necessary services are lacking, it means you will have to find a reliable, independent service firm yourself.

It should be quickly noted that a good marina need *not* have (in fact few do) technicians on staff to perform all necessary repair services. Many fine marinas have working relationships with independent mechanics, electricians, and carpenters. Such arrangements are usually quite satisfactory for most repair needs. The question becomes whether your prospective marina has a good working relationship with these freelance service technicians.

If a particular marina affords a goodly amount of business to its independent service people, they will most likely feel an obligation to "hurry over" and address your problem, rather than risk damaging their relationship with the facility. No mechanic, electrician, or carpenter who is worth his salt is going to allow a marina that sends a lot of work his way to slip through their fingers. This means he must please you!

You will find it most convenient if your marina can supply all necessary hull and bottom maintenance. In most waters, fiberglass-hulled boats must have their bottoms scraped and then painted with an anti-fouling coating at least once a year. This protects the hull against excess barnacle and weed growth, which can rob your craft of speed and fuel efficiency. Of course, this task requires that the boat be hauled out of the water, which, in turn, means that your marina must have a travel-lift, marine railway, or crane to do the job. Boaters who berth at marinas without these facilities must make arrangements with an independent boatyard to perform the necessary service work. While this is a normal and acceptable practice, it does require the boat owner to make arrangements for delivering his boat to the yard and then returning the craft to its home slip. Sometimes particularly helpful yards will come and get the boat for you and then deliver it to your marina when the job is completed. This is not always the case, however. Contrast this procedure with simply picking up the phone and telling your marina to have the boat hauled and the bottom painted by a mutually-agreed-upon date. The bottom line is, if you can find a marina with its own haul-out and bottom painting services, it is a big plus in that facility's favor.

Some marinas are very much in the service business, while others have just enough facilities to attract potential dockage patrons. To determine which category your prospective marina falls under, seek out the following information:

1. Is there one service technician or several on staff at the marina?

2. Does the facility have a marine railway, travel-lift, or crane? If so, does it appear to be in regular use or the relic of bygone days?

3. Does the marina maintain a large, well-stocked workshop or just a small tool shed? (Incidentally, don't be put off by any seeming disorder in a marina tool shop. I have yet to see a "neat" facility of this type at a boatyard.)

Talk to the marina manager or dockmaster, at length if possible, about service. Find out what relationships he has with independent professionals who can perform the necessary services that the marina's own personnel can't handle. After observing the facilities and picking the manager's brain, ask yourself whether this marina is really serious about repair work or whether it is primarily a dockage facility. As a first-time owner of a larger power boat, you will be much happier in a service-oriented marina. Only later, after you have established your own working relationships with several independent service technicians, should you consider a "dockage only" marina.

Security

Be sure to make a detailed inquiry about security arrangements at your prospective marina. It is an incredibly frustrating moment to arrive at your craft, looking forward to a leisurely weekend, only to find some of your valuable equipment has been stolen. The best insurance against such theft is to berth your boat in a marina that has adequate security procedures.

The most secure marinas have a "live-in" owner or dockmaster. With such an arrangement, you can be certain the docks will be checked at regular intervals during the nighttime hours. Thieves and vandals are very wary of facilities where they might be unexpectedly interrupted. If the owner does not live on the premises, is there an all-night security guard or someone who at least checks the boats on a regular basis? If no one is responsible for nighttime security, it is an invitation for theft.

There is at least one exception to the rule described above. At my marina, no one lives on the premises and there is not a regular security guard, but there is *never* a problem with theft. Why, you may ask? Our marina is a family operation. The owner and his bevy of sons check the docks on a hit-or-miss basis. However, it is *well known* that they all carry stainless-steel .44 magnum handguns and are not afraid to use them. It is understandable why potential thieves have given their facility a very wide berth.

Fuel

For convenience and practicality, your prospective marina should offer a fueling dock with either gasoline or diesel fuel, depending on your craft's requirements. Ideally, the dock should be as sheltered as possible and situated for easy mooring and casting off. Be sure to inquire about the fuel pier's hours of operation. It's always best if the facility is manned by the marina personnel from dawn to dusk. More restrictive hours can sometimes necessitate changing a day's cruising plans.

Ship's Store

The truly "full-service" marina maintains a well-stocked ship's and grocery (convenience) store. The stock should include a wide assortment of marine parts and equipment as well as basic food items. While such a store is not absolutely necessary, it is undeniably convenient. I cannot tell you how many times I have been working in the bilge of my boat, only to discover that I need one or two stainless steel screws. Of course, I have every other size that I might ever need, but not the size this particular job requires. It is wonderful to just trip a few steps up to the marina store, snatch what I need, and be back to work in less than five minutes. Contrast this easy procedure with having to jump in your car, drive to the hardware store, and then spend thirty minutes trying unsuccessfully to clean off the grease on your car seat.

On-Site Restaurant

Many otherwise first-rate marinas do not have a restaurant on the premises. However, while not a real necessity, there are times when the convenience of having a good spot to dine immediately at hand is worth its weight in gold. After a hard day polishing and waxing the fiberglass or working in the bilge, it's a great feeling to simply wash up and then walk a few paces to a familiar restaurant with good food. Just be sure to sample the offerings *before* you count the restaurant in the plus column.

BOATING MEMBERSHIP ORGANIZATIONS

Within the past decade several large boating membership organizations have sprung up in the United States. As these groups have grown, so have the many services they offer to their members. The best of these groups now feature boating equipment, nautical books, and government charts at *substantial* savings. Best of all, these products usually receive extensive testing before they are offered to members. Boaters ordering from these reliable organizations can be assured of receiving the best products available.

In addition to the equipment offerings, members can voluntarily participate in such programs as group marine, life and accident insurance, boat and personal loans, consumer protection agencies, and federal documentation services. As is the case with marine equipment, members can save a lot of money by cashing in on the group's huge buying power, particularly in the field of marine insurance.

Some of these organizations even have monthly newsletters that apprise you of recent political and product developments in the boating field. There is often a listing of used boats for sale by other members.

Probably the best-known boating membership group at the present time is Boat Owners Association of the United States (usually abbreviated Boat/US), headquartered in Alexandria, Virginia. This organization, of which I am a proud member, offers all of the services outlined above, and more. It is a great source of information, equipment, and essential services for new boat owners.

If by now you have detected a certain rampant enthusiasm on this writer's part for boating membership organizations, then you are indeed on the right track. I suggest assigning top priority to contacting and joining one of these groups after (or maybe even before) you have purchased your first larger power boat. Then, while awaiting delivery of your new craft, you can order necessary equipment and charts. By all accounts, *be sure* to get a quote on marine insurance from the membership organization before committing yourself with any other insurance carrier!

BOATING EDUCATION

It always shocks me how many new boat owners imagine that merely purchasing a larger vessel somehow instantly qualifies them to be a knowledgeable pilot. Nothing could be further from the truth. Everyone should have a working knowledge of coastal navigation and basic piloting techniques *before leaving the dock.* A great time to acquire this basic boater's education is now, while you are awaiting delivery or outfitting your new craft.

Many first-time owners of larger power craft who have previously owned smaller boats believe their past experience with an outboard

"We tried waving, yelling, and even calling the boat on the VHF, but all to no avail."

or I/O will stand them in good stead now. In a word or two, forget it! To take only one instance, many smaller boats operate almost exclusively in large lakes or reservoirs. Once you are over fifty yards from the shoreline in these sorts of waters, there is generally plenty of depth for safe boating. Coastal waters are *very* different. There are shoals and sandbars, sometimes miles from shore, waiting to trap the unwary navigator.

Consider the following real-life story. Some ten years ago the "first-rate, first mate" and I were piloting our small boat in a remote section of North Carolina coastal waters adjacent to a body of land known as Harkers Island. Near the western tip of the island, there is one spot where the otherwise broad channel narrows down to a funnel spout, only fifty feet in width. Anyone who bothered to look at a chart of these waters and knew how to read it, would see this danger section clearly noted. As our craft neared the mid-point of the narrow channel, we observed a thirty-four-foot power cruiser bearing down on the shallows north of us at breakneck speed. We tried waving, yelling, and even calling the boat on the VHF, but all to no avail. The doomed craft hit the sandbar at full speed. We eased our boat over onto the shoal and waded across the sand to render what aid we could. Fortunately, no one was injured. However, the grounding completely stripped away both rudders, props, struts, and propeller shafts. The boat was so hard aground that the Coast Guard finally had to dispatch a forty-three-foot vessel three days later to tow it off the bottom. Repairs ran in the five- to six-thousand-dollar range.

After meeting the captain, we learned that he had just purchased his vessel the preceding weekend. He had never taken any boating courses but had operated an outboard on a lake near his home for many years. He made the fatal assumption that since he was almost half a mile from the shoreline, the water was plenty deep. That turned out to be a very expensive assumption.

Let this story be a word to the wise. If you have not had any previous training in coastal navigation and piloting, you need it. If you took a safe boating course some years ago, it might be a good idea to review what you learned. In the following discussion, we will explore some of the nautical skills you need to know and the best means to acquire a good marine education.

Piloting

Piloting is a broad nautical term that refers to operating your vessel in a safe manner. Piloting skills can range from docking techniques to the "rules of the road." These "rules" are internationally recognized strictures to avoid collision. They specify which vessel is to give way in a crossing situation, when meeting, or when one boats overtakes another. Additionally, you need to know about aids to navigation (markers), good anchoring techniques, and required safety equipment. Students learn how to calculate an estimated time of arrival and speed made good. A good piloting course will also give you a working knowledge of boat handling in various conditions, particularly foul weather. A smattering of first aid would also be a good idea. The list is quite long. Take heart; in this chapter you will learn how to acquire all the necessary knowledge.

Navigation in All Its Forms

There are three basic types of navigation practiced by modern boaters. Of these three varieties, coastal, electronic, and celestial, you will be most concerned with the coastal and electronic ilk. Students of coastal navigation learn how to read a chart and recognize the meaning of the various colors and symbols that appear on this cartographical aid. You will also learn to chart a compass course between two points and how to measure the distance between your departure and destination. A qualified coastal navigator knows how to recognize aids to navigation on the water and what the various shapes, colors, and lighting characteristics of these sentinels have to tell about channel conditions. In short, you, as a student of coastal navigation, will learn to tell where you are and where you are going by the use of charts, compass, navigational aids, and various other tools. Boaters lacking this absolutely essential knowledge are asking for trouble by merely untying their dock lines!

Electronic navigation has undergone an astonishing revolution during the past several years. With such modern wizardry as GPS, laptop computers, color Radar, synthesized VHF radio, SSB radio, and video depth sounders, the flybridge of a well-outfitted power cruiser often seems reminiscent of a *Star Wars* movie set. Fortunately, except for the basic VHF and depth sounder, you need not acquire the necessary skills for all this equipment until after your budget allows you to purchase the various devices. A good, basic boating course, such as those described below, will give you an introduction to electronic navigation. There will probably be just enough information to whet your appetite. For a more complete discussion of modern electronic navigational equipment, see Chapter 4, "Practical Accessories."

Celestial navigation is least important to the new power boat owner. In fact, you may never need to learn this ancient science. This art form (and that is exactly what it is) is normally employed only by sailors who are engaged in offshore passage-making. Just so you can amaze your friends at parties, here is a quick discussion of this somewhat obscure form of plotting your position. Celestial navigation involves the use of a sextant. This rather exotic-looking instrument simply measures the angle of rise between a particular celestial body, such as the sun, and the horizon. Then with an exact reading of the time, you can enter some very complicated tables and, if you are lucky, eventually extrapolate a line of position. This process is known as "sight reduction." During what is called, "local apparent noon" you can, theoretically, plot your exact position anywhere on the globe. Since the early 1980s, solar-powered celestial calculators have vastly simplified the process of sight reduction, but it is still not for the faint of heart.

United States Power Squadron

So, now you know what you need to know. Well, you may be wondering, "How do I acquire all this knowledge?" Fortunately, there are two national boating organizations, a number of correspondence courses, and untold nautical books to help you along the way. Perhaps the best-known source of basic piloting and navigational skills is the free public boating course offered by the United States Power Squadron. This worthy organization is comprised of cruisers who are very serious about safe and knowledgeable boating. Some Power Squadron members spend years acquiring various degrees in advanced navigation, boat handling, and mechanical repairs. Fortunately, you need not go this far at first. In fact, you do not even need to join the USPS to take the basic boating course.

The USPS public boating safety course is offered at least twice a year in most larger cities and towns across the USA. There are usually announcements in the local papers publicizing the event. Try calling the outdoor editor at your local paper. He or she may well be able to direct you to a Power Squadron member. They will, most likely, know the date of the next offering. The course is taught during the evening hours, usually one night a week for twelve weeks.

The USPS course is *great!* It is undoubtedly the single best overview of piloting and coastal navigation that I have ever encountered. The text is thorough, complete, and precise, and the classroom instruction is exemplary. By the way, while the course itself is offered without charge, you will need to purchase some basic navigation tools such as a plotter and divider, and there is a small charge for the instruction manual. All this gear is offered by the squadron in a quality kit at very reasonable prices. There is a tough exam at the end of the course. Those who graduate (and believe me this is no "give me") receive an attractive certificate. Most marine insurance carriers offer a significant saving for those who can show that they have passed the Power Squadron or Coast Guard Auxiliary course of instruction. I highly recommend the USPS public boating course to my fellow cruisers. You cannot go wrong by using this instruction as your basis of boating knowledge.

U.S. Coast Guard Auxiliary

The United States Coast Guard Auxiliary is an organization of private citizens mandated by Congress to aid the Coast Guard professionals. In many ways similar to the USPS, this association also offers a free boating course to the public. Personally, I have always perceived the USCGA program as being a bit more oriented to lake-type recreational boating than its USPS counterpart. However, there is no denying the validity of the USCGA course of study. Millions of boaters have taken this course over the years, and, as they saying goes, all those cruisers can't be wrong.

Local newspapers are also used as information outlets for the USCGA boating course. Again, try contacting the outdoors editor at your local daily newspaper to get a line on a member of the nearest USCGA chapter.

The USCGA also performs one other notable service to pleasure boaters that should be mentioned in passing. Often, members of this fine organization will donate their time on the weekends to give voluntary inspections of pleasure craft. These most worthwhile examinations check for proper safety equipment and the general operating condition of the vessel. It's a lot better to have a member of the auxiliary point out the absence of a required piece of safety equipment than to have an officer of the U.S. Coast Guard issue you a costly citation. If an opportunity presents itself to have your new vessel inspected by the USCGA, I urge you to take advantage of this valuable service.

Correspondence Courses

If you happen to live in a region where neither the Power Squadron nor Coast Guard Auxiliary courses are readily available, piloting and coastal navigation correspondence courses are a good alternative. I have found these sorts of instruction to be well planned and quite valuable. Unfortunately, while all the courses with which I am familiar offer individualized help by mail, usually through a series of chapter-length exams, this instructional method does lack that classroom give-and-take that is such a valuable part of the USPS and USCGA courses of study described above.

Correspondence studies can also be used as a valuable supplement to the USPS or USCGA courses. Most marine correspondence companies offer advanced courses that go far beyond the skills taught in either of the two classroom sessions.

If either the USPS or USCGA courses of instruction are available in your area, I would suggest these studies first. Then, you can look at the descriptions of various correspondence courses and decide whether you want to sharpen your skills further. If, on the other hand, you can't take one of the classroom sessions, then a correspondence course is your next best bet.

Nautical Books and Magazines

There are many nautical books and magazines that cover every aspect of piloting, navigation, and maintenance. While there are a few volumes among this list that may as well be written in Greek, most are valuable sources of nautical knowledge.

Now, far be it from me to put down nautical books and publications. After all, that's how "yours truly" earns his livelihood. However,

I would not be fair to my readers if I did not point out a few shortcomings of this type of instruction *for first-time power cruisers*.

Obviously, books and magazines lack the one-on-one instruction available in the classroom and even the individualized help that comes with most correspondence courses. Thus, your nautical studies are totally in your own hands. If you don't understand something in the text, there is no one ready at hand to ask for an explanation. On the other hand, the best nautical books offer specialized training in a particular set of skills. This "narrow and deep" approach can be a great adjunct to your knowledge in a particular portion of nautical lore.

I would again suggest that you first take either a classroom (preferably) or correspondence course to serve as a base reference of nautical knowledge, and then begin to supplement your skills with the many fine books and magazines that are available. As time passes and your own store of nautical lore grows, the individualized instruction of a classroom or a correspondence course will become much less important. When your nautical education reaches this point, you will find books and magazines written from the nautical point of view to be increasingly important.

BOAT INSURANCE

First-time cruisers who have never before priced marine insurance are in for quite a shock. If you expect to find premiums similar to your homeowners policy, let me be the first to offer my condolences. Quite simply, boat insurance is *much* costlier than its shoreside counterpart. Insurance companies justify this wide disparity in premiums by pointing to the increased risk involved in boating. This may be true, but I for one think marine insurance rates are entirely too high and only wish there was a wider forum in which I could propound my views.

After that mild word of protest, it can only be noted that most boat owners *should* have their vessels completely insured. If you finance your boat, your creditor will insist that you insure the vessel up to the amount of the loan. Even if you own your boat outright, the danger of hurricanes (particularly on the Atlantic and Gulf coasts) and other potentially expensive catastrophes (such as a hose slipping off a thru-hull fitting, leading to a premature watery grave for your "pride and joy"), dictate that most thoughtful owners will opt for full insurance. Captains who choose to insure their boat should acquire the necessary coverage before taking delivery on their vessel, or immediately thereafter. That leaves the questions of what type of insurance and from whom you should purchase your coverage.

Seasoned boaters will tell you, quite truthfully, that there is only one wise choice in marine insurance. No matter what some hot-shot salesman tries to tell you, the only coverage you should consider is "All-Risk Hull Insurance." Basically, this type of policy covers just about every catastrophic event that could befall your boat, whether it's your fault or not. Of course, in spite of the "all" in this coverage's name, there are exceptions, and you should take the time to read the fine print in your policy to determine just what is not covered. For example, most of the contracts with which I am familiar do not cover damage from ice. In northerly climes, spring ice flows can be a real hazard, and this exclusion would certainly be a concern for boaters on these waters. Captains south of Norfolk, Virginia, on the other hand, can be cavalier about such an exception. If the exclusions seem reasonable or not particularly pertinent to your situation, the policy is probably right for you. If not, keep looking.

Coupled with "All-Risk Hull Coverage" insurance companies, almost without exception, include liability and medical payment coverage. This is only as it should be. In fact, in a society that seems obsessed with legal litigation, the more liability coverage your policy carries, the better. If the budget allows, you might consider asking for more liability coverage than is normally offered for your policy. Often, for just a few dollars more, you can receive greatly expanded liability protection.

Some policies also include protection for personal injury. This feature supplements your personal health insurance and is a valuable addition to your coverage. If your policy does not include this feature, you may want to purchase an additional accident policy. While, with care, boating is perfectly safe, the possibility of injury does exist. The few extra dollars for accident insurance could really pay off if the unexpected should happen.

Finally, you must decide from whom you should purchase your marine insurance. This choice is not nearly so straightforward as deciding what type of coverage you should obtain. You will be faced with three basic choices, all of which have merits and disadvantages.

First, you might choose to acquire your coverage through a local, independent insurance agency. These firms can usually be depended upon for superior, personalized service. When filing a claim, the advantages of having your agent available locally to help with the necessary paperwork is not something to be taken lightly. Unfortunately, the premiums paid through a local agent are undoubtedly higher than those of the alternate choices. You must decide for yourself whether this increased cost is offset by the advantages of local, personalized service. For my money, if the differences in premium rates are not too great, then I would pick the local agent every time.

Insurance companies that specialize in marine coverage are a second option for you to consider. Pick up any boating magazine and leaf through the advertisements. Unless the sun failed to rise this morning, you will discover any number of ads for these specialized firms. The advantages and drawbacks of this sort of marine insurance are exactly the opposite of the good and bad aspects of local agent coverage. Premiums through marine insurance companies will almost always be less expensive. However, when it comes time to file a claim, you must call a toll-free number. The voice on the other end is the only connection with your coverage. While many marine insurance companies make sincere and dedicated efforts to provide their clients with the best service, there are still stories of claims that take months and months to process. If you should decide to purchase a policy from a marine insurance company, I suggest asking around at local marinas and boat dealers for a recommendation. If you find other boaters who have had a good experience with a particular company, it's a good bet you will have the same good luck.

Finally, there is a third option that may offer some of the best of both worlds. Boating membership organizations, as previously described in this chapter, offer their members group plan marine insurance. Premiums for these policies are often *even lower than those available through companies specializing in marine insurance.* The group buying power of the membership organization allows the association to negotiate superior rates with private insurance companies.

One word of caution: be sure to read the fine print of these boating organization policies. Recently, it has come to this writer's attention that some of these policies are not as all inclusive as they might at first appear. *Be sure* to read the fine print!

ORDERING EQUIPMENT

If you've already picked out a marina, taken a boating course, read a few good cruising books, joined a membership organization, acquired the right insurance, and are still awaiting delivery of your new craft, there is still one thing you can do to relieve the painful anticipation. I know of nothing that relieves the "boating blues" better than to order nautical equipment. In the next chapter we will examine the nautical gear that every boat should have aboard before leaving the dock. After reading this section, you might consider ordering some of the gear that is not being included with your boat as standard (or add-on) equipment. Then, when your new boat does arrive, you'll be ready!

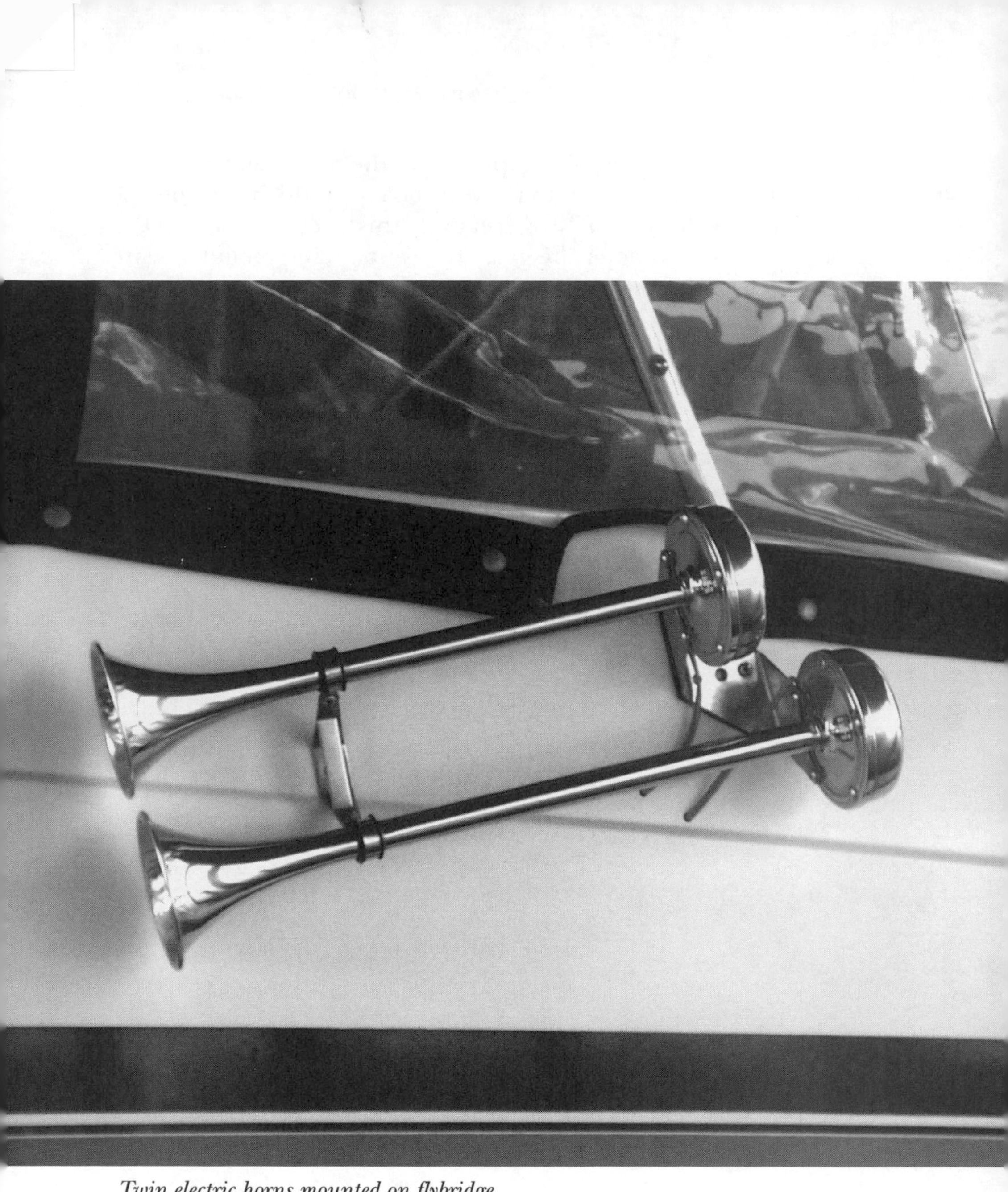

Twin electric horns mounted on flybridge.

CHAPTER 3

Outfitting Your New Craft

EVERY BOAT SHOULD HAVE certain pieces of nautical equipment aboard before ever leaving the dock. Some of this gear is required by Coast Guard regulations while other paraphernalia is demanded by simple common sense. In either case, responsible new captains must acquire, and in some cases install, this necessary equipment before beginning their first cruise. This chapter will cover this essential ordinance in detail. Optional gear that an owner may consider, but which is not absolutely necessary for safe boating, will be discussed in Chapter 4.

DOCKING EQUIPMENT

Clearly, no boat can take to the water without docking equipment. It's about as basic as you can get. After all, without the necessary lines, the only alternative is to just let your new vessel float away. Some new boats and practically every used craft will come equipped with at least a portion of the required docking gear. Even so, you will want to review the items listed below to be sure that your boat is equipped with everything that might be required.

Docklines, Lines, and Rope

Docklines are not just rope. They are specialized lines that have been prepared specially for docking purposes. One end is braided into a large eye that can slip over a piling or be used as a ready-made slip knot to fit around a post that is too tall or large for the eye. The opposite end is carefully "whipped" to avoid any unraveling of the rope.

Whipping is an old nautical art. In days gone-by, it was accomplished by winding numerous turns of strong thread around the rope end and then tying it off. With modern nylon and Dacron line, a candle or match can usually accomplish the same job. In this process, the end of the rope is actually melted by the flame. The liquid nylon or Dacron hardens, thereby holding the various rope strands together. Practice with a few small pieces of nylon rope and you will soon be an expert at modern whipping. With large diameter rope, the flame-melting process is sometimes not sufficient to keep the rope ends together. In such cases, you can take a shot at old-style whipping, or wrap plastic electrical tape around the ends.

Most boaters, particularly those new to the sport, will want to buy pre-made docklines. While you could probably whip the straight end yourself, braiding the loops (or eyes) is a job better left to machines and experts.

A set of pre-made dock lines usually consists of four heavy-gauge lines with eyes and one smaller size "spring line." The four larger ropes are used for mooring the boat at both corners of the stern and on either side of the bow. In some docking arrangements, the stern and bow lines cannot prevent the boat from sliding too far forward or backward. Spring lines are used in this instance to restrain the fore and aft motion of the boat. (Please see Chapter 6 for a complete discussion of docking techniques.)

This seems like a good time for a general discussion of "rope" and "line." Many new captains wonder about the difference between these two terms. They are something of an artificial distinction. When you buy rope off a coil in the store, it's called rope. When the rope is put to use on a boat, then it becomes line.

Modern nautical rope is usually made from either nylon or Dacron. Both of these synthetic materials are strong and durable but they differ in their flexibility. Nylon stretches quite a bit. This makes it ideal for jobs that require shock absorption. Anchoring lines (or rode) are a good example of this use. On a windy night with the boat swinging to and fro, an anchor rode needs all the shock absorbency it can get. Nylon lines are also good for towing vessels, *when they are free to move.*

Dacron is almost as strong as nylon, but it has very little flex. Dacron is the ideal rope material when trying to tow a grounded vehicle off the bottom. It is also heavily used by our sailing brethren. In a heavy pull, such as that encountered when freeing a grounded

Two types of line—braid on braid is multicolored and nylon twist is white.

vessel, cleats, binding stanchions, and other deck hardware have been known to pull completely free. The slingshot effect created by stretchable nylon rope can make the errant cleat a lethal missile.

Most cruisers use nylon rope for docking and anchor lines while keeping a heavy-gauge Dacron line aboard for hauling purposes. This is a good, sound boating plan.

Nylon and Dacron rope is available in both three-strand twist and braid-on-braid style. The three-strand twist, as its name implies, is composed of three smaller nylon fiber ropes twisted tightly together to form a larger diameter line. Braid-on-braid is many smaller strands braided together. This produces a much smoother rope, which some claim to be more flexible and easier on the hands. You will discover that many power boaters discount these claims and opt for the three-strand twist variety.

Bigger boats require stronger, larger diameter dock lines, while smaller vessels can make do with smaller rope. The following chart gives a good rule of thumb for boat size vs. rope diameter using *nylon* docking lines. These recommendations are not guaranteed to hold

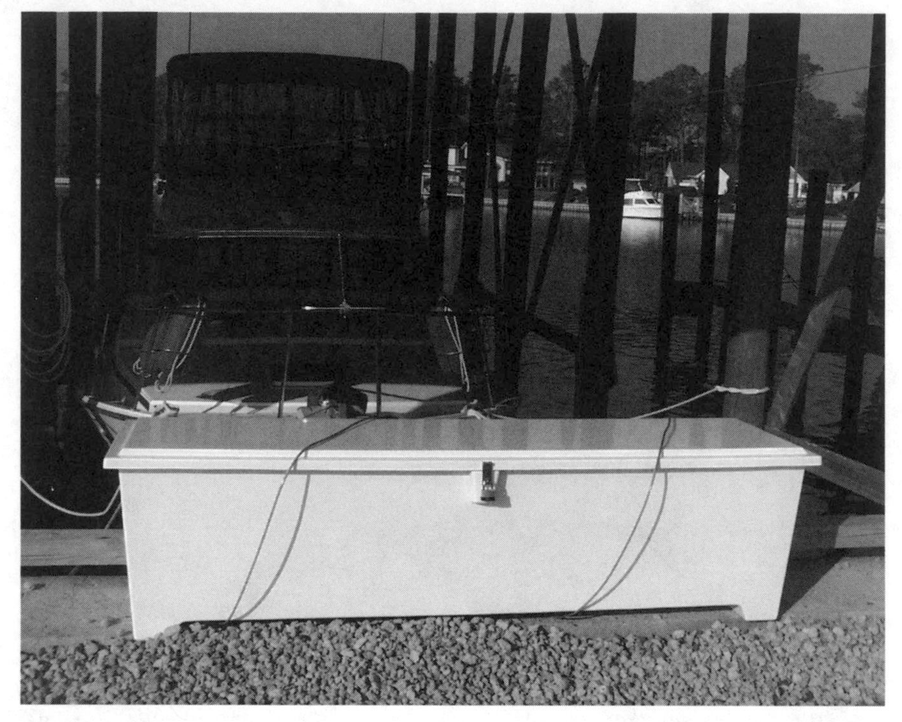

Dock box.

up in a hurricane or whole gale. In really nasty weather, you will want to use heavier-gauge lines.

Boat Size	*Recommended diameter nylon line*
25' to 30'	3/8"
30' to 35'	1/2"
35' to 45'	5/8"
Over 45'	3/4"

Two other rope materials are sometimes seen around boatyards and marinas. Old-style manila and modern polypropylene line should be avoided by captains of larger power craft. Manila rope is made from natural materials and was the only line available before modern synthetics appeared. While there is really nothing wrong with this type of line, it is not as strong as nylon or Dacron, it deteriorates faster, and is almost as expensive. Manila is now seen less and less around boating supply stores.

Polypropylene or plastic rope should *never* be used to moor or anchor larger vessels. This type of line is often utilized in smaller craft, particularly as ski ropes. It is ideal for this purpose as it floats in the water and is less likely to foul outboard or I/O props. The line is usually bright yellow, though other equally vibrant colors are employed from time to time. Polypropylene rope is *much* weaker than any other variety of line discussed above. A ½"-diameter polypropylene line used to moor a large vessel can part in a moderate wind. Around marinas there is a standing joke about the inexperience of a boater who uses yellow line.

Fenders

Docking fenders are soft, cylindrical-shaped devices designed to protect a boat from scraping against pilings or docks. They are strung either horizontally or vertically along the side of a boat at a point where the hull is likely to rub against a piling or seawall. Most fenders have a white vinyl exterior and are filled with either soft synthetic rubber or slightly compressed air. Whatever they are covered by or filled with, fenders must be large enough to protect your vessel in spite of any curvature in the boat's hull. They must also be tied securely at the point of contact to be effective. Ideally, fenders should be secured to the boat. This procedure will allow the fender to rise and fall on the tide along with the boat. Unfortunately, power boats are notorious for a lack of belaying points from which to tie fender lines. Consequently, it is sometimes necessary to secure a fender to a piling. You must then move it periodically as the water level changes.

Fenders come in a variety of shapes and sizes. Some have holes on each end to tie securing lines, while another popular variety has a hole through the center. Small-gauge rope is passed through this hole and a knot is then placed at either end (larger than the passage hole) so the line will stay put. In looking through catalogs, you may find charts that recommend certain size fenders for certain length boats. In my opinion, these recommended sizes are too small.

When we began boating I purchased four 12"-by-4" fenders, thinking they would certainly be large enough for a thirty-one-foot vessel. After mooring to a lock wall for the first time, I consigned those fenders to the garbage heap. With the curve in our bow, it was necessary to string the fenders every few feet for adequate protection. Inevitably, one would not be in the right place and excessive chafe was the less than ideal result. Now, we cruise with two very large, hole-in-the-middle fenders. I have never had occasion to question

Fenders mounted in twin fender baskets; plow anchor mounted on bow pulpit with electric windlass.

this choice. I recommend oversize fenders, no matter what your size craft may be.

Fender boards are vinyl-covered planks that are placed in front of two fenders to serve as extra protection between the boat and pilings. This arrangement is more commonly observed on sailcraft as these sorts of vessels have numerous tie-offs available. Powerboats do not often have enough ready cleats to conveniently secure two fenders and a fender board at one location alongside the hull. However, if you are docked on a long-term basis at a face dock, rather than a slip, you might want to consider a fender board. Face docks greatly add to the possibility of chafe, and to protect your boat, it just might be worth the trouble to find or install enough cleats and tie-offs to make use of a fender board.

Recognizing the difficulty in securing fenders to power craft, several nautical supply houses have begun manufacturing various forms of fender hooks. Some of these handy tie-offs are designed to attach to bow rails, while others are permanently mounted in the fiberglass.

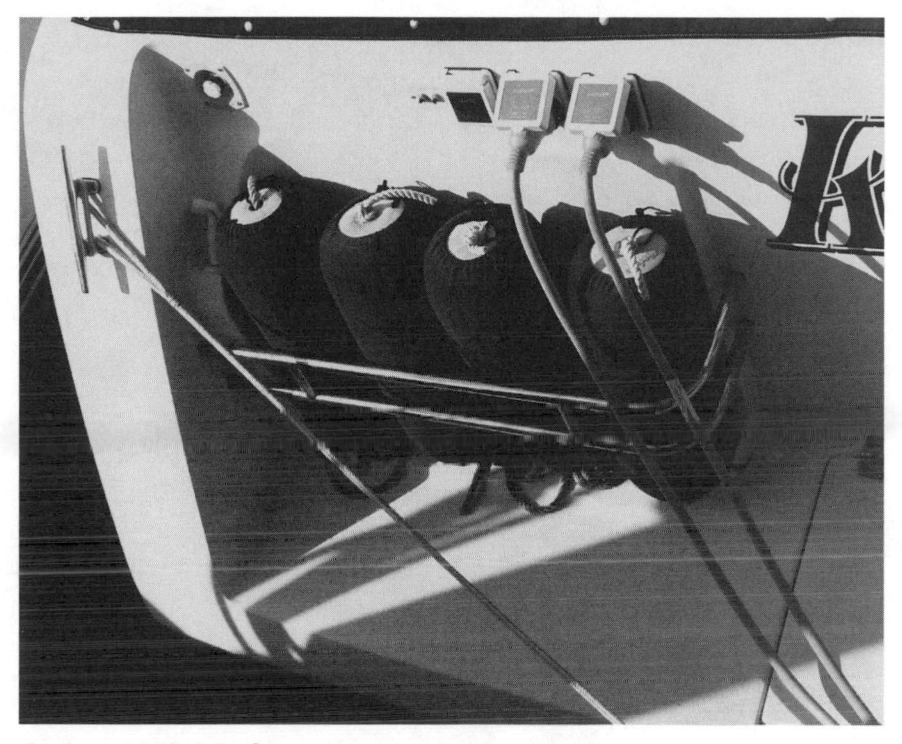

Fenders with cloth fender covers mounted on boat's stern.

If you are in need of additional tie-offs, these small, inexpensive devices can be lifesavers.

Storing fenders in a convenient, accessible location was a real problem until just a few years ago. During our early cruises we simply laid them in the cockpit where they proceeded to roll this way and that during rough weather. Later I tried storing them in one of the V-berth lockers. While we finally squeezed them in, it took about ten minutes to extract the fenders when it came time to dock. That was an unacceptable situation, so it was back to the cockpit. Fortunately for us power boaters, somebody came up with the idea of fender baskets. While not an essential piece of equipment, these handy receptacles allow you to conveniently store your fenders in a readily accessible location.

Fender baskets are cylindrical mesh containers with an open upper end. The mesh is made from either stainless steel or reinforced plastic. This assembly is bolted to the bow rail and the fenders are inserted from the top end. Boaters with a flair for style usually tilt their fender baskets at the same angle as the bow rail stanchions. The

Telescoping boat hook.

fenders are secure and ready at hand for any docking emergency. It's one of the most attractive storage ideas imaginable for those bulky, but necessary pieces of docking equipment. While the plastic variety is less expensive, the stainless steel models last indefinitely. Neither model is particularly cheap, but if you can fit this novel accessory in your boating budget, it is highly recommended.

Over the years I have observed many boaters installing cloth covers on their fenders. This seems to be a trend in modern power boating. The more expensive models are made from acrylic while the less costly variety is composed of cotton terry cloth. In theory, these covers will prevent marring and staining of the fender surface by creosote-coated pilings and barnacle-encrusted lock walls. In practice, the covers are usually removed when the fender is in use. It's not difficult to imagine the risk of tearing fabric while the fender is rubbed back and forth against a piling. Cosmetically speaking, fender covers look great while underway with the fenders stowed securely in their basket along the bow rail. If you are interested in spiffing up your craft, I suggest pricing acrylic covers and then consulting your budget.

Boat Hooks

Boat hooks are composed of a pole with a hook attached to the end. Modern models feature a telescoping inner shaft with a vinyl-tipped hook. Fully equipped boats will also have a fixed boat hook for those rare occasions when the telescoping pole fails to operate properly. Even the most experienced captain will occasionally miss the pier a bit when docking. If the first mate has a telescoping boat hook ready to hand, it is often a simple matter to grab onto the dock and pull the boat up to the pier. Boat hooks are also very handy for grabbing dock lines from a piling that is just out of reach. Finally, they are also quite useful for retrieving the hat that just blew overboard off your head. Succinctly, you shouldn't leave the dock without one.

GROUND TACKLE

The nautical term, "ground tackle" refers to anchors (also called hooks) and all the necessary adjuncts that go with them such as anchor lines, anchor chains, chocks, and deck pipes. First-time boaters who plan to dock exclusively at marinas may wonder why they need a quality ground tackle system. The question will be answered the first time an engine fails and it becomes necessary throw out the hook to prevent drifting towards a sandbar.

It is also a nautical truism that "anchoring off" while cruising can lead to some of the most unforgettable times any captain and crew can experience. I well remember one research trip when I was compiling information for my North Carolina cruising guide. We had spent the afternoon exploring the beautifully undeveloped Bay River. As evening approached we carefully maneuvered into a small cove at Chapel Creek. The shoreline was lined with lush greenery, completely unbroken by human development. As night came on, the array of stars we could see in the clear coastal air was something you had to experience to understand. After a hearty dinner of broiled steaks, mashed potatoes, and fried squash, Bud, my ace research assistant, hauled out his portable radio and tuned in the Yankees baseball game while I retired to the flybridge and contemplated the state of the heavens. As long as I go "a-cruising," I will never forget that night of watching all those stars with the sound of Yankees baseball in the background. With planning and a bit of meteorological cooperation, you too can look forward to many such experiences while swinging tranquilly on the hook. However, without the proper ground tackle, this whole scenario is out the proverbial window.

Danforth-style anchor mounted on chocks.

Some new boats are factory-equipped with one anchor, an anchor line, a chock, and a deck pipe. Purchasers of used craft may find all the necessary ground tackle already aboard. *Every boat should have two functioning anchors and related ground tackle before leaving the dock.*

Why two anchors, you might ask? There are many reasons. In an anchorage with restricted swinging room you may need to put out two anchors at 180 degrees from each other. This is known as a Bahamian moor (see Chapter 6). If you should be caught out in high winds, you might well decide to put out both anchors for extra holding power. Sometimes an anchor becomes stuck on the bottom and it simply can't be retrieved, even by employing the power of your engines. If you are not inclined to dive over the side to retrieve the hook, your only alternative is cutting it loose. Without a second anchor, there will be no functioning ground tackle aboard.

Many captains choose to carry two, sometimes three different size anchors. The smaller (and lighter) anchor is often euphemistically known as the "lunch hook." This unit is perfect in good weather for a quick lunch stop or an afternoon exploring the shoreline. You also

Danforth-style anchor mounted on bow pulpit.

need a larger, heavier, working anchor that you can depend upon to hold in most any weather short of a full gale. Finally, some long-range cruisers also include a so-called storm anchor. This heavy-gauge hook is used in really foul weather as an added measure of security.

Most power boaters will only need a lunch hook and working anchor. Some boaters prefer to have two working hooks. As you cruise farther from your home base a heavy weather (storm) anchor becomes more of a consideration, but most power craft captains will probably want to head for the nearest protected marina if high wind and waves are in the forecast.

If it becomes necessary to add to or replace your ground tackle, there are a number of options that you must select from when purchasing all this essential gear.

Anchor Types

First, of course, you have to choose what type and size anchor(s) to purchase. From a bewildering selection of designs and variations, there are two, possibly three, basic varieties of anchors that modern power boaters may consider. The most popular anchor style, by far, for power craft is the Danforth. This design features two large triangular "flukes" between a movable neck. Two metal plates known as a crown sit between the flukes behind the base of the neck. The

Plow anchor mounted on bow pulpit.

anchor line is attached to the far end of the neck. When pressure is applied from the line, the angle of the crown forces the flukes to dig into the bottom.

Danforth anchors are great for sandy bottoms and acceptable in heavy mud. They are less effective in heavily vegetated bottoms and rocky strata. Even with these limitations, the vast majority of power craft confine their ground tackle to this anchor design.

It should also be noted that Danforths are easily stowed on deck in "anchor chocks" and are relatively easy to handle when anchoring. Many newer models of power craft in the 30- to 45-foot range now come with Danforth anchors mounted in a slot on the bow pulpit. This clever design makes for much simplified anchoring. The easy storage of this type of hook is in marked contrast to the next design we will discuss.

CQR or Plow anchors are designed for strength. The head of the anchor looks exactly like a miniature version of a plow. The head is attached to a movable neck. As pressured is applied from the anchor line, the plow digs deeper and deeper into the bottom strata. This hook style is ideal for any bottom except a very rocky strata.

In spite of the CQR's strength, this anchor design is usually seen aboard sailcraft rather than power boats. The plow is difficult to stow properly. It does not lend itself to deck chocks. Sailors often have a slot cut out of their bow pulpit and the anchor is left hanging by its line, ready to be dropped. This arrangement is sometimes seen on trawlers as well. Due to the storage problem, as much as any other factor, most (though not all) power captains choose the traditional Danforth design and leave the CQR to their sailing brethren.

Finally, boaters may come into contact with a third type of anchor known as the "mushroom." As its name implies this design looks like nothing so much as an inverted mushroom. This anchor is not really a hook. It depends more on its weight to hold a boat secure rather than any "digging in" effect. Mushroom anchors are often used for permanent moorings. If you have ever visited a seaport and seen mooring buoys clustered in a particular area, many of those markers were undoubtedly secured to mushroom anchors.

Mushrooms are fine if the fickle wind does not become too enthusiastic. In heavy blows, boats tied to mushroom anchors have been known to be pulled off station (known as "dragging anchor").

Very few boaters actually carry a mushroom anchor aboard. You should be familiar with the design, however, in case you ever encounter it while cruising.

Size, Weight, and Holding Power

Many new boaters try to buy the proper anchor for their size craft based on the weight and size of the hook. While this would, at first, seem the obvious strategy, it is fatally flawed. Variations in the design and size of the anchor flukes or plow, as well as the particular material from which the anchor is constructed, can actually give a smaller, lighter hook more holding power than a heavier unit. For this reason, anchors are now rated for "holding power" in pounds. Below you will find a chart that represents the *average* holding power necessary to secure a certain length boat in winds up to twenty knots. In stronger gusts, you may need even more:

Boat Length	*Holding Power Required*
25' to 30'	950 lb.
30' to 34'	1,300 lb.
34' to 38'	1,600 lb.
38' to 44'	2,000 lb.
44' to 54'	3,000 lb.

Consult the holding power of your prospective anchor as specified by the manufacturer, equate it with your length vessel, and you should come up with the proper hook. If you choose to purchase a lunch hook as one of your anchors, you can decrease the holding power specified in the chart above by 25 percent.

Anchor Chains

All too many owners simply shackle their anchor lines to the hook and assume (incorrectly) that they have the proper ground tackle. Anchor rodes attached directly to the hook are subject to chafe from underwater rocks and coral. In extreme conditions the lines can part completely. Additionally, anchor rodes by themselves do not provide any weighted buffer for the boat's motion. Enter anchor chains to solve this problem.

An anchor chain is about six feet long and is attached between the end of the anchor line and the hook. The best variety is vinyl coated to prevent rust and facilitate cleaning. Besides protecting the anchor line from underwater chafe, the weight of the chain itself tends to reduce the strain on the anchor when the boat is moved by the wind or tide. Imagine, if you will, a sudden gust of wind moving your boat to one side. There is a momentary slack, and then the tension on the anchor line increases. The chain is then picked up from the bottom. The weight of the chain tends to slow the boat's motions, thereby reducing the shock on the anchor.

Most boaters should select an anchor chain with links at least 5/16" in diameter. Skippers of larger craft may want to consider a 3/8" chain. You will also need an additional galvanized shackle to secure the chain to the anchor.

Anchor Line

Nylon anchor lines (also known as anchor rodes) are very specialized units. The line is fitted with an eye on the anchor end, which is stretched tightly around an oval metal support, pinched at one end, known as a thimble. The line is then secured to the anchor chain by a device known as a shackle. You can think of a shackle as a link of chain with a removable side for connecting. Practically all boaters, even seasoned professionals, purchase anchor lines as pre-made units. Sizing requirements are somewhat different for nylon anchor lines than their docking counterparts:

Boat Size	*Recommended Diameter*	*Recommended Length*
25' to 30'	3/8"	180'
30' to 35'	1/2"	200'
35' to 40'	1/2"	250'
Over 40'	1/2"	300'

For really heavy weather, you will want a heavier anchor rode. On my thirty-one-foot vessel, I always use 1/2"-diameter anchor line.

Looking at the chart above, you may wonder a bit at the recommended lengths. After all, most of the coastal waters in which you will cruise never exceed fifty feet of depth. The answer to this question lies in the requirement of using far more anchor line than just what is necessary to reach the bottom. In fact the more line you pay out, the better the anchor will hold. This ratio of water depth to length of anchor line is known as "anchor scope" and will be fully discussed in Chapter 6.

Anchor Chocks

If your craft is equipped with the popular Danforth anchor, you can easily secure the hook to the bow portion of the deck with a set of anchor chocks. These units come in various designs and configurations, but all are designed to hold your anchor firmly and securely while underway. Besides presenting a neat and tidy appearance, chocks allow the anchor to be ready at hand whenever it comes times to drop the hook. If you install the chocks yourself, *be sure* to use a waterproof caulk to seal their base to the deck surface.

Deck Pipes

Deck pipes are to anchor lines what chocks are to the hook. You will find one or two of these units on the bow of practically every power craft. This stainless steel or chrome pipe is simply a throughdeck fitting or pipe that has a cap set over the top. On one side of the pipe and top, a hole is cut out to allow the anchor line to be fed into a rope locker below decks.

If you install a second anchor, you will need another deck pipe. Two anchor lines to a pipe just doesn't work. You can install the unit yourself with a good quality hole cutter, but, again, *be sure* to seal its base completely with good quality, waterproof, marine caulk. It is also a good idea to fabricate a divider in your rope locker. This simple precaution will keep the two anchor lines from becoming snarled together.

Deck pipes, as already noted, come with tops to prevent the entry of rain or seawater into the rope lockers below. On some designs, the caps are secured to the pipe by a chain. My experience suggests that these chains weaken and break after several years. A "better mousetrap" design is a deckpipe with a hinged top. With this variety, you won't have to go forward in a heavy seaway, as I once did, to try and rescue a cap that just bounced off, broke its chain, and is slowly sliding towards the water.

Depth Markers

While not essential, vinyl depth markers attached to the anchor line are a great addition to any set of ground tackle. These inexpensive tags are inserted between the strands of three-twist nylon anchor lines. After installation, it is a snap to tell how much anchor rode has been let out. This measurement is essential in determining "anchor scope" (see Chapter 6).

BOATING SAFETY EQUIPMENT

PFDs

Life jackets or Personal Flotation Devices (PFDs in nautical jargon) are the most basic personal safety equipment aboard any seagoing vessel. They are essential! If a boat should be sunk or a crew member thrown overboard, PFDs are the best first line of defense against drowning, a fate that can really ruin a boater's whole day. You are *required* to have at least one life jacket for each person and one throwable device (such as a life ring) aboard at all times. The Coast Guard takes a very dim view of the excuse that such and such couple were only aboard for this one trip. If you don't have a PFD for *each* person aboard *every* time your boat leaves the dock, heavy fines and other, longer-term tragedies are the likely result.

When purchasing PFDs, check first for the U.S. Coast Guard stamp of approval. If you can't find it, don't give the brand a second look.

Modern life jackets are filled with either vinyl-enclosed kapok, polyethylene, ensolite, or altrex. Kapok is the oldest of these materials. In times now long gone, kapok was used without any vinyl protection. Life jackets made this way tended to become waterlogged after a time. Thankfully, these old, unreliable units are now gone from today's market.

Even kapok enclosed in vinyl has its problems. If the vinyl is pierced, moisture can leak in and rot the kapok, causing a very perceptible loss in buoyancy. Also, kapok-filled life jackets are stiff and do not conform well to the body. This means that a swimmer with this type of PFD has very little protection from cold water temperatures. In spite of these shortcomings, many modern life jackets, particularly of the Type I variety (see discussion below) are filled with vinyl-protected kapok. They are perfectly acceptable *if* the jackets are rigorously inspected twice a year for rot and deterioration.

Polyethylene-filled PFDs also have their problems. This material is also stiff and suffers from the same lack of temperature protection as its kapok counterpart. Another problem peculiar to polyethylene is the loss of buoyancy caused by squeezing the life vest. Compressing polyethylene can burst some of the internal cells that hold air and give the material buoyancy, Consequently, you never really know whether the life vest is at full efficiency. Personally, I wouldn't want one of these PFDs aboard my boat.

Ensolite is a soft, flexible foam filling that is ideal for life jackets. It is rot-resistant, conforms well to the body, and does not lose it buoyancy with age or squeezing.

Altrex, a type of Poly Vinyl Chloride is the newest of the PFD fillings. It has qualities similar to Ensolite but is even more durable.

Obviously, these latter two materials are ideal life jacket fillers, particularly for Type II units. Either would be a wise choice for any boater.

Life jackets or PFDs are categorized into five distinctive groups by the U.S. Coast Guard. Each has a particular application as specified below:

Type I—also known as "Offshore Life Jackets," provides the maximum safety and buoyancy. This unit is designed to turn an unconscious swimmer into an upright position. Despite such obvious safety factors, this type of life jacket is seldom used by coastal cruisers. Type I PFDs are usually stuffed with vinyl-enclosed kapok and are quite stiff and bulky. If you intend to cruise extensively in offshore waters, it would be a very good plan to have some Type I's aboard.

Type II—similar to Type I but lacks some of that design's buoyancy. Type II life jackets will usually turn an unconscious person upright, but the action is not as reliable as with Type I. This style of PFD is less bulky than Type I and is probably the most common variety of life jackets found on power craft.

Type III—a far more comfortable life jacket. Type III PFDs are usually made from one of the newer materials such as Ensolite or Altrex. Unfortunately, someone falling overboard must be conscious for this type of life jacket to be effective. Despite this shortcoming, Type III PFDs have been gaining popularity during the last decade.

Type IV—This variety of PFD is usually known as a "throwable." It is designed to be thrown to a crew member who falls overboard without wearing any flotation. A life ring or the old reliable vinyl seat cushion with handles are the two most common varieties of this PFD type. You are *required* to have at least one Type IV device aboard.

Type V—the newest category of PFDs. These life jackets are often called "hybrids" and come in many shapes and sizes. The most common variety is the life jacket vest. Made from the most modern materials, it is extremely comfortable to wear and provides sufficient flotation for conscious swimmers. Type V PFDs are probably the most expensive of the lot, but due to their comfort, boaters are more liable to wear these devices when underway. This safety factor often justifies the additional expense.

When underway, we usually cruise with half Type II and half Type III (or V) PFDs. This gives a good mix and allows us to react to a variety of weather and cruising conditions. Remember, you must have at least one PFD for each and every person aboard whenever your boat leaves the dock!

First Aid Kit

Every cruising craft of any size should be equipped with a well-outfitted *marine* first aid kit. You never know when you might need a bandage, smelling salts, or even a Tylenol when afloat. If the need for first aid arises on the water, far from any marina or other shoreside aid, an onboard kit is worth its weight in gold.

Marine first aid kits differ from their shoreside equivalents by including more of everything. A good nautical kit contains such diverse items as adhesive strips, alcohol wipes, ammonia inhalants, antiseptic wipes, cold packs, sterile cotton, elastic bandages, eye irrigation packets, burn cream, gauze bandages, sting relief wipes, lip balm, motion sickness tablets, scissors, triangular bandages, tweezers, and non-aspirin headache pills.

Be sure to purchase such a *marine* first aid kit and have it close at hand before beginning your first cruise! Failure to meet this minimum safety requirement can only be considered foolhardy!

Fire Extinguishers

Your new craft, whether purchased new or used, will probably come with enough fire extinguishers to meet USCG regulations. On the off chance that a miserly factory did not include the necessary units, or some former owner makes off with the onboard extinguishers, let's take a moment to review the Coast Guard requirements.

Boat Length	*Extinguishers Required*
Less than 26'	One type B-I
26'–39'	Two B-I's or one B-II
40'–65'	Three B-I's or one B-I and one B-II

The B-I and B-II rating refers to flame retardant type and capacity of the extinguishers measured in pounds. The chart below rates the most popular varieties of marine fire extinguishers:

Type	*C02*	*Dry Chemical*	*Halon*
B-I	4 lb.	2 lb.	2.5 lb.
B-II	15 lb.	10 lb.	N/A

Most boaters will want to choose "Dry Chemical" type fire extinguishers as their onboard, portable fire control units. This variety of flame retardant is effective on all types of fires. Carbon dioxide (C02) and Halon, on the other hand, are not recommended for paper, wood, or cloth fires, though they are effective for gasoline and electrical-type blazes.

Captains of gasoline-powered craft may want to seriously consider installing an *automatic* Halon fire extinguisher system in the bilge. Halon is colorless, odorless, and won't damage electrical or mechanical systems. Should a fire break out in the bilge, the system would be automatically activated. There is a good chance the blaze would be extinguished before igniting the main gasoline supply. If such an unlikely event ever occurred aboard your craft, the three or four hundred dollars spent for the automatic Halon system would seem like a bargain indeed.

While experienced captains sometimes install a Halon system themselves, I suggest first-time power boat owners employ a boating professional for this purpose. As always, watch the technician as he goes about his task, and you may be able to do the job yourself next time.

Signaling Equipment

All power boats over 16 feet in length are now *required* by Coast Guard regulations to carry a designated quantity and variety of safety signaling equipment. For craft that will only operate during daylight hours only, three orange, 50-second smoke signals or one 3"-by-3" specially-marked flag is acceptable. For nighttime operation *only,* an automatic, electric SOS light will fulfill the requirement. Most boats should be equipped with acceptable day/night signals. The day/night requirement can be satisfied by either three red handheld two-minute flares, three red six-second meteor flares, three red parachute flares, or any combination totaling three flares.

Your best bet is to purchase one of the many pre-made signaling kits. These practical units are designed to fulfill all the Coast Guard signaling requirements for any time of day or night. You can find such kits in most nautical stores or they can be purchased from any marine equipment catalog.

ELECTRONICS

Most marine electronics can be considered optional equipment and, as such, will be discussed in the next chapter. There are two important exceptions to this rule, however. No boat should so much as untie a dockline without a well-functioning VHF, two-way marine radio, and a depth sounder (or finder) aboard. These two pieces of electronic gear are fundamental to the safety of any vessel! To paraphrase a popular television commercial, "Don't go cruising without one."

VHF Radio

VHF (FM) marine radio provides instant contact with the U.S. Coast Guard on any coastal waters of the continental United States. In case of emergency, a VHF radio is your best source for requesting aid and assistance! Since the 1970s the government has constructed numerous VHF frequency listening stations on both shores of the U.S. to insure that any vessel in distress can reach the Coast Guard on channel 16. It is your responsibility to purchase, install, and obtain a license for a VHF radio. Obviously, only those boaters with a VHF aboard can take advantage of the Coast Guard safety net.

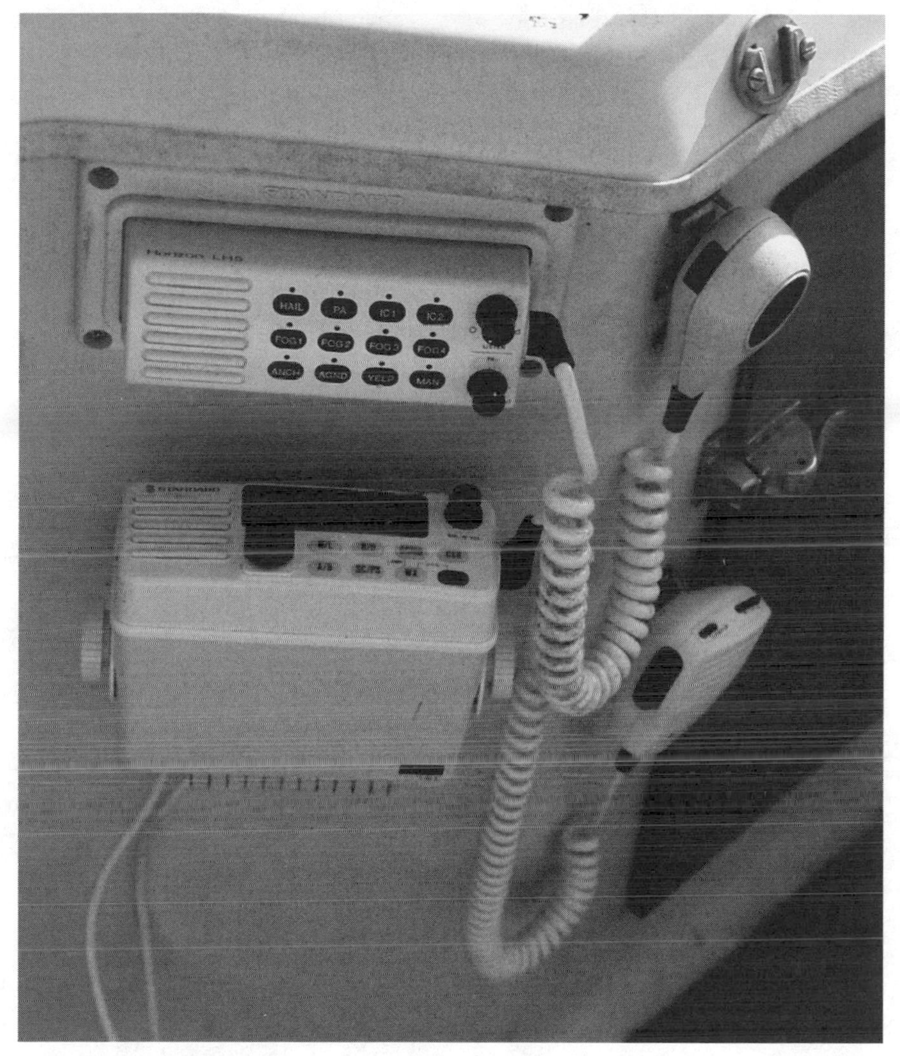

Twin VHF marine radios.

While they come in a mind-boggling variety of brands and models, all VHF marine radios share some basic features in common. The maximum allowed output is 25 watts. All shipboard units can be expected to transmit up to this legal maximum while handheld varieties are usually limited to a 3- to 5-watt output. Additionally, all VHFs have a low-power switch that reduces transmitting output to 1 watt. In a crowded port with cluttered radio traffic, you are required by regulations to attempt contact on the low-power setting *first,* before making the attempt at full output. This is a rule that is often ignored, much to the detriment of marine communications.

All marine VHF radios have certain transmitting and receiving channels. Some units have far more choices than others. VHF radios of the 1970s and older vintages were usually restricted to only five or six channels while modern synthesized models can offer 78 (or more) receive and transmit frequencies. Each channel is assigned a *very specific* purpose. You must use the channel that is appropriate to your intended use.

For instance, channel 16 is now the emergency channel, which is supposed to be used exclusively for true, on-the-water perilous situations. In practice, this is, unfortunately, not always the way it works. In any case, you should use channel 16 to raise the U.S. Coast Guard or other emergency assistance agencies when the situation requires such a call for help. Recently, channel 9 has been set aside as the calling channel on which vessels can contact each other, or make calls to shoreside marinas and bridges. On this frequency, you can quickly make contact, and then shift to a "working, non-commercial channel." Channels 68, 70, 71, and 72 are used for non-commercial, inner ship (and ship-to-marina) communications. There are many other channels such as 6, the safety channel, which can be used by pleasure boaters for the appropriate purpose.

Selecting the right channel, as well as proper calling and answering techniques are all part of the science of correct VHF operating procedure. Whole books have been written on this subject, and the sum total of all the rules and regulations goes far beyond the scope of this work. Most new VHFs come with a brief discussion of the pertinent regulations. While this may be sufficient to get you up and going, I suggest purchasing one of the inexpensive guides to marine VHF radio that are available at most nautical book stores. These handy reference works will have you operating your VHF like a pro in no time at all.

In times past, it was also necessary to obtain an operator's and a ship's VHF license before making use of your marine radio license. Thankfully, both of these requirements have now been dropped.

Marine VHF radios, as already mentioned, come in a wide variety of brands and models. As recently as the 1970s, all VHF radios were "two crystal" sets. With this variety, two crystals (send and receive) had to be installed in the radio for the unit to be active on a particular channel. This limited the number of available channels. Crystals are also subject to breakdown. This type of VHF radio is now almost extinct.

Enter the synthesized VHF. This type of radio, introduced in the late 1970s, uses a solid state circuit rather than crystals to synthesize all send and receive channels. With the introduction of synthesized VHFs, 78+-channel models began to appear on the market, and are now commonplace. Without a doubt, this variety of VHF is a most superior design. It's what you want! If you should purchase a used craft that has an ancient crystal VHF, I suggest dumping the old unit and purchasing a synthesized radio. For flexibility and reliability, you'll be glad you did.

There are several other features you might want to consider when purchasing a new VHF radio. Digital readout of the current frequency is much to be preferred over a dial selector. Just try reading a dial in direct sunlight, particularly after the numbers have faded a bit, and you will see what I mean. The vast majority of current VHF radios now offer "channel scanning." When this feature is in operation, the radio scans all the selected channels (much as a shoreside police scanner) for transmissions. This can be very helpful for fishermen who are trying to listen out for the best spot on any particular day.

As mentioned briefly above, handheld VHFs have made a determined appearance on the marine scene. The most obvious use for these units would seem to be shoreside transmission to a boat on the water. Unfortunately, the FCC takes a very dim view of this sort of operation. In fact, it is prohibited by regulation. Consequently, handheld VHFs have been relegated to a backup status or even as a primary transmitter-receiver on small craft (usually less than 26 feet). The lower transmission output of handhelds (3 to 5 watts) make them inappropriate for use as a primary station on larger vessels.

A VHF marine radio is practically worthless without a well-functioning antenna. While there are some portable models available, captains of larger craft will want to opt for the permanently installed variety. However, it's a good idea to have one of the small, emergency antennas aboard, should the main unit fail. VHF antennas are rated in db (decibel) gain. The higher the db rating, the better the antenna will pull in and transmit a signal. I suggest a minimum 6 db rating for a boat over 28 feet, with a 9 db unit preferred. While, as a rule of thumb, the higher the db gain, the taller the antenna, you should make your antenna purchase on the rated gain, not just its height.

Installing an antenna is *not* a job for the new power skipper. It is often necessary to reattach a male jack to the end of the antenna cable. This task should be left to a professional. Even if you buy your VHF and antenna through a discount catalog or membership organization, I suggest spending the extra money for a professional installation. You might want to watch the technician as he goes about his business. Ask plenty of questions and you might be able to handle the job yourself next time.

Virtually all modern VHF marine radios are now equipped with the three primary NOAA (National Oceanographic and Atmospheric Administration) weather channel frequencies. For those of you who are not already aware of this service, NOAA now maintains continuous weather broadcasts in almost every corner of the good old USA. Having this sort of information at your fingertips is an incredible advantage for cruising boaters. By simply pushing a button, you can determine whether this would be a good day to leave the dock or a time to batten down the hatches. While there are separate weather radios available, and it is a good idea to have one of these inexpensive units aboard, there will be times when it is more convenient to have the weather channels on your VHF. Sometimes the taller, more sensitive, VHF antenna will pull in a distant weather channel that the smaller units cannot receive.

Finally, there is the question of whether one VHF radio is sufficient. Once, on a cruise from the North Carolina shore to Washington, D.C., our VHF packed it in. There was really nothing we could do except continue our cruise, but it was with some genuine concern that we did so. Had our engines failed, or a fire broken out aboard, we could have done nothing except abandon ship. Upon returning to home port, we purchased a handheld unit as a backup and have cruised with it ever since. If your craft has both an upper and lower helm station, you might want to consider having two full-power VHFs, one at each location. You can install two antennas, or purchase a simple switch available from any marine electronics dealer that allows both radios to transmit (one at a time) over the same antenna.

Depth Sounders

There is an old maxim in boating that goes something like this: "tearing the bottom out of your craft can ruin your whole cruising day!" While careful navigation and good planning with the latest charts reduces the likelihood of this unhappy event, the only sure prevention is the addition of a reliable, well-functioning depth sounder to your craft's arsenal of navigational aids.

Depth sounders (or "finders" as they are sometimes called) have been around in one form or another for many years. I ran across an article written in a 1944 edition of the *State* magazine in which the author described seeing a depth finder for the first time. It is only since 1983, however, that computer chip technology has allowed the modern sounder to really come into its own.

A depth sounder consists of two pieces of equipment. A "transducer" is affixed to the boat's transom or through the hull while an "instrument head" is located next to the helm station. The head provides a readout of water depth in feet or meters. When underway an electronic signal is sent through the transducer and bounced off the bottom. The instrument head meters the time interval between the signal and its return and automatically calculates the depth from this data. In theory, you will have an accurate representation of the actual distance from your keel to the bottom always ready at hand.

In practice, some bottom strata (particularly soft mud), strong water currents, debris, and other factors can cause a depth sounder to give false readings. Modern, solid-state circuitry has greatly enhanced the operation of newer sounders. False readings and inaccurate information are not the problems they were just a few years ago. Today, most sounders can be relied upon to give accurate information about 80 to 90 percent of the time.

Proper installation is the most important factor in accurate depth sounder operation. While mounting the instrument head is no great trick, the location of the transducer is critical. Until recently, I would not have considered a depth sounder without a thru-hull transducer. While this type of transducer installation is more difficult and expensive, it can be relied upon to relay accurate information to the instrument head. Now, however, transom mount transducers have been improved to the point where they are an acceptable alternative. Again, as a new power boat captain, you should give serious consideration to professional installation of your first sounder. *After* gaining experience in marine electronics, you might consider mounting a finder yourself.

Be on guard against "to-hull" transducer installation. Some dealers who are not concerned with quality work have been known to seal the transducer to the inner hull surface with silicone caulk or a so-called "water box." This method is certainly the least expensive way to install a transducer, but it's also the least effective. Don't be fooled! No matter what anyone tells you, this sort of installation will reduce your sounder's sensitivity. It is *not acceptable!* Insist on either a thru-hull or transom-mount transducer. New boat buyers should be particularly alert for this corner-cutting practice by penny-pinching dealers.

There are four basic varieties of depth sounders. The oldest, probably the same model that the author of the 1944 magazine article observed, is the so-called flashing sounder. This type of sounder (now rarely seen) has a round dial marked with water depths. When operating, a flashing line of light appears on the inner part of the dial. The corresponding depth figure next to the line is the water depth. While this variety of sounder was used for years, it is undoubtedly finicky, and the information display cannot hope to compete with the modern digital and video models.

A second older variety of depth sounder (also rarely encountered today) is known as the chart recorder. This unit makes a carbon sketch of the bottom strata on a piece of moving paper. The paper feeds out of the end of the instrument head and gives a permanent record of the bottom over which the boat has traveled. Chart recorders are notoriously unreliable, and best avoided.

Digital depth sounders display the depth of water in feet (or meters) by an easily read digital display. The older varieties used a LED (Lighted Electronic Display) while present day units feature a LCD (Liquid Crystal Display) read-out. The LCD sounders draw much less battery current and are easier to read in direct sunlight. For nighttime operation, most LCD units have a backlit display. The only disadvantage usually attributed to digital units is their lack of bottom trend information. Even so, by watching a digital sounder closely, you can quickly spot rising water levels. On the *Kaycy* we have logged hundreds of miles with our digital sounder with never a complaint.

Video depth sounders are the flashy kid on the block. These units give you a video picture of the changing bottom strata, along with a digital read-out in feet (or meters). The less expensive video sounders have an LCD display while the more costly variety feature a high resolution, video picture. Both kinds are reliable and have the added bonus of showing large schools of fish. LCD units are considerably less expensive, but they do lack the high resolution of the true video units. The price of video sounders can be expected to

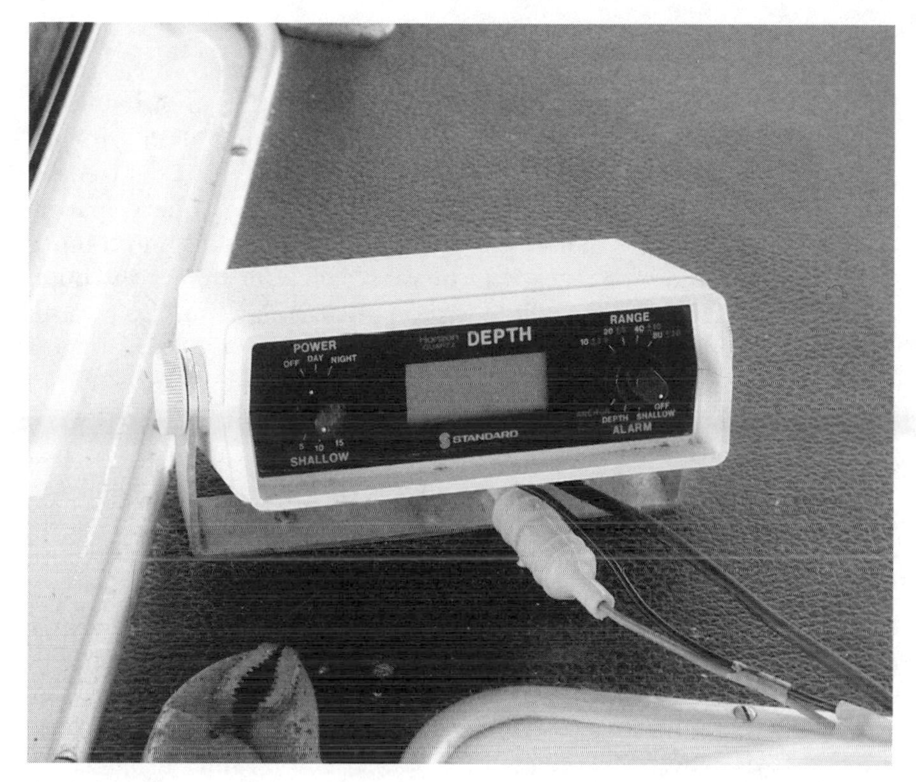

Digital depth sounders.

increase in direct correspondence to the number of colors shown on the display.

Video and LCD depth finders are truly the best of both worlds. They give you a quickly read digital read-out of water depth while also allowing ready identification of bottom strata trends and fish. You may have to pay a bit more for this type of depth sounder, but this is one case where the additional expenditure may be justified.

NAVIGATIONAL EQUIPMENT

In Chapter 2 we discussed the need for a working knowledge of piloting and coastal navigation before taking your first cruise. All those hard won skills will be of minimal benefit if you don't have the proper navigational equipment aboard. A compass, charts covering the waters you intend to cruise, and appropriate cruising guides are the most basic equipment acceptable for navigational cruising safety.

Compass

For those true landlubbers who don't already know, a compass is simply a device with which one can determine a direction known as magnetic north. Inside a compass, a strong magnet is mounted on a needle, or more usually a card. When this structure is allowed to float freely it naturally aligns itself with the earth's magnetic field. Modern marine compasses are filled with a so-called damping fluid. This liquid tends to stabilize the pointer or card in heavy seas. Nevertheless, in rough conditions, it can be a real pill to stay on a particular compass course.

Degree markings appear on either the compass card or the border of the instrument (with needle-type compasses). In learning about coastal navigation, you will discover how to use these degree designations to follow compass courses. By plugging this information into a current chart, you can theoretically find your way from point A to point B completely in the dark. On the water, it's a little more complicated, but, even so, you can certainly understand how important a compass is to coastal navigation.

Compasses come in many shapes and sizes. There are even electronic compasses, but they are *usually* so expensive as to preclude their use by many first-time power boaters. Generally speaking, the larger, more expensive traditional compasses are constructed to more exacting quality standards than their smaller counterparts. Larger units usually have better damping for operating in rough seaways as well. Consequently, I would advise purchasing a good-sized, quality compass. It need not be the largest, most expensive model available, but neither should it be the economy prototype meant for outboards and I/Os.

If your boat is equipped with both upper and lower helm stations, you should have a compass installed at both locations. Boats with a compass mounted only on the flybridge can be hazardous to operate from the lower station in foul weather. Think for a moment. If the boat is operated from the lower helm, how can you navigate without a compass by which to steer?

Compass installation calls for care and caution. Most units can be self-installed by following a few simple rules. For worry-free operation, however, you might again want to consider employing the services of a professional.

Metal and electronic equipment can cause a compass to deviate from correct course readings. If, for instance, a depth sounder is mounted too closely to a compass, the instrument might read as much as ten or fifteen degrees from actual magnetic north. Consequently, care must be taken to locate your compass as far from metal and electronic equipment as possible. Looking at it another way, you should have electronic gear installed as far from the compass as is practical. With these precautions in mind, you need only bore the appropriate holes and connect the night light to a switched twelve-volt source. Finally, before screwing down the unit permanently, every effort should be made to line the instrument's front-to-back axis with your boat's centerline. I've never found any way to do this except by eye. Take a careful look at the compass, and jockey it back and forth until it seems to be lined up with your boat's stern-to-bow centerline.

Even if you install a compass with the greatest of care, it's almost a sure bet that some metal object or electronic gear aboard will affect its accuracy to some degree. Recognizing this possibility, compass manufacturers include an internal compensation device. By using a non-magnetic brass screwdriver (provided with almost every compass), you can adjust both the north-south and east-west axis.

Well, you may ask, how do I know how much to adjust the compass? Good question. I have read many exotic procedures for accomplishing this task which seem to be devised in fairyland rather than from a practical boating viewpoint. Let me simply relate how I go about compensating a new compass. Take out a chart of your home cruising grounds and find a pair of buoys or daybeacons (or other aids to navigation) that are located less than a mile apart, and are as near to a magnetic north-south line as possible. Now find a similar pair of aids for an east-west axis. Plot the actual course between the two aids of each pair with great care (you will learn how to do this in coastal navigation). Now, take your boat out on the water. Carefully put the first marker of the north-south pair directly to stern (in the middle of your stern line) and point straight for the marker ahead. When you are lined up directly between the two markers, read your compass course. If it deviates from the predicted line (and it probably will) turn the north-south adjustment screw with the brass screwdriver until the error is gone. Now, proceed to the far aid, and then reverse your course. Put the second aid to stern and point directly for the marker you just left behind. Once you are aligned, check your compass again. If it shows an error, use the adjustment screw and correct for *half* the deviation from the expected track. Repeat this process for the east-west buoy pair, and your compass will be adjusted as closely as possible to actual magnetic north. Be warned, this process can be time consuming and more than a little frustrating, but the end result is certainly worth the effort.

So, you've installed your compass with care and have compensated it as closely as possible. This means that the instrument will now read *true* geographic north accurately, right? As an old cartoon character once said, "Wrongo." The first problem is that the *magnetic* North Pole has perversely located itself quite some distance from the true *geographic* North Pole. The difference between "true north" and "magnetic north" is known as *variation.* Nautical charts *always* show the variation for their particular locale. By plugging this figure into your magnetic courses, you can convert them to true directions.

It should be noted that variation is not a constant reading. As you move from one cruising area to another, the amount of variation changes. You must consult the differing charts to discover the compensation necessary for any particular area.

Many boaters never bother with the conversion from magnetic to true courses. Since you are always following magnetic courses anyway, via your compass, so the logic runs, why not just plot magnetic courses in the first place. While some of the navigational purists among us may disagree with this approach, I, myself, have used this plan with great success for many years.

Now that you've compensated for variation, you may think that your compass is at least aligned with true north. Again, such an assumption would be in error. Even though a compass is installed with care, and it is compensated properly, chances are that metal objects and onboard electric equipment will still affect the instrument to some extent. The difference between actual magnetic north and what you might call "compass north" (north as shown on your compass) is termed *deviation.*

Some 95 percent of all power boaters never worry with deviation. With coastal cruising, you will seldom follow a course exceeding twenty or thirty miles between aids to navigation. Most runs will be considerably shorter. The tracking error engendered by your compass being off two or three degrees (the norm for a properly installed, adjusted compass) will be negligible. Of course, if you were making an offshore passage from the USA to England, the situation would be very different indeed.

If for one reason or another you decide that you must compensate for deviation, the best bet is to obtain the services of a professional compass adjuster. In addition to compensating your compass with a greater degree of accuracy than you can obtain, he will formulate a "deviation table," which will show the compass deviation error for each ten-degree segment around the compass card. To repeat myself, most coastal power cruisers will read this paragraph and then forget about deviation tables entirely.

Charts

Allow me to be blunt. Any boater who leaves the dock without the *latest* NOAA charts for *all* waters in which he plans to cruise is being irresponsible. Coastal navigation and piloting courses teach you how to use the charts. Graduating students will be able to discern what types of buoys and daybeacons to expect from their particular chart symbols. There are also unique colors to designate certain water depths and different landward colors to specify solid ground, marsh, and populated areas. Charts are, quite simply, the single best source of cruising information.

As discussed in Chapter 2, you can obtain a map-type chart catalog from almost any nautical store or mail-order marine discount dealer. You can then order the individual units you need accordingly.

In reviewing the chart catalog, you may notice several charts covering a single area. The smaller charts are more detail-specific, and should definitely be included in your cruising gear. The smaller scale, larger-area charts are also quite useful for planning a cruise and are sometimes essential for plotting long-range courses between widely spaced aids to navigation.

NOAA charts are updated regularly. In waters with swift tidal currents, the changes after only a few years' time can be surprising. Make every effort to keep the most recent editions of all charts covering your cruising area aboard.

The U.S. Coast Guard publishes a monthly newsletter called *Notice to Mariners*. Besides specifying any temporary or long-term changes in aids to navigation, this publication also gives you a checklist of recently updated charts. The *Notice to Mariners* is available without charge to all pleasure boaters. You can request the notice from the nearest regional Coast Guard headquarters. Contact your nearest Coast Guard facility for more information.

Cruising Guides

While NOAA charts are a very valuable source of cruising data, they cannot be solely relied upon for all the information you will need. Even with periodic updates, nautical charts are sometimes in error, particularly in waters that are far from the beaten path. Even accurate charts do not reveal such necessary data as marina locations and services, restaurants and other shoreside attractions, safe anchorages, and recent danger areas. You can also improve your cruising enjoyment with an appreciation of the heritage of the land and the waters through which you are traveling. Cruising guides fill this information gap nicely.

There is no denying my prejudice in this regard, but I recommend cruising guides that only cover one specific coastline. This limited format (which I term "narrow and deep") allows the guide to present far more detailed information than that available in guides that attempt to cover several states' shorelines in one publication. Some of your most enjoyable "armchair boating" can be accomplished while reading a good cruising guide.

TOOL KIT

Finally, captains should have a well-planned tool kit aboard before beginning their first cruise. Even if you aren't yet ready for major onboard repairs, there are always screws and bolts to be tightened. As you come to know your craft better, the tools listed below will allow you to undertake many small jobs yourself. This will save both time and money. On the water, having the right tool can often mean the difference between fixing the problem yourself or having to call for a tow.

The various tools with which you might choose to outfit your kit are almost endless. The list below represents only the bare minimum, and you should feel encouraged to add to these items as your circumstances and budget dictate.

A well-outfitted nautical tool kit should include:

1. Socket Wrench Set(s)—You should have at least one set of wrenches ranging in size from $^1/_4$" to 1" or their metric equivalents (both long and short sockets) with a $^3/_8$" drive. Be sure to select standard or metric sizes depending on your boat's sizing for nuts and bolts. When your budget allows, a $^1/_2$" drive with sockets to match would be a very good addition.

2. Regular Wrench Set—There are places and circumstances where a socket wrench is not appropriate. You should also have a set of fixed wrenches in your kit. I prefer those which have an open wrench on one end, and a closed, box wrench of the same size on the other. This type will cover every conceivable application. Again, be sure to select standard or metric sizes depending on your boat's requirements.

3. Adjustable Wrenches—You should always include one small and one larger adjustable wrench in your tool kit. These units are invaluable for removing or installing that odd-sized nut for which you do not have a fixed wrench or socket.

4. Vise-Grips—If you have never seen a vise-grip before, they took somewhat like a large pair of pliers. They are designed to lock down tight on a nut or bolt. This unique action allows for removing many bolts whose edges might be too worn to use a standard wrench. If your boat is like mine, you will find 101 uses for a vise-grip and will never leave the dock without one.

5. Allen Wrench Set—On boats many engine parts and accessories are held together with Allen bolts. These reliable fasteners have a six-sided hole in their heads. An Allen wrench will fit snugly into this enclosure allowing you to insert or retract the bolt. While you might not use them too often, *don't* overlook this necessary item. When you need an Allen wrench, *nothing* else will do.

6. Large and Small Pliers—When all else fails, drag out the good old pliers. Some jobs demand these old-fashioned helpers, but remember, use a wrench when at all possible.

7. Large Set of Screwdrivers—No matter how many screwdrivers are aboard, you will eventually find that you need another size. I suggest purchasing a large set of screwdrivers with both straight and Phillips heads. They should range from a very small unit for use with (for example) electrical gear to a large handled screwdriver to handle the big jobs.

8. Hammer—It is surprising how many uses you will find for this indelicate instrument while afloat. Select a medium weight head for best results.

9. Wire Stripper and Cutter—A combination wire cutter, stripper and crimping tool is a real necessity for any floating tool kit. Repairing electrical wire can become a regular job for power captains. This useful piece of equipment beats the old knife cutting and stripping approach hands down.

10. Six-foot (at least) Roll of 12-Gauge Multi-Strand Wire—You never know when you might have to replace a piece of electric wire when you are far from a port of call. Having a ready piece of cable aboard can make all the difference.

11. Solderless Wire Connectors—Many "old salts" will tell you that all connections between two wires on a boat should be soldered. That may be true, and I usually try to solder all permanent connections. However, for a "quick fix," nothing beats crimped, solderless connectors. The wire stripper-crimper discussed above can be used to install these connectors firmly and quickly.

12. Stainless Steel Screws and Nuts—All screws, bolts, and nuts used aboard a cruising boat should be made from stainless steel *only*. Conventional zinc-coated screws soon rust and corrode in a saltwater environment. Having a good selection of S/S screws aboard will prevent many a run to the marina store every time you need a bolt or nut.

While they cannot be considered as essential, you will probably want to include a 3/8" power drill along with a good selection of high-speed metal/wood bits and a set of screwdriver bits. I use mine as often as any tool we have aboard. A high-output soldering iron and a coil of resin core solder would be another good addition to your kit.

FINAL THOUGHTS

Well, now you have your new craft outfitted. The boat is ready to leave the dock for her first cruise. Before you go though, you might want to consider some additional nautical accessories that will enhance your life aboard. The next chapter is devoted to these considerations. If you are bursting at the seams, however, to take your new craft for a quick spin before considering accessories or maintenance, allow me to recommend a quick read-through of Chapter 6 before you leave the dock!

CHAPTER 4

Practical Accessories

ONE FINE FALL EVENING the "first-rate, first mate" and I were enjoying a delectable pig picking at our home marina. As I contemplated another bite of barbeque, or possibly one more beer, my eyes strayed to a beautiful fifty-five-foot Hatteras motor yacht docked across the way. It was with some amusement that I inspected the bevy of antennas that adorned the cruiser's flybridge. It was easy to pick out two VHF antennas, one for SSB, another for Loran, and a fifth for FM, but there was one short unit that eluded easy identification. I mentioned this to John, the marina service specialist, and he roared with laughter.

It seems the captain of this particular vessel was one of those individuals who sits around all day trying to figure out what else he can install aboard his vessel. The "short antenna" in question, it turns out, was intended for use *when passing under a bridge and it became necessary to lay the larger VHF antennas on the side of the boat.* Not only was there scant opportunity of missing a radio call during such a short period of time, but, John told me, he had never had the heart to tell the boat owner in question that the larger antennas received a better signal, even lying down, than the smaller unit standing up. I guess you might say that was a boat with "everything," even if all those things were not really needed.

Now, I don't mean to suggest that you become as engrossed in accessorizing your craft as the captain described above, but you will soon discover that buying attractive, interesting, and, above all, practical accessories for your new craft can be one of the most enjoyable of boating activities. A *huge* array of equipment and accessories is

"It was with some amusement that I inspected the bevy of antennas that adorned the cruiser's flybridge."

available to the new boat owner. Within the scope of this work, we cannot possibly hope to cover all the varied gear. I have endeavored to present information concerning the more popular and exciting boating accessories currently available. You may use the following discussion confidently as a basis for the many additions and modifications that might be envisioned for your new craft. Just don't be surprised to pick up almost any marine equipment catalog and run across some piece of equipment that I omitted (intentionally or not) from the list.

MARINE ELECTRONICS AND LAPTOP COMPUTERS

No other single category of marine equipment has engendered so much excitement and genuine interest during the last several years as marine electronics. The advent and subsequent sophistication of computer chip technology and reliable laptop computers has fostered a wholesale revolution in electronic navigation, communication, and general cruising equipment. Just a few years ago this sort of sophisticated gear might have been relegated to a *War Games* movie set. Not only is this equipment eminently practical, it's just plain fun. Many modern boaters enjoy the technical challenge of learning to

Searchlight mounted on bow pulpit; fenders in fender basket in background.

use such diverse gear as GPS, computer navigation software, SSB, and color radar, to name only a few. All this equipment is now far more affordable than it was just a few short years ago, and this writer, for one, would not leave the dock without some of these marvelous gadgets.

Loran C

Loran C, the successor to the older Loran A, was the first really practical modern, onboard electronic navigation system for coastal vessels. While you will still find many boats with Loran aboard, this system's task has been pretty much overtaken by the new GPS system (see below). Besides being a bit bulkier and definitely harder to install than GPS, there is some talk that Loran service may be discontinued by the government by the early part of the next century. Maybe not, but I think most boaters, particularly first-time captains, would do far better to consider purchasing an inexpensive GPS. As such, there will be no further explanation of Loran C within this book.

GPS

It is really not overstating the case to say that the introduction and (now) full implementation of the Global Positioning Network (GPS for short) has utterly revolutionized coastal navigation for pleasure boaters. Now, with a $200 portable unit, you can know pretty much know where you are anywhere on earth. Wow, how's that for impressive! Interface a GPS with a laptop computer containing appropriate navigational software and full-color nautical charts in digitized form, and you can actually see your boat's position on the charts as you cruise along. To say this is revolutionary simply falls short of the mark. You have to see this technology to believe it, and, quite simply, things will never be the same again.

The heart of the GPS system is a series of satellites stationed around the earth in geosynchronous orbit (which is to say they stay in the same place relative to the earth's surface all the time). These satellites transmit data continuously that is received by GPS units on the ground. Through some sort of electronic alchemy, the units measure these signals and display (at least) the latitude and longitude of your present position.

Before going forward with all the exciting news, it should be noted that the GPS system is not perfect. To protect our nation (at least that's the claim), the military (which owns the GPS satellites) purposely scrambles the signals a bit. What this means is that civilian GPS receivers suffer somewhat in the accuracy of their fixes. While military units can routinely fix their position within fifty feet, the sort of GPS units that we pleasure boaters make use of are only accurate to within some fifty meters (though it is usually more accurate than this).

Also, weather conditions can sometimes affect the quality of GPS reception, though this has become less of a problem as more sophisticated and sensitive units have become routinely available. Additionally, at certain times of the day and year, some of the satellites seem to be mysteriously blacked out, probably for maintenance or security concerns. During these periods, you may have trouble obtaining an accurate and timely fix.

All this is really quibbling. For the vast majority of your time on the water, a good quality GPS receiver will work well and will give you acceptable accuracy for all but the most critical, narrow channel navigation. You should also know that there is currently serious discussion in governmental circles as to whether the military scrambling of GPS signals is really warranted. It is possible that this accuracy-reducing practice may be completely abandoned in the future.

Fenders in fender basket.

So, having said all that about the GPS system, let's spend a few minutes looking at the various alternative routes you might choose to go with GPS receivers. Pick up any discount equipment catalog, or enter virtually any marine store and you will find a goodly selection of GPS units. Basically, these wonderful machines break down into two categories—handheld and fix mounted. These descriptions are pretty self explanatory. The handheld units have the advantage of being portable, which means that they can be moved from boat to boat, or even used for landside navigation. These units normally operate for many hours on a set of AA alkaline batteries. For use aboard, inexpensive mounts are available to secure the unit temporarily beside your helm station. Another cheap accessory cable allows these portable units to operate off your onboard 12-volt battery power when they are plugged in, rather than their own batteries.

Fixed-mount GPSs usually feature a larger screen and are (usually) permanently connected to the boat's 12-volt batteries. This larger screen can be a considerable advantage if you are not interfacing your GPS with a laptop computer (see below).

Until recently, another considerable advantage of fixed-mount GPS receivers was the option (in the more expensive units) of incorporating a chart cartridge. With the use of this clever device, a small portion of the waters and adjacent coastline on which your boat is operating is depicted on the GPS screen, and your boat's moving position on the chart is also clearly noted. Many of these displays are black and white, and can be a bit difficult to read. For my money, I would use an interface with a laptop computer every time rather than the chart cartridge system (again, see below).

In the last few months, some handheld GPS units have appeared that also allow the use of a chart cartridge. Personally, I consider these units of limited value, as the small, black-and-white display is rather difficult to read and employ for successful navigation.

GPS receivers differ in their sensitivity and their ability to receive navigational data from more than one satellite at a time. It doesn't take too much imagination to guess that the more sensitive the unit the better, and that it's better to be able to receive data from several satellites at once rather than one at a time. Equally obvious, the more expensive units usually feature better sensitivity and multiple satellite inquiries. Don't despair. Just as an example, the handheld Garmin 48XL has superb sensitivity, multiple satellite channels, and yet it can be purchased from discounters for about $250. Is that a good deal or what?

Laptop Computers, Navigational Software, and Electronic Charts

If you are lucky enough to already own a laptop computer that is capable of using the Windows 95-98 operating system, then you won't believe how inexpensively you can bring the very best of electronic navigation to your craft. Now, you old salts out there are probably muttering in your beer at this point and thinking that you've been using DR coastal navigation successfully for years, and what do you need all this new gear for anyway. Well, let me tell you. I used to be among your ranks, but just last summer it was brought home to me how much this new form of electronic navigation can radically affect your time on the water.

The cruise in question found this writer and my ace research assistant, Bob Horne, exploring the waters lying about Panama City, Florida, in preparation for an updated edition of my *Cruising Guide to the Northern Gulf Coast.* To the east of Panama City, there is a wonderfully isolated anchorage on a body of water lying directly off the ICW known as California Bayou. There is just one big problem. To successfully enter this anchorage, you must navigate a completely unmarked, twisting channel. Shallow water lies on all sides of the otherwise deep cut, and a piloting error can all too easily lead to that sad sound of your keel meeting up with the bottom.

In times past, it has always taken fifteen to twenty minutes of white knuckle, nerve wracking, ultraslow speed cruising to make good our entry into California Bayou. On this particular occasion, however, we were using, for the first time, a new navigational software program plus the latest edition of digitized NOAA nautical charts on my laptop computer. The computer was appropriately interfaced with our onboard GPS by an inexpensive, easy-to-install serial cable.

The laptop's screen depicted our vessel's current position by way of a "boat" symbol, which moved over the electronic portrayal of the chart as we moved on the water. It was a mind-blowing revelation to simply watch the screen, correcting our course to port or starboard a bit as we got a little too close to one side of the channel or the other. In some five minutes' time, our hook was safely down on the sheltered, inner reaches of California Bayou. It was with more than a little astonishment that I reflected on the vast difference between this entry and all my past visits to this anchorage. It was suddenly very clear to me that my on-the-water coastal navigation had taken a most definite turn for the better, which would never be abandoned.

So, by now you are probably asking yourself how you can become a part of this electronic revolution, and what it will cost. As was stated at the beginning of this article, if you already own a laptop computer capable of running the current version of Windows 9x, then the financial burden will be relatively light; but if you need a computer, that is a bit of a different story.

When it comes to a discussion of what laptop computer to purchase, you should check out any of the excellent computer magazines that are available at every newstand in the world these days. It goes far beyond the scope of this book to present more than a cursory discussion of what is available in the way of laptop computers in these quickly changing technological times. Nevertheless, with that said, here are a few of my ideas on the subject. First of all, don't even consider any system that does not run the Windows 9x operating system. You will find that 99.99999999 percent of all up-to-date navigational software available today runs on Windows 9x.

Your next consideration should be just how much horsepower is needed to run Windows 9x. When it comes to computers, horsepower is broken down into two components, processor speed and RAM (Random Access Memory). Without getting into any discussion of what these two components actually are, I recommend at least a Pentium II 233 processor (a Pentium II 266 is even better) and at least 32 megabytes of RAM (64 megs is better). As computer technology goes forward, these numbers will undoubtedly change. You would do well to educate yourself a bit about laptop computers before making your purchase.

As to price, it is an unfortunate fact that laptop computers cost more than desktop computers. This problem can be alleviated to some extent by ordering your new machine from one of several outstanding mail-order vendors that at least to some extent dominate this market today. Dell and Gateway 2000 are excellent choices in this regard. Even so, expect to spend at least $3,000 for a computer that will really do the job.

You will also discover ads for so-called "marinized" laptop computers as you look through boating magazines and other nautical literature. This writer is unqualified to judge just how much this marinization is worth on the water. I can only tell you that I have cruised for two years with my unmarinized Dell laptop and, with the precaution of quickly getting the machine into a watertight compartment as soon as weather and waves turn nasty, I've never had a problem. To be sure, "marinized" computers are more expensive than their landlubber cousins, but you will have to judge for yourself whether this cost differential is justified.

OK, so now you've finally got your laptop. What else do you need? Three things, actually—navigational software, digitized nautical charts, and an interface with your GPS. First, let's consider navigational software. There are many excellent packages available today that will do the job for you. Knowledgeable mariners will spend more than a few minutes discussing the merits of each software system with the computer guru at their local marine store. If you need to stretch a bit farther from home to find this advice, this writer highly recommends the good people at Bluewater Books and Charts (phone: 954-763-6533).

In the most general sense, if your purpose is to simply follow your boat by way of a digital representation of the nautical charts on your computer screen, then the Nav-Trek Solo program by Nobletek at a measly $200 simply cannot be beat. If you want to engage in sophisticated route planning before your time on the water, consider

Nobletek's Visual Navigation Suite ($495), or ChartView by Nautical Software ($469).

Next up are digitized nautical charts. This one is easy. A company known as Map-Tech (formerly BSB or BBA) is exclusively licensed by NOAA to reproduce all the official nautical charts in digitized form from the original negatives. This results in very high-quality on-screen reproductions, and Map-Tech can generally be relied upon to have the latest editions of charts readily available. Again, this writer highly recommends Bluewater Books and Charts as your source for Map-Tech products.

The Map-Tech charts are available on CD-ROMS (about $200 each). Each disk contains *all* the NOAA charts for a particular portion of the U.S. coastline. Unless you are going to be cruising a broad range of coastal waters, you may be able to get by with a single disk.

Finally, you will need to acquire a cable to connect your GPS to a serial port on your laptop computer. These inexpensive units are usually available from the manufacturer of your navigational software. Typical cost is between fifteen and twenty dollars. Then, you will have to wrestle with making sure your GPS output and your computer serial ports are set up properly. This can be more than a little frustrating for first-timers. Try following the interface instructions included with your navigational software package. If all else fails, you may well need to employ the services of a local computer technician for first-time set-up.

At last! You have it—a good laptop computer, navigational software that meets your particular needs, the Map-Tech digitized nautical charts on CD-ROM that cover your particular part of the world, and a working interface between your GPS and computer. I know it sounds like a lot of effort, but once accomplished, your practice of coastal navigation will never be the same again. Trust me, seeing is believing!

Radar

Radar, another byproduct of the Second World War, has become a darling of modern pleasure boating. Radar units transmit a signal from a rotating antenna. When the radar beacon encounters a solid object, a shoreline, or another boat for instance, it is reflected back to the unit, which now becomes a receiver. The strength and position of the "contact" is interpreted by the machine and represented on a video display (sometimes called a CRT—short for cathode ray tube). That's the theory, but, in this case, the practical operation is even more impressive.

Marine radar transmitter and receiver with enclosed dome.

Radar the has been called the ultimate navigational tool. With a well-functioning system, the coastal navigator can easily view a video image of a particular shoreline, aid to navigation, or other boats. More importantly, it requires only an additional glance to determine how far you are from a particular point and what the compass course would be to that location. If all this sounds impressive, it is, but, stand by—there's more.

Radar units used to be massive affairs that required a great deal of space. Worse still, the video image required extensive training to interpret accurately. As such, these old systems were usually confined (in pleasure craft) to large yachts with professional captains.

Computer technology has changed all that. Modern radar units are vastly smaller and lighter than their predecessors. Furthermore, with the introduction of color radar displays (known simply as "Color Radar"), an accurate interpretation of the radar image is now within the grasp of any boater who is willing to take some elementary instruction. Even non-color systems can be translated by the amateur with a bit more practice.

Marine radar transmitter and receiver with swinging head.

By changing radar "ranges" you can close in for a detailed display of what's close by, or punch up a longer-range scan to see what might be approaching. This capability allows radar to render the most effective aid available to help prevent on the water collisions. The tricks you can do with radar are endless, and fun to boot.

Modern non-color, LCD (liquid crystal display) radar systems are available for as little as $1,200 while color units require an additional expenditure of several thousand dollars. Professional installation is a necessity for first-time power captains (and most veterans as well). If you can fit this piece of modern electronic wizardry into your boating budget, it is highly recommended for all cruisers.

Autopilot

An autopilot interfaces with your onboard steering system to keep your boat on a particular course without having to touch the helm. There are many autopilot models and brands, ranging from the simple to the sophisticated. Some coastal boaters, under particular circumstances, will find autopilots quite useful, while others will never miss it.

If you cruise in waters where there are frequent, long runs through deep water between various destinations or aids to navigation, then an autopilot might be for you. These systems shine when you must remain on a particular course for long periods of time. Autopilots relieve the captain from long, boring sessions at the helm. Of course, you must still keep alert for potential collision or other on the water obstructions.

Boaters who plan to fish offshore often are also prime candidates for an autopilot. With this accessory in place, the captain can take a welcome break from the helm or help his guests land fish or bait hooks while the boat continues on its trolling run. Autopilots are invariably found on professional sportfishing craft.

On the other hand, if your cruising waters call for frequent course changes, then an autopilot will be of very limited value. Intracoastal waterways, small sounds, and rivers with abundant shoals are examples of these navigationally complicated waters. In such a cruising environment, it would be necessary to reset the instrument every time you round a point or set course for a different aid to navigation. All boaters, without exception, prefer to handle the helm manually in these sorts of cruising conditions.

SSB

Back in the 1950s and before, all boaters used to employ a marine radio system called DSB (Double Side Band). This radio operated on the AM (amplitude modulation) frequencies and often transmitted with up to 200 watts of power. This system had more than a few drawbacks. A shrimper operating on the coast of North Carolina could call a fellow captain and his broadcast might sometimes be heard in Louisiana (particularly at night). With the introduction of FM (frequency modulation) during World War II, the U.S. Coast Guard began implementing a change to VHF (FM) marine radio during the 1950s and 1960s. VHF has a maximum output of 25 watts and is usually limited to an effective range of 25 to 30 miles. By creating a net of coastal listening stations (described earlier in Chapter 3), the USCG was then able to give complete protection to the coastal mariner without the problem of long-range broadcast overlay.

Of course, VHF does not provide effective communications for boats that cruise more than 30 miles offshore, or those who need longer-range coastal transmitting capabilities. Thus SSB (Single Side Band) radios were introduced. Available with various transmitting power levels, ranging from 50 to 200 watts, this sort of two-way radio allows for long-range communication. With some frequencies and maximum power levels, transoceanic exchanges are possible.

First-time power boaters who only cruise on coastal waters can probably take the money they might fork out for an SSB and spend it elsewhere. It is seldom that you will ever require such long-range communications. However, if you plan to fish more than 20 to 30 miles offshore, SSB could become a genuine consideration. Also, SSB does provide a very reliable backup for VHF. Should you find yourself in the unlikely (but remotely possible) situation where you can't raise the Coast Guard on VHF Channel 16, then an SSB radio could be priceless. Those lucky captains who have a prodigious boating budget might want to consider SSB for this reason.

As you might expect, SSB radio requires a separate antenna and professional installation. The price for this long-range accessory ranges from one to several thousand dollars. Obviously, it's not inexpensive and most boat owners will want to identify a definite need before laying out that kind of cash.

Cellular Telephones

Since the 1980s, cellular telephone technology has taken the USA by storm. A cellular telephone is actually a low power (3-watt maximum) transceiver (transmitter plus receiver) that can be installed in your car or boat. Battery operated, handheld units are also available. The landside cellular receiving system consists of several towers or "cell sites" interconnected to a very sophisticated computer system. When you make a call, the central cellular computer immediately determines which cell site antennae will best service your transmission. As you begin to move away from the tower in your car or boat, and enter another cell, the central computer senses the change in signal strength. Your call is handed off to the next cell site tower *without any noticeable interruption in service.* Thus, you can make a phone call in one cell and travel through two, three, four, or more cell sites without any discernible disturbance to your conversation.

Most cellular telephone companies have so-called "roaming" agreements with other systems. This means that you can use your phone, not only in your home system but in any other city or coastal area that has cellular service. With the advance state of cellular service available today, owners of these technological marvels can now pretty much use their phones coast to coast. A few unserviced areas still remain, but their numbers diminish daily.

Cellular telephones (both fixed and portable) can now be purchased for less than fifty dollars including professional installation. Many cellular companies run specials on the necessary hardware to encourage customers to sign up for their system. A careful shopper can often take advantage of these special deals and save big time.

Permanently mounted cellular phones usually feature a 3-watt output, while the handheld varieties have a less than 1-watt power. Cellular coverage is so pervasive now that on most occasions, even the lower power units give acceptable reception. However, for maximum clarity of signal, the higher-powered, fixed installation units are still to be preferred.

Professional installation is a *must* for fixed mount cellular telephones. The sophisticated programming of the phone requires extensive training. As already mentioned, most cellular companies include the cost of installation in the purchase price.

Considering the inexpensive cost of their acquisition, this writer would highly recommend a cellular telephone for virtually everyone taking to the water. Not only will it allow you to communicate via the best informational network in the world, but a cellular phone is a great back-up to the VHF for emergencies. If you are worried about your secretary calling while you are on the water, don't give her your number!

Engine Synchronizer

Boats with twin power plants have a special problem with engine synchronization. If both motors are not turning at the same RPM (revolutions per minute), uncomfortable vibration and loss of fuel efficiency are the result. RPM meters are not accurate enough for fine tuning of the engine's speed. So, how do you set the speeds together? Enter the engine synchronizer.

An engine synchronizer tests the RPMs of both power plants and then allows the operator to set the speeds accurately via a visual display. Some models consist of a single light. As long as the light is flashing, the speeds are different. Once the light is constant (or almost constant) the engines are synchronized. Another version consists of three lights. When the left is lit, the port engine is running faster than the starboard. When the righthand light is on, the condition is reversed. The center light indicates a synchronized condition.

While there are many captains who would disagree with me, I prefer the "three light" variety of synchronizer. With the single indicator version, you never know which engine is fast or slow.

Engine synchronizers are almost a necessity aboard twin engine boats. After carefully reading the instructions, adventurous new captains *may* be able to install the unit themselves. However, most first-time power boat owners will probably opt for that old reliable professional installation.

Fuel Totalizers

A fuel totalizer meter is a really "neat" accessory. This electronic marvel relies upon a sensor placed in the fuel line between the gas tank and the engine. The metered instrument head monitors the amount of gasoline flowing through the line. This information is presented in two forms. With most models, a round gauge meters the "gallons per hour." This is a rating of fuel economy. It can be quite useful in finding your boat's most efficient trim (see discussion of "Trim Tabs" later in this chapter). Even more useful is the readout of total gallons consumed. You can plug this information into the total capacity of your fuel tank and quickly calculate exactly how much fuel remains onboard. This sure-fire metering of gasoline or diesel reserves is quite useful on long cruises.

Fuel totalizers are available in single and twin engine models. The twin variety totals the fuel burned by *both* engines. A switch allows you to monitor the gallons per hour of either the port or starboard engine.

Knotmeter/Log

I have always contended that it is almost as important to know how far you have gone as it is to know what course you are on, or how deep is the water. The simple modern expedient to this question is the combination knotmeter/log.

A speed/distance instrument of this type consists of a thru-hull or transom-mounted transducer (often called a paddle wheel). The faster the boat goes through the water, the more quickly the paddle turns. A small magnet is attached to one fin of the paddle. A sensor mounted above the paddle counts the number of revolutions.

This information is electronically passed to an instrument head where the speed of the boat is indicated on the knotmeter. Much as an odometer operates in a car, the "log" calculates the miles traveled from the speed through the water. Thus you have two pieces of vital information: how fast you are traveling and how far you have gone. While, as you will learn in your studies of piloting, it is possible to calculate distance from speed and time, a functioning log simplifies this process greatly.

Knotmeter/logs present their information in a variety of ways. The traditional model (now seldom seen) is very similar to an automobile speedometer/odometer. The boat's speed is represented on a round dial, while the total miles traveled is clocked on a mechanical circular counter. Typical present-day units present an LCD digital display of speed and/or miles. A few have separate instrument heads for distance.

Whichever type you choose, and they are all almost equally effective, be sure to select a model with a *resettable* log. This feature allows you to set the distance read-out to zero when passing a certain point in your cruise. If you know from your chart work that the next daybeacon is supposed to be twenty miles away, then a quick glance at the log will indicate when the aid should be in sight. If the log cannot be reset, you must make note of the reading when you pass your point of departure and calculate what the reading would upon arriving at your intended destination. While this is, of course, quite possible, a resettable log removes one more thing that you have to be concerned with while underway.

Another modern trend in knotmeter/logs is to combine the speed/distance information with water depth and even water temperature. These "all in one" instruments are quite practical and their price is often less than a depth sounder plus knotmeter/log purchased separately.

Finally, let's have a quick word about the "knots" in knotmeter. When calculating distance by automobile, we speak of miles traveled. In nautical jargon, this variety of land distance measurement is known as a *statute mile.* On-the-water navigation uses a different unit of measurement known as a *nautical mile.* This type of mile is 15 percent longer than its landside brother. One nautical mile an hour is known as a knot. Hence the term *knotmeter.*

You may wonder why navigators would go to all the trouble to use a different measurement for on-the-water distance. The answer lies in the fact that a nautical mile is exactly equal to one minute of latitude. If those terms are not familiar, you will learn about them at length in your studies of coastal navigation.

ONBOARD APPLIANCES

Marine Air Conditioning

Marine air conditioning systems are almost a necessity for anyone who cruises the waters of the southeastern or southwestern United States. Without some way to cool your boat, the months of July and August are almost off limits, at least for comfortable live-aboard cruises. An efficient marine air conditioner can make all the difference.

There are a wide variety of air conditioning systems available on the marine market. The best models are water cooled! In this one area, the marine environment is much superior to the landside home.

If you ever took a scuba class, the instructor probably warned you about wearing a wet suit to keep warm. He might have gone on to say that water conducts heat away from the body five times faster than air. This same principle allows marine air conditioning to be much more efficient than its landlubber counterpart. With a ready supply of sea water at hand, a pump in the bilge can direct a stream of cooling water through the system and then discharge the heated water overboard. Thus, water-cooled marine air conditioners can be much smaller and more compact than home (air cooled) units while still providing the same BTUs (British Thermal Units) of cooling power.

Another option worth considering is "reverse cycle." Systems equipped with this feature can draw heat out of the water during cold weather and provide a ready central furnace for your boat. This operating principle is very similar to a home heat pump.

Some smaller, semi-portable marine air conditioners are air cooled. While this variety is not as efficient as its water-cooled counterpart, they do provide cooling on some small vessels that might not be appropriate for the larger, fixed units.

By now, you may be tired of hearing me say this, but, again, professional installation of a water-cooled marine air conditioning system is almost a necessity. It sometimes requires more than a little imagination on the installer's part to hide all the various pieces of equipment associated with the air conditioner. Practice and training are absolutely necessary for a good installation. Contact a marine air conditioning dealer in your home port for a "turn key" estimate (equipment and installation).

If your boat is equipped with a single, 30-amp, 120-volt electrical service, a second shorepower cable and connector will be necessary. Your dealer should provide all the necessary materials and make the appropriate installation.

Generator

There will be many occasions during your cruises when it will be a distinct advantage to have a 120-volt generator aboard. When anchoring off, you can charge your battery (if you have an automatic battery charger), cook on an electric stove, watch TV, or run a VCR. Once we were caught at our marina for three days during a freak, 13-inch snowstorm. The power went off midway through the first day. Our generator was a lifesaver on this occasion.

Generators are rated in amps. As a new power boat owner, you should consult a marine generator dealer to determine what power level would be appropriate for your boat and its 120-volt accessories. As long as you are going to the expense of installing a generator, you might as well purchase one that is powerful enough to handle all your onboard 120-volt chores.

It's only fair to note that generators, particularly the gasoline-powered variety, are habitually temperamental. Mine gives more trouble than any other single piece of equipment aboard. Regular maintenance is the key to minimizing generator problems. Plan on a vigorous maintenance schedule for your unit, including an annual professional servicing.

Generators usually come equipped with a water muffler to minimize operating noise. Even so, an unshielded unit is much too noisy for normal operation. Before we acquired our sound shield, it was impossible to hear one another in the cockpit without yelling while the generator was operating.

Recognizing this problem, all generator manufacturers offer sound insulation boxes. Plan on laying out the extra cash and ordering one of these necessary items at the time of installation.

Proper installation of a marine generator can be an exacting job after the boat has left the factory. Be sure your dealer has full and adequate provisions for complete, professional installation *before* closing the deal.

Marine generators are not inexpensive. You can look forward to a bill ranging from three to as much as eight or nine thousand dollars. The first time you crank up the TV and VCR while swinging tranquilly on the hook miles away from the nearest marina, the expense just may seem justified. On the other hand, if you cannot fit a generator in your boating budget at first, it's certainly an accessory you can live without for a few years.

Before leaving our discussion of marine generators, take heed of one *important warning!* Occasionally, defective generator exhaust systems leak carbon monoxide. Operating such a flawed unit overnight *can lead to suffocation by all aboard.* Even if I think my generator is in top working condition, we make it a rule never to operate the unit while sleeping.

ENGINE ACCESSORIES

Certain engine accessories can help your power plants run cooler and last longer. If any of the items listed below were not included on your craft at the time of purchase, you should make every effort to install them as soon as possible.

Raw Water Filters

Even freshwater-cooled engines must draw in seawater for a "heat exchanger" to dissipate heat from the motors. Raw water-cooled engines circulate the saltwater directly through the transmission, block, and manifold. Foreign bodies such as sand or seaweed can clog or damage the water pump and interrupt this vital cooling flow.

Filters in the cooling water intake line can prevent just this sort of trouble. Raw water filters contain a wire mesh that screens out foreign bodies before they can reach the engine's water pump.

Some raw water filters are housed in a plastic body while others have a bronze casing. We installed the plastic variety aboard our craft, only to have one filter crack after a single month of operation. As you can guess, we immediately switched to bronze filters and have stuck with them ever since. Some models have a glass sleeve surrounded by the bronze supporting structure. This allows for easy inspection of the filter to determine if cleaning is necessary.

To perform properly, raw water filters must be installed between the thru-hull water intakes and the engine's water pump. Practical, but inexperienced boat owners can often perform this task themselves. First, determine the inner diameter of your cooling hose. Then, journey down to the local plumbing supply house and purchase all the fittings you need (including two hose clamps) to mate your particular filter with the hose in question. Cut the raw water hose where the filter can lay on or against some solid object for support. If this is not practical, you must tie the filter up with some sort of strap support. Once you have mated the filter with the hose, screw down the hose clamps on either end and the job is done. If this sounds a bit complicated, ask one of the service technicians at your marina to install one filter for you. Observe the process, and, if you have twin engines, perhaps you can install the next one yourself.

Freshwater Cooling Kits

Raw water-cooled engines that have less than one hundred engine hours (hours of actual operation) are candidates for freshwater conversion. There is still a great debate in boating circles as to how much longer a freshwater engine will last versus the raw water-cooled variety. There is no question in my own mind. In 1988 we had to replace both motors in our cruiser to the tune of $8,700. 1 watched the yard personnel as they removed and disassembled the old power plants. Evidence of internal rust and corrosion was everywhere. Never again will any boat of mine be equipped with raw water-cooled engines.

Freshwater conversion kits are available for almost any marine engine for about $500 to $1,000 per power plant. These kits are often available in on-engine (the parts are bolted directly to the motor) and off-engine (separate mounting is necessary) varieties. If available, the on-engine kits are much preferred.

New skippers *with previous mechanical experience* can install a freshwater conversion kit themselves. Everything you need is usually provided in the kit, and the step-by-step directions are, in my experience, quite clear. Nevertheless, it's not a quick or uninvolved job. If you don't know a water distribution block from a manifold, better have a qualified mechanic make the installation and check the system thoroughly.

Flush System

If your new "pride and joy" is equipped with raw water-cooled engines that have more than two hundred hours of actual operation (engine hours), then you should probably not spend the money for a freshwater conversion. The theory is that after pumping so much saltwater through an engine, the porous metal will retain enough salt to partially negate the improved longevity afforded by freshwater conversion. However, there is still something you *can* do to improve your power plant's useful life.

Consider for a moment, if you could leave your engine filled with *fresh* water while it was sitting at the dock, saltwater would only come in contact with the blocks and manifolds during actual operation. An easily installed flush attachment provides just this benefit.

This is one engine accessory that you can certainly install yourself. First, close the raw water intake and remove the cooling water hose. Use a ruler and determine the inner diameter of the cooling line. Pay a visit to a plumbing supplier and purchase a "T" fitting that will fit your diameter cooling hose. Now, ask the clerk to fit the odd (or upper) end of the "T" with a valve and male garden hose fitting. To this assembly, attach a ½" plastic reinforced hose with a female garden hose fitting. The opposite end of the plastic hose will be connected to a pressure regulator-female garden hose fitting such as that discussed in the Freshwater System section later in this chapter.

Return to your boat and cut the freshwater cooling line (be sure the thru-hull intake is still closed) at some convenient place well back from the water pump. Using two hose clamps, install the "T" fitting at this point. Connect the plastic hose to the upper end of the "T" (be sure to use rubber washers on all garden hose connections), and route it to some convenient location on deck where the pressure regulator/connector can be secured.

Now, when you operate your engines while cruising, open the thru-hull valve and *close* the valve on the upper end of the "T" fitting. Raw water will then flow normally through your cooling system. After returning to the dock where your boat will reside for several days (at least), close the thru-hull water intake and attach a freshwater hose to the on-deck pressure reducer. Be sure the water is turned on! Have your mate start the engine while you quickly open the valve at the top of the "T." Look over the stern to make sure you have water flow through the exhaust ports. If you don't see what appears to be a normal amount of water, shut down the engines at once and find out what's wrong.

If all is well, run the engines for five minutes with the freshwater feed. As this process goes forward, the fresh water will help to flush the salt from your engines and manifold. After the flush process is complete, have your mate stop the engines while you quickly shut off the "T" valve.

The high pressure of city water systems necessitates this quick turn-on and turn-off of the "T" valve. Should you allow the water pressure unrestricted access to your engine, it could damage some of the power plant's seals.

With a little experimentation, you should find this a fun, first do-it-yourself project on your new vessel. If you are not clear about any portion of the described installation, be sure to consult a boating professional *before* proceeding!

Oil Changing Pumps

Shoreside mechanics have a considerable advantage over their nautical counterparts when it comes time to change the oil. With a car, the vehicle can be raised, the plug removed, and the old oil simply drains into a convenient container.

With marine engines, the situation is very different. In the first place, the drain plug on the bottom of the oil pan is often virtually unreachable. Even if it can be removed, the boat owner is faced with the problem of how to keep the old oil from spilling all over the bilge. Unless you want to jack your engines out of the bilge whenever the time comes for an oil change (not a practical alternative), a pump must be employed to suck the old lubricant out through the dipstick passage.

Various pump kits are available to accomplish this task. Some connect to an electric drill (as a power source) and have one hose designed to be pushed down through the dipstick hole, while a second hose carries the old oil to a bucket or other container. The better models are self-contained units with a complete 12-volt pump permanently attached to a bucket that serves as a container for the used oil. I prefer this variety but it is more expensive (usually about $75), while drill pump models go for a little as $20.

Whichever model fits your boating budget, this is an accessory that you will *want to have.* Eventually, most captains change their own oil. It doesn' t make sense to pay a mechanic $25+ per hour for this simple task. To do the job right, you *must* have an oil pump system of one form or another.

PROTECTIVE COVERINGS

Canvas Covers and Tops

New boat owners invariably discover that their new craft needs several marine canvas covers, tops, and/or enclosures. These sorts of coverings can range from a bimini top for the flybridge to a protective jacket for the searchlight. Equipping your craft with the appropriate canvas covers can accomplish two very different tasks. First, they will help to protect the boat from the damaging effect of sun and rain. Any boater who has tried to clean and polish an uncovered flybridge can attest to the truth of this assertion. Secondly, with a bimini top or full flybridge enclosure, you can accommodate cruising in less than ideal weather. Meeting these two objectives calls for careful selection of covers, based upon your particular boating needs.

Most coverings must be custom-made by a nautical canvas shop. First-time power boat owners will be surprised (possibly shocked) at the cost of these covers. I know I was (and still am). For instance, a simple bimini top for the flybridge of a thirty-two-foot power cruiser can run up to $500. A full enclosure can set you back $1,500. Not small potatoes, I'm sure you will agree. Unless you are a captain with an unlimited boating budget, it will be necessary to pick and choose which coverings are necessary, and which can be installed at a later time.

Within the last decade the marine coverings industry has been turned upside down by the introduction of the “Sunbrella” fabric. Manufactured in North Carolina by Glen Raven Mills, this marvelous product (available in a whole rainbow of colors) is incredibly durable and it simply *will not* mildew. You will quickly discover that the vast majority of marine coverings are now made from Sunbrella. You would be well advised to take a quick ride on this bandwagon. No matter whether you are adding a bimini top, flybridge storage cover, or simply a covering over your cockpit wet bar, this fabric will more than fill the bill.

Sunbrella coverings can be used in a wide variety of applications. As you become familiar with your new craft, many different uses will become apparent. Some of the most popular types are discussed below. However when your budget allows, you will undoubtedly find many additional uses for Sunbrella that have never even occurred to this writer.

Bimini Tops

A bimini top can be thought of as a roof over your flybridge. It is open on all four sides and, as such, provides only overhead protection from sun or rain. Bimini tops are undoubtedly the most popular marine canvas coverings. Walk around any marina, and you will discover that four out of five flybridge-equipped boats sport a bimini top.

A bimini consists of a sloping canvas roof buttressed by a system of aluminum tube-type supports. It is usually held in place by nylon straps at each corner. In good weather you can unsnap the belts and lay the cover forward or backward to facilitate a good sun tan. This feature is in marked contrast to a full flybridge enclosure, which requires a real effort to disassemble.

Unfortunately, bimini tops do have some disadvantages as well. In a windy rainstorm, the helmsman is liable to get just about as wet as if there were no covering over his head. Also, at cruising speeds over 15 knots, the bimini can act as a wind catch, vastly increasing the wind and noise buffeting those riding on the flybridge. For this reason, in good weather, we often cruise with the bimini laid back.

In spite of these shortcomings, a bimini top is perhaps the most basic canvas cruising aid. Without one, you will be limited by the effects of sun and even a mild rainstorm. With the possible exception of a flybridge storage cover, I would suggest putting a bimini top at the head of your vinyl wish list.

Full Flybridge Enclosures

Flybridge enclosures are bimini tops with curtains on all four sides of the cover. Most of the curtains are made of transparent plastic to allow for easy viewing from all angles. Numerous zippers allow for

Bimini canvas top over flybridge.

entry from the flybridge ladder and airways during hot weather. While a driving rain can make it somewhat difficult to see, a full enclosure does allow the helmsman to operate the boat from the flybridge in almost any weather. Unfortunately, as mentioned earlier, this type of covering is expensive and difficult to disassemble. However, many professional fishing captains and long-range cruisers choose full enclosures for their vessels. You must weigh the advantages and disadvantages against the depth of your pocketbook to make an intelligent decision. Most new boat owners will probably choose to begin their cruising life with a bimini and then perhaps step up to full enclosure at a later time.

Flybridge Storage Cover

If your boat has a flybridge and is docked at a slip or pier exposed to the weather, an upper station storage cover is certainly first priority. Just imagine all the complex wiring and engine instruments on your flybridge subject day after day to sun and rain. It does not require too much imagination to foresee that

Canvas hatch covers.

numerous electrical problems will be the quick result of such exposure. A flybridge storage cover is the best answer to this serious problem.

During installation, the canvas maker will mount snaps around your flybridge to secure the cover. I have found that many installers tend to place the snaps so that the cover is too tight. Of course, it must be taut enough to allow for rainwater runoff, but not so tight that it becomes necessary to strain and curse every time you snap it on. I suggest checking your new cover after installation and reporting any problems to the canvas shop immediately.

Other Canvas Covers

Movable stainless steel hardware such as searchlights, permanently mounted deck chairs or exterior teak furniture (such as wet bars) are all candidates for canvas covers. In our own case, we built a cockpit wet bar from teak plywood several years ago. After only a year it was necessary to clean the teak extensively (and laboriously), and then recoat with teak oil. It wasn't long before a cover was ordered and installed to protect the wood.

Canvas cover protection can significantly reduce the maintenance on most any piece of nautical equipment exposed to the elements. Stainless steel, teak, and other vinyl (such as seats) can all benefit from such treatment. As always, you must balance your needs against the old boating budget.

12-VOLT ELECTRICAL SYSTEMS

Many veteran boat owners seldom think about their twelve-volt electrical systems until it's time to replace their expensive marine batteries. Then, they often wonder why the batteries didn't last longer. Several electrical accessories can lengthen the life of your onboard power sources and provide electrical flexibility when living aboard.

Automatic Battery Chargers

Unless your vessel comes equipped with a 120-volt AC battery charger, you should put this piece of equipment at the top of your accessory list. Without one, the engine's alternator is your only power source for recharging the batteries. If you stay aboard your boat for several days without starting the engines, the 12-volt power will soon be exhausted.

Another possible scenario can be even more damaging. Suppose your dockage basin experiences heavy rains. The automatic bilge pump will cycle on and off to evacuate the rainwater. What happens, though, if the pump eventually drains the battery? Rainwater will continue to collect in your bilge, possibly causing damage.

A *marine automatic battery charger* is the answer to all these problems. The average cost ($250-$400) is easily justified by the benefits. A good quality unit can charge three to five banks of batteries without damage from overcharging. This is where the ranks of auto and marine battery chargers part company. The landside units must be physically removed from a battery after a full charge condition is achieved. If the charger continues to operate, the battery is literally "fried," often ruining the power source permanently. Marine battery chargers, on the other hand, sense a full charge and shut off *completely*. This is *very different* from so-called trickle chargers, which always maintain a small amount of current to the battery. Don't accept anything but a fully-marinized battery charger with *complete shutoff*. As you might expect, marine battery chargers should be professionally installed in practically every instance.

Deep-Cycle Batteries and Battery Isolators

To understand the importance of a deep-cycle 12-volt power source, you must first learn about the two fundamentally different types of marine batteries. The most common variety is known as a cranking battery. These units are designed to give a quick, high amperage burst of power in order to start the engine. For long life, they should *seldom (if ever) be discharged completely*. Most factory boats are delivered with one or more (usually one per engine) cranking batteries. All the onboard 12-volt accessories are powered from these units. Even with an automatic battery charger, complete discharge will sometimes take place, particularly at anchor. Now, you can begin to understand why the captain down the dock has to replace his batteries so often.

Deep-cycle batteries, originally developed for golf carts, are very different animals. They are designed to give an even flow of power over a long period of time, and, most importantly, they can be discharged and recharged repeatedly without undue damage. Thus, they are a perfect power source for all your onboard 12-volt electrical equipment.

Given these facts, you might want to consider employing a marine electrician to install one or more deep-cycle batteries, and wiring all onboard 12-volt equipment to this power source. With this arrangement, the cranking batteries will always be fresh and ready to start your engine. Meanwhile, the deep-cycle battery will have a long life in spite of repeated discharges.

An additional accessory that fits well with such a 12-volt electrical system is a battery isolator. These clever devices allow a single engine alternator to charge several batteries without overcharging any of the units. Thus, when any of your engines are in operation, the alternator can charge your cranking and deep-cycle batteries in one fell swoop. Couple the isolator with an automatic battery charger

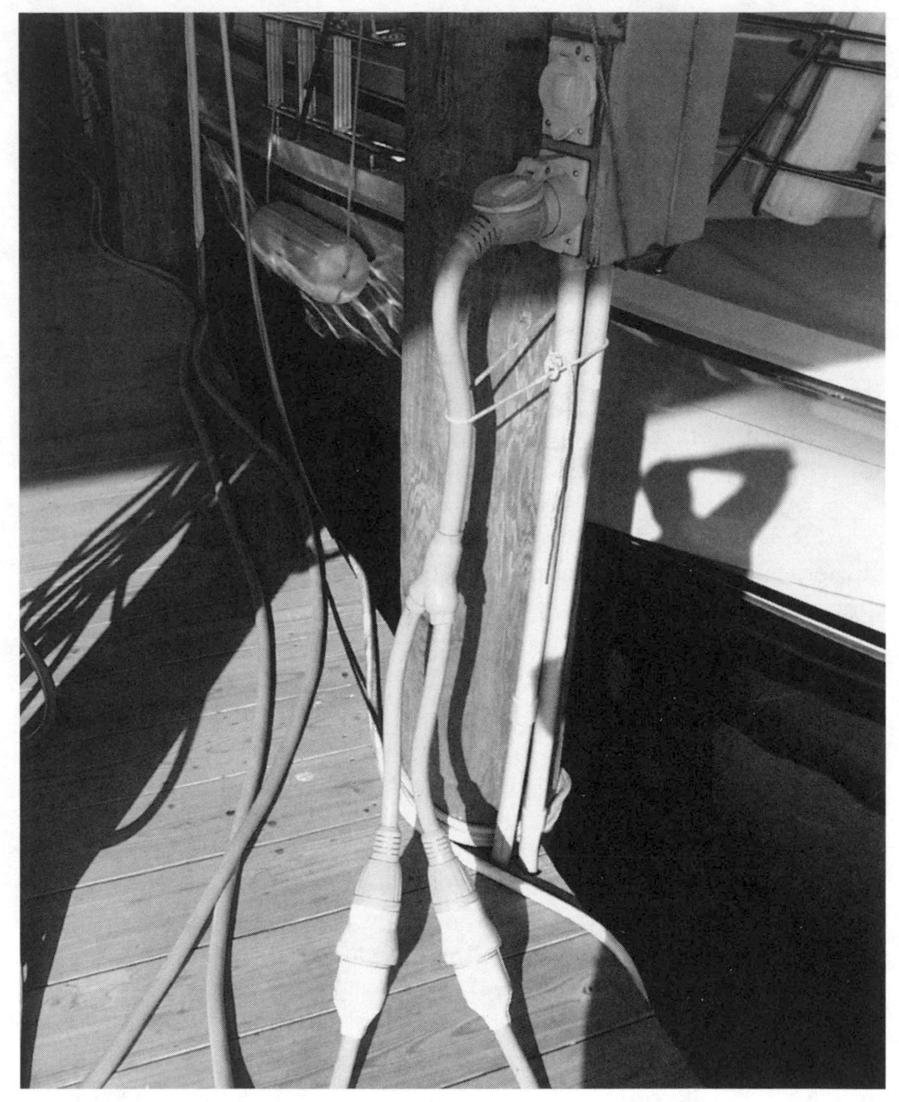

Twin 20-amp splitter connector.

(described above) charging all your batteries at dockside, and you have the near-perfect 12-volt system.

Shorepower System Adapters

While we are on the subject of electrical power, let me mention a very important accessory. As discussed in Chapter 2, different boats have differing amperage electrical systems. Similarly, marinas have different electric services. The normal ratings for both shoreside and onboard systems are 20, 30, 50, and (for *large* pleasure craft) 100 amps. Each of these power ratings employs its own unique style plug. To further complicate the situation, fifty-amp services have two different types of connections. If you happen to have a 30-amp onboard system, and the marina where you stop to spend the night has only 50-amp and 20-amp service, you can't plug into shorepower. Cold sandwiches for supper, not to mention a cold shower, can be the result.

To guard against this occurrence, cruising boats should be equipped with a selection of shorepower adapters. Whatever the amperage of your onboard system, select the necessary adapters to hook up to the power level above and/or below your system. For example, if your boat has an onboard 30-amp system (the most common rating), then you should consider purchasing a 50-amp to 30-amp twistlock (or range plug) adapter, and a 20-amp to 30-amp unit. Be advised that a 50-amp shoreside service might require a twistlock or a so-called range plug. We usually travel with a range plug, rather than a twistlock adapter, and have never regretted this arrangement. However, new marinas may require the twistlock type of plug.

Fifty-amp shoreside services can power *two* onboard 30-amp (or 20-amp) systems and 50- to 30-amp adapters are normally outfitted with two 30-amp female connectors. This setup is often called a "pigtail" adapter. A 50- to 30-amp adapter is an ideal arrangement for two 30-amp shorepower cables (one for normal service and one for air conditioning).

Sometimes marinas will loan visiting boaters any necessary adapters, but cruising captains can't count on this helpful service. It's far better to spend the money for any adapters you might need rather than suffer a disappointment while cruising.

CRUISING ACCESSORIES

Certain non-electronic cruising accessories can help to make your waterborne trips a safer and more enjoyable experience. The well-outfitted cruising boat will have most of the items listed below aboard.

Second Bilge Pump

If your boat is equipped with only one bilge pump, the installation of a second unit is an excellent safety precaution. If one pump should fail, or, more likely, if the pump's automatic switch should malfunction, a second unit can make all the difference between a minor problem and a major incident. New boat owners often suppose that bilge pumps are used only to counteract major leaks that result from the hull being pierced or a thru-hull giving way. Actually, even the highest capacity bilge pump can only keep up with such a catastrophic accident for a short period of time. Most of the time, bilge pumps drain away water from minor leaks, spray and overwash from rough cruising conditions, and rain leaking through the various bilge hatches.

Planing-hulled boats can benefit from placing the second pump near the stern. On long cruises, bilge water collects at the rear of the bilge while the boat is on plane. Factory-installed bilge pumps usually reside near the center of a vessel. This is the lowest point when the boat is level. However, if you stay on plane, hour after hour, a bilge pump placed in the usual position will not have a chance to siphon off any excess water. By locating a second pump with an automatic float switch near the stern, this problem is immediately solved.

There is really only a small difference in price between a high-capacity bilge pump and its low-volume counterpart. I suggest purchasing a pump with at least a 1,500 gallon per hour rating. By all accounts, you should only install a unit that includes an automatic float switch. This necessary adjunct automatically activates the pump when the bilge water reaches a certain level, and cuts the pump off after the excess has been removed.

With a lifetime of boating experience under my belt, I got the bright idea of installing a second bilge pump myself. After sweating and cursing for an entire day, the unit was at last in place. I was exhausted. If you decide to equip your boat with a second pump, do yourself a big favor and have your marina install the unit.

Trim Tabs

Trim tabs are a great addition for any boat with a planing hull. These units consist of two flat metal surfaces that are affixed to the bottom of the stern transom. The metal planes are attached to a hydraulic cylinder that can force the flat surface down into the water or withdraw it toward the surface.

Most planing hulled boats are designed to ride with their bows out of the water. This is only as it should be for rough weather. However, it requires additional power to keep the bow up, and fuel efficiency suffers. In calm waters, trim tabs allow the captain to force the bow down at cruising speeds. By touching an electric switch, a hydraulic pump forces the cylinder to push the flat metal plane further into the water. The resulting upward push from the water flow onto the metal plane forces the stern up and the bow down. When properly adjusted, this "bow down" position results in lessened water friction and can improve fuel economy as much as 10 percent.

An additional benefit of trim tabs is their ability to balance a listing (leaning) boat. Most trim tab controls allow you to push one tab or the other further into the water. Thus, if a boat is overloaded on the port side, for example, and the vessel is listing to that quarter, you can depress the port tab further, and the resulting water pressure will force that side of the boat upward into a level posture.

Trim tabs are not inexpensive and they should most certainly be installed professionally. They are useless for displacement hulls and normally not required on semi-displacement boats. However, if your craft is of the planing variety, then you will certainly want to give every consideration to this most practical accessory.

Binoculars

Modern binoculars are a near necessity for cruising craft. During daylight hours, daybeacons, buoys, and other aids to navigation often blend in with the background. A good pair of binoculars can help any navigator find a hidden marker or landmark. At night, binoculars act as "light gatherers." Captains studying the water through these instruments can see buoys, other boats, and (most importantly) obstructions that are too dim for the naked eye. To be succinct, I wouldn't leave the dock without a good pair of binoculars.

Be sure to select a waterproof model. These fortunate units do not normally fog internally during damp conditions. Nitrogen-filled binoculars are practically immune to fogging and offer protection from internal fungi and bacteria, which can eventually clog the lenses of inexpensive marine binoculars. Some more expensive models also come equipped with a compass that is readily visible when looking through the instrument. Binoculars equipped with this feature double as a hand-bearing compass (discussed below). While you can look forward to spending as much as $500 for compass-equipped binoculars, the extra expense might be justified in navigationally tricky waters.

Binoculars come with various magnifications. Some are even "zoom" models, which allow for variable enlargement. The best all-round magnification and lens size is 7 x 50. Magnifications higher than "T" introduce too much motion into a floating environment, and you need an objective at least 50 mm in size for its light-gathering qualities.

Searchlights

It can be an unnerving experience when you first venture out upon the water at night. Everything looks different! New boat owners should wait until they gain experience with daylight cruising before attempting their first nighttime sojourn. Locating channel markers, even lighted ones, can be more than a little difficult. You need a good quality, bright searchlight to rescue you from this gloomy condition.

Practically every navigational aid now features a strip of reflective material similar to that used on highway signs. This allows the marker to be spotted from as much as a mile away with a powerful searchlight. Obviously, the light will aid in spotting obstructions and other boats as well.

Searchlights come in various designs and candlepower. I recommend a light with at least 200,000 preferably 300,000 candlepower. You must also choose between the handheld vs. the fixed variety. On larger vessels and boats without flybridges, fixed searchlights are the obvious choice. These model are more expensive, and more difficult to maneuver, but the disadvantages are certainly acceptable. When piloting from a flybridge, I prefer a handheld searchlight. Usually, the "first-rate, first mate" searches out the various aids to navigation while I watch the compass and the water directly ahead. The handheld light allows her to search the horizon quickly from port to starboard.

Fixed searchlights are, of course, permanently wired into the boat's twelve-volt electrical system. Handheld lights are usually configured to plug into a chart (cigarette) lighter plug or a waterproof, two-prong deck plug. Boat owners with electrical experience can install either plug easily.

Chart Lighter

Another nighttime cruising accessory that I have found useful is a small, cylindrical chart lighter. This unit is composed of a brass tube, somewhat smaller than a normal flashlight, which contains two AA batteries. The red shielded bulb is activated by a spring-loaded push bottom on the opposite end. For those of you who have never watched World War II submarine movies, red light does not destroy your night vision as does normal white light. Hence red is the illumination of choice for after-dark cruising.

Chart lighters come with a lanyard, so the unit can be hung around your neck. It has little weight and is always ready at hand if you need to check the chart. Chart lighters are a small, inexpensive accessory, but they can be a real life saver when the situation calls for a quick nighttime check of the charts.

Hand-Bearing Compass

In your studies of coastal navigation, you will learn how you can fix your position (find out exactly where you are) by taking compass bearings on two charted landmarks or aids to navigation. On many occasions, it's not convenient or practical to use the shipboard compass for taking the necessary bearings. A handheld compass can solve this dilemma.

Handheld compasses are very much like their fixed counterparts, except they are mounted on a handle and have an optical sight that allows you to take bearings on a specific object in the distance. Mine is housed in an attractive wooden storage case, and even features night lighting for after-dark navigation. While not essential, hand-bearing compasses can be very useful, particularly if you cruise waters where the aids to navigation are widely spaced.

Swim Platforms

If you plan to anchor off and dinghy ashore often (dinghies will be discussed later in this chapter) or if scuba diving is part of your cruising itinerary, then a swim platform is an accessory that demands your consideration. Swim platforms are slotted, stable platforms that are mounted just above the waterline on a boat's stern. They are usually about 2 ½ feet wide and stretch from one side of the stern to the other. When it comes time to launch and load the dinghy, it is most convenient to have this stable surface just above the waterline from which to work. It is a relatively simple matter to mount a small outboard on the dinghy, load your gear, get everyone onboard and head for the shore. Similarly, scuba divers will appreciate this ready depository of tanks and other gear.

Swim platforms are usually made from either fiberglass or teak. The fiberglass variety is less expensive and does not require as much maintenance. Teak platforms usually need at least one rigorous cleaning followed by multiple coats of teak oil per season. Many owners, nevertheless, prefer the teak style for the warm, non-plastic appearance it confers on the craft's stern.

Foul Weather Gear

No matter how carefully your cruises are planned to coincide with good weather, the day will come when a thunderstorm or unexpected cold front will rain on your parade. With a good set of foul weather gear onboard, you can continue to pilot the boat from the flybridge in relative comfort.

Teak swim platform.

A set of foul weather gear consists of a waterproof coat and a pair of trousers or a bib. Our sailing brethren often add boots and a hat to this ensemble, but most power boaters forego these additions. Some suits are made from vinyl or PVC while the best sets derive from a very closely woven, nylon fabric that is somewhat akin to an umbrella.

Of course, there has to be a down side. A really good set of rainware will cost several hundred dollars. Try purchasing your foul weather gear at one of the large boat shows. Several reputable manufacturers of this type of clothing usually have booths at these shows, and they usually offer a special "boat show" price.

DINGHIES

What would you do if you anchored in a picturesque harbor where there were no available docks and smelled the tantalizing aroma of fresh seafood being cooked at a restaurant across the way? Without a dinghy, your only alternative would be swimming. Since this situation, and many others like it, occur frequently when cruising, most power craft carry a dinghy of one variety or another aboard.

Fixed dinghy mounted on sun deck of motor yacht.

For those landlubbers who are not familiar with the term, a dinghy (or "tender") is nothing more than a small boat (6 to 10 feet usually) whose sole purpose is to serve the mother ship. It can be used to ferry captain and crew ashore whenever there is no convenient dockage for larger craft. Isolated beaches and anchor-only harbors are the two best examples of this cruising event.

Dinghies may be almost indispensable for cruising, but they can be a real pain to store. The traditional fixed dinghy has always been an accessory looking for a place to stay. Some captains mount their dinghy on the bow, where it always seems to be in the way. Other use dinghy hooks and clip the boat over the stern. While practical, this is about as unsightful an arrangement as you will ever see.

On boats over 36 feet in length, fixed dinghies are acceptable. There is usually enough room to mount dinghy chocks on the bow or cabin roof, and store the small boat securely. Captains with craft over 45 feet sometimes use a davit (crane) with an electric winch to lower the dinghy and retrieve it. Some of these impressive yachts sport a tender in the 16-foot range.

Fixed (hard) dinghy lying hull up.

Dinghies are surprisingly expensive. A good wooden or fiberglass model can run between $500 and $2,000. Obviously, this is an expense that must be carefully taken into account by almost every boating budget.

Within the last two decades, another tender alternative has appeared over the horizon. Inflatable dinghies have finally come into their own and taken the pleasure boating world by storm. Once looked upon as a swimming pool plaything, sophisticated inflatable dinghies now feature outboard motor mounts, fixed floorboards, and good stability in choppy water. They also sport the obvious advantage of easy storage. When deflated, this sort of tender can be quickly stowed in a locker or compartment.

Of course, what goes down must come up, which is only to say that an inflatable dinghy must be blown up every time it is put to use. There are various devices available to facilitate dinghy inflation. A foot pump is usually supplied with most dinghies. While this is an inexpensive alternative, blowing up the dinghy on a hot summer day with a foot pump can result in most any captain losing

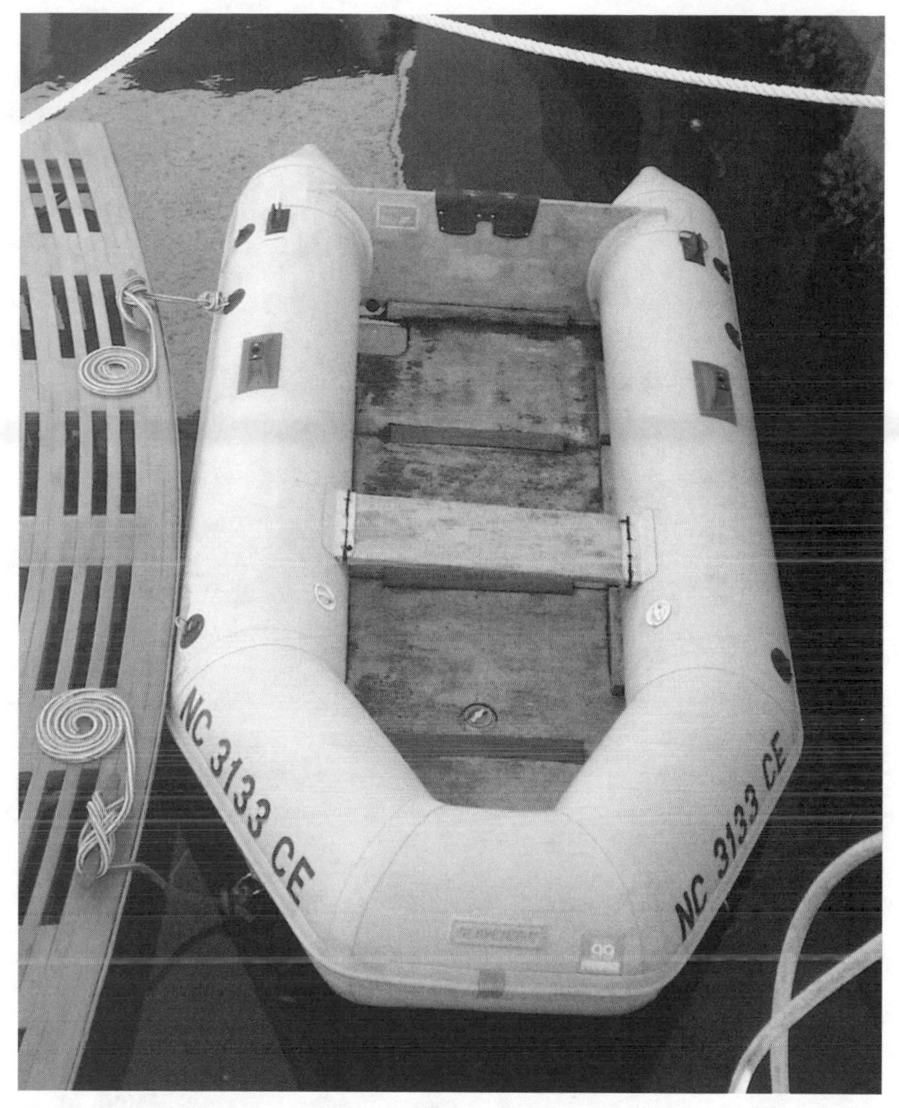

Inflatable dinghy moored to swim platform.

his religion. High speed, 12-volt pumps are now available. While these units will set you back another $75 or so, the savings in toil and temper may justify the additional expense. Finally, I know of several boaters who have adapted a scuba tank and regulator to blow up their dinghies. This is an ideal arrangement, except that you can only expect to inflate the dinghy once or twice before taking the tank in for a refill. If this system sounds interesting, make

Inflatable dinghy mounted on sun deck of motor yacht.

Inflatable dinghy.

Dinghy outboard mounted on stern.

inquiries at a local dive shop. I do not know of any "off the shelf " kit that accomplishes this objective, but a good scuba technician should be able to put something together for you.

Inflatable dinghies are not inexpensive either. In fact, some of the more sophisticated models are even more costly than their traditional alternatives.

Then, there is the question of powering your dinghy. Unless your tender is large enough to accommodate a three-horsepower outboard, I recommend a good pair of oars (these can be ordered at additional cost with most fixed and inflatable dinghies). The one- to two-horsepower outboards intended for small dinghies are *notoriously* unreliable. After cussing out three such units, I've consigned them all to the junkpile and polished up my oars.

FRESHWATER SYSTEM ALTERNATIVES

Cruising power boats allow you to take your living quarters with you. Such creature comforts as a good hot meal, television, and even a hot shower are simply more enjoyable while swinging at the hook in an isolated anchorage. A freshwater system with all the extras is an integral part of this comfortable live-aboard environment.

City Water Hookup

Most factory-installed marine freshwater systems consist of a water tank, pump, hot water heater, and any number of outlets including a shower. The water is routed to its various destinations by flexible

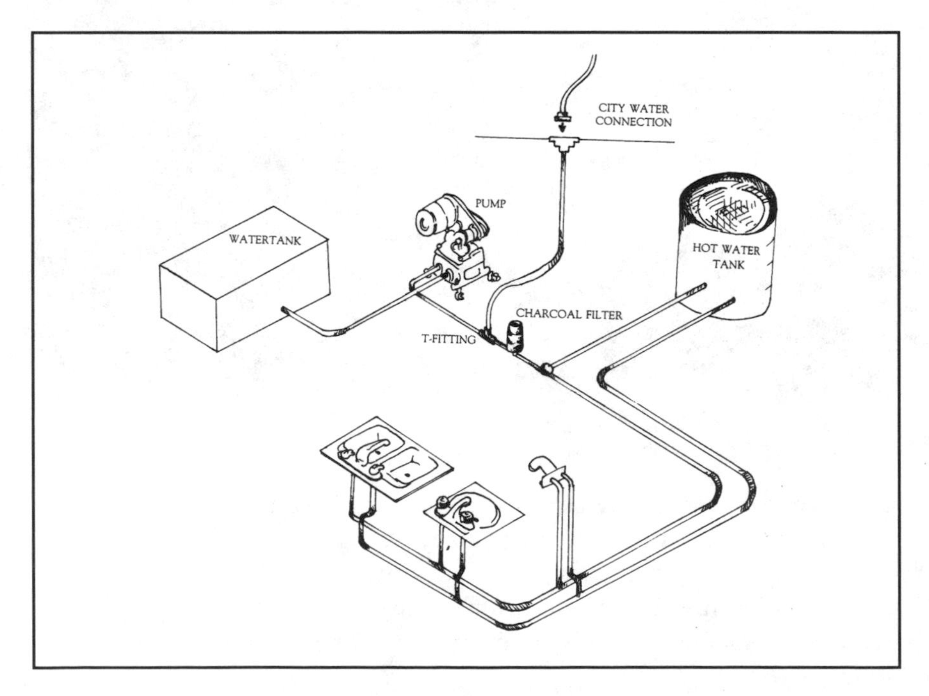

Marine freshwater system with city water hookup.

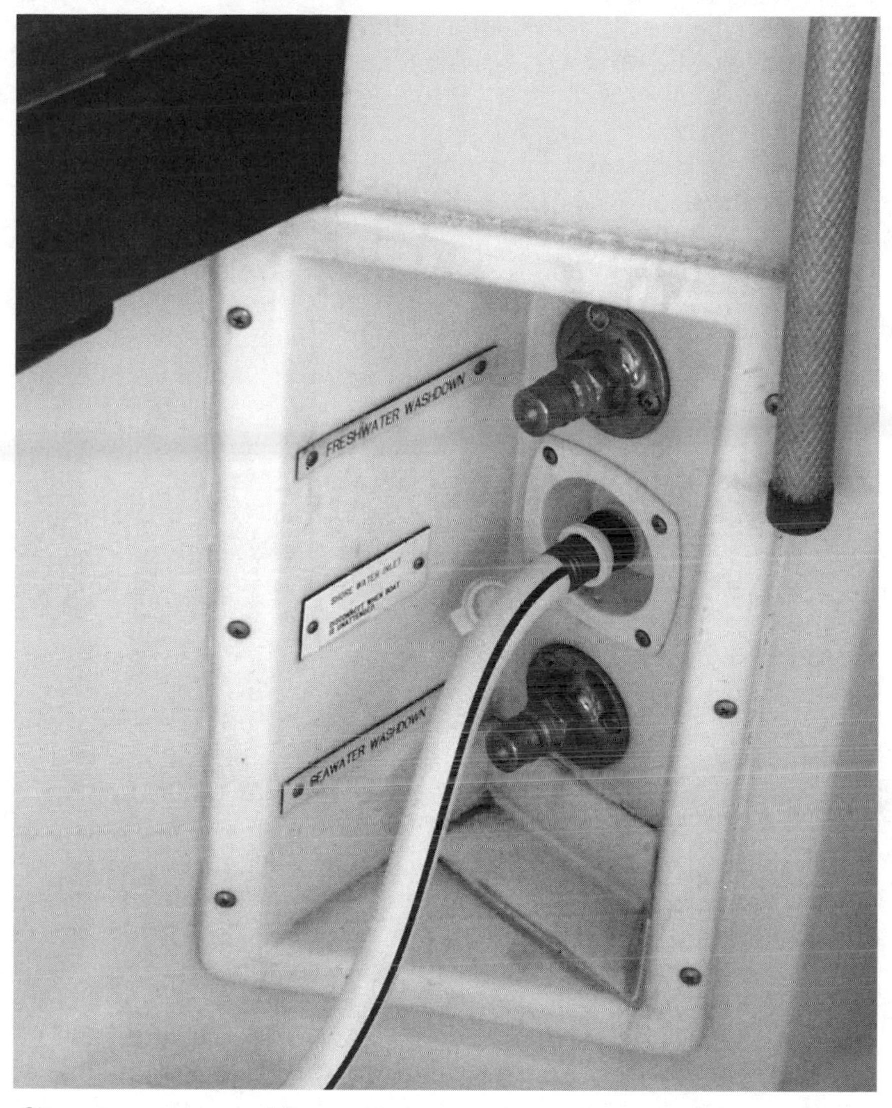

City water connector and hose.

plastic hose, usually reinforced with an inner nylon mesh. This system has one large flaw: it can run out at the most inopportune moments.

Once, when docked at Wrightsville Beach, North Carolina, the "first-rate, first mate" decided to take a stroll on the dock while yours truly washed off the day's salt and grime. I had just gotten my hair good and soapy when the water flow stopped abruptly. Only then did it occur to me that I had failed to refill the freshwater tank before beginning my shower. I waited, waited, and waited. Karen had apparently taken a long stroll. At Wrightsville, they are probably still talking about that crazy boater who popped a soap-encrusted head out of the hatch and yelled at the top of his voice for the first mate to come and refill the water tank! It was then and there that I decided it was time for a city water hookup.

Par (and several other companies) now offers a combination pressure reducer/anti-backflow valve, female garden hose connector that is ideal for adapting boats to city water. Simply pick out a likely spot in the cockpit or on deck to mount the fixture. Be sure there is ready access from the rear of the fitting to the bilge. Then, route a piece of freshwater hose from the deck connector to a position in front of the water pump. You will then need a "T" connector that will fit your freshwater hose. Cut the existing freshwater line (with the pressure off!) and install the straight portion of the "T" fitting in the line. Connect the freshwater hose from the new deck fixture to the tail end of the "T." Secure all hose ends with appropriate hose clamps.

Purchase a garden hose that is rated safe for drinking water. Connect the hose to a shoreside water source and the opposite end to the just-installed deck connector. Cut the water on, and you need never worry about running the tank dry. As long as city water pressure is maintained, your onboard pump will sense the presence of adequate pressure and remain dormant. While underway, and drawing fresh water from the onboard tank (and using the internal pump for pressure), the anti-backflow feature of the freshwater fitting will prevent any leakage of water through the new hose fixture.

This is a good first-time project for new boat owners. Just be sure you have all the right equipment (including hose clamps) before beginning. If you are unsure about the location of your water lines or pump, ask a technician at your marina or dealership for advice. He should also be able to help with the proper connections and the placement of the on-deck water connector.

Quick Hose Connectors

Boats owners who install a city water hookup, as described above, can make life aboard even easier with quick hose connectors. These devices consist of a male and female fitting that quickly connect and disconnect by simply moving a collar or lever on the female portion of the device. When first introduced, these devices were known for their leaks. Now they have now been perfected, and unless undue pressure is applied to the hose, boaters can be assured of a watertight connection. Quick connectors are available in brass or plastic models. For nautical purposes, the brass variety is to be much preferred.

The male end of the quick connector is permanently installed in the female freshwater connector (described above). Smart boaters will then insert an in-line shutoff valve at the end of their freshwater hose, followed by the female portion of the quick connector fitting. Now, to remove the hose, you need only cut the pressure off at the in-line valve, move the quick connector collar or lever back a bit, and the end will come free. To reconnect, the procedure is simply reversed. This system sure beats fighting with an ornery screw-in hose every time you connect to or disengage from city water!

Charcoal Filter

Fresh water in coastal communities is notorious for its bad taste. In a worst case scenario, it can resemble a sulfurous brew more than water. Some marinas install elaborate filtering systems to improve their water's taste and, thankfully, many coastal cities have now taken steps to solve the problem.

Even if your city water does not have an objectionable flavor, water drunk aboard most boats still tastes a bit like plastic. This condition is caused by long-term contact between your water supply and the onboard plastic hoses and/or water tank. If you should be hooked up to city water as described above, it is a good practice to let the water run for thirty seconds or so before filling your cup. Unfortunately, this wise procedure won't help the taste of onboard water.

Whether because of problems with city water treatment or their own freshwater system, many boaters wisely choose to install a charcoal filter between the water pump (and city water connection, if so equipped) and the remainder of the system, including the hot water heater. These inexpensive units are available through any plumbing supply house, marine catalog, or nautical equipment dealer.

Installation is a snap. Make sure you have the necessary fittings and hose clamps to adapt the filter to your size freshwater hose. All you need then do is mount the filter at an accessible spot in the bilge next to the freshwater line. Next, cut the line (again with the pressure off) and connect the ends at the appropriate points. Tighten up the hose clamps and that's all there is to it.

Sophisticated Freshwater Filters

Freshwater filters that actually treat drinking water are also available. These extensive filtering systems remove harmful bacteria and pollutants. With trustworthy freshwater available at practically every marina, most boaters will not find it necessary to install one of these expensive systems.

Hot Water Heaters

If, for some reason, you purchase a boat without a hot water heater, take heart. It is still possible to install the device. With all the necessary 120-volt wiring, this task should most certainly be left to a boating professional.

Marine hot water heaters are usually smaller than their landside counterparts. Crew members who use up all the hot water are subject to walking the plank. Standard and stainless steel models are available. As you might guess, the stainless variety lasts longer but is initially more expensive.

Unless the generator remains in constant operation while underway, the hot water in your tank will eventually cool. While many boaters report still having enough for a quick shower after a day spent on the water, a "heat exchanger" can assure enough hot water for the entire crew. This clever device circulates hot sea water from the engines around the heater's inner tank, thereby keeping the fresh water hot. Heat exchangers must be ordered *along with* a hot water heater. This device cannot be installed on an existing unit at a later time.

GALLEY ADDITIONS

The galley is an integral part of any cruising boat. After a long day on the water, nothing tastes better than a good, hot meal. Most boats come factory equipped with just about everything you will need to perform nautical culinary magic. There are a few additions, however, that may help the process along.

Stove

If your boat is equipped with an alcohol-only rangetop stove (particularly if it is one of the older, pressurized models), you might want to seriously consider upgrading the unit. While alcohol is clean and safe, it is rather inefficient. The pressurized types, as mentioned earlier, are difficult to light and maintain pressure.

There are several choices available when upgrading the galley stove. Vessels equipped with pressurized alcohol units should seriously consider substituting the newer wick-absorption models. You might choose an all-electric range, but this alternative would tie all onboard cooking to dockside power or the temperamental generator. There is also LPG (propane) but, as explained in Chapter 1, there is a small risk of explosion from this sort of unit. A good choice is a CNG (compressed natural gas) stove. With its lighter-than-air gas, this cooking fuel is dependable and lacks the pressure and lighting problems of an alcohol unit.

My personal favorite is the combination alcohol/electric stove discussed in Chapter 1. With this device, you have the best of both worlds. At dockside or when the generator is operating, the electrical elements can be used. At anchor, you can use the alcohol burners if you don't have a generator, or if you just want peace and quiet.

Installing a new galley stove requires a marine electrician and careful carpentry. Experienced captains might undertake this chore themselves, but first-time power boat owners should certainly seek out a professional.

Oven

Larger power boats are usually shipped from the factory with an oven, while smaller craft are often equipped with a rangetop stove only. If your boat falls into the ovenless category, it is sometimes possible to have an oven installed *if* you are willing to give up some of your precious galley storage space.

New ovens are normally located below countertop level. This is the usual position for drawers and galley cabinets. Obviously, if an oven is installed at a later time, some of this storage space will be lost.

For my money, I would always choose either an electric or CNG oven. While an LPG unit would probably be safe 98 percent of the time, the constant worry and sniffing for a leak could intrude on the otherwise pleasant galley duties.

Oven installation requires even more carpentry and electrical wiring than a range top. I would not advise any power boater to undertake this project themselves without *extensive* experience in both fields. In most cases, stove installation is a case of inquiring at the marina office or dealership for a qualified professional.

Marine Microwave Oven

If your boat is one of those craft on which a built-in stove is impractical, or if you simply want the quick convenience of non-thermal cooking, a marine microwave oven is just the ticket. These small, compact cooking units can sit on top of almost any counter and are easily moved from place to place to accommodate different cooking requirements. Of course, you will need shoreside or generator power to operate the oven, but, with most cruising boats, one power source or the other will be available much of the time.

While they are somewhat more expensive than their landside counterparts, marine microwave ovens are built with durable materials that are designed to withstand the saltwater environment. Doesn't it make sense to spend an extra hundred dollars now rather than have to replace the entire system three years down the road? I think it does, and consequently, this writer recommends the marine version of this popular cooking alternative.

Nautical China

I suggest investing in a set of nautical china. These plates, cups, and saucers are constructed of an almost non-breakable plastic that will bear washing after washing. Additionally, most brands come equipped with a non-skid, rubber ring on the bottom. This slippage protection is very important in rough weather or when trying to eat while underway.

HEAD ACCESSORIES

Most accessories for the head are small affairs. You might install a deluxe, finger cutoff shower head or spiff the head up with a nautical soap dish and tumbler. There is one major exception to the incidental quality of most marine head additions.

Most boats come from the factory with a manual flush, holding tank waste disposal system. As discussed in Chapter 1, it is now quite illegal to dump untreated waste overboard. Your craft must be equipped with some sort of system to avoid this illegal activity. Holding tanks are often a less than ideal choice, even though they are the least expensive of the various alternatives. The objectionable odor, not to mention the difficulty in finding pump-out stations, have motivated many a boat owner to install an onboard waste treatment system.

While there are several fine brands and models currently available, probably the best known marine treatment plant is the "Lectra-San." This system treats waste through an electric-saltwater interaction and renders it harmless for overboard discharge. If you operate a Lectra-San in fresh water, you must physically add salt, but coastal applications require nothing more than turning the treatment timer knob and flushing the head.

Boats equipped with a manual flushing head will need to convert to an electric flush toilet when adding a waste treatment system. The Par company offers an "electric conversion kit" that easily changes many manual toilets to electric flush. If this kit will not work on your particular unit, the entire bowl assembly must be replaced.

Onboard waste treatment plants are not cheap. Lectra-San systems currently list for some $650, but can usually be purchased through a marine discounter for about $525. Expect to spend another $200 to $300 for conversion to an electric flush toilet.

It goes almost without saying that professional installation of an onboard waste treatment plant is a near-necessity. Your largest problem may be in finding a technician in your home port who is willing to undertake such a chore. As can be easily appreciated, this is a sensitive task that is fraught with the possibility for mistakes.

ENTERTAINMENT AND COMFORT

Visitors to coastal seaports are likely to see any number of sailcraft running along on a close reach, drenching the cockpit occupants with cold, salt spray. You might conclude from such observations that boating is a "roughing it" game. Well, maybe at times that's true, but power boaters seem to think differently of cruising and living aboard than their sailing brethren. When visiting other power craft, new boat owners are likely to spot any number of accessories devoted exclusively to live-aboard and cruising comfort. While all of the items discussed below may not fit in with your idea of nautical comfort, some of this gear can certainly contribute immeasurably to the quality of life afloat.

Deck Chairs

If your boat is equipped with a cockpit or sun deck, you will probably want to invest in several deck chairs. There are few more enjoyable boating activities than taking one's ease with a cold drink and a good book while sitting tranquilly in the cockpit and watching the world flow by.

Deck chairs can be divided into two fundamentally different categories. Some are covered with canvas stretched between wooden or aluminum frames. Canvas chairs are durable and far less expensive than the alternative. Vinyl cushioned deck chairs, on the other hand, are much more comfortable, but require additional maintenance and make a much larger dent in your pocketbook.

Every variety of deck chair, in my opinion, is surprisingly expensive. Canvas units, even at discounted prices, run from $30 to more than $100 each. Vinyl cushioned chairs start at about $75 and continue on up out of sight. Even so, most power craft captains will want to grin and bear the expense of at least a few of these expensive accessories.

Cockpit Table

Should you decide to invest in deck chairs, you may decide to purchase a small cockpit table as well. These units are ideal for serving drinks or snacks while relaxing on deck. Most are small, vinyl covered affairs with various nautical motifs decorating the table surface. You can purchase a good quality table for about $25 to $50.

Icemaker

Take my word for it, there never seems to be enough ice on a boat. Hot days inevitably bring forth a steady stream of thirsty crew members traipsing to the refrigerator for relief. It's not long before the ice trays are exhausted, and the captain inevitably gets the blame. Boat owners with an affluent budget can alleviate this problem with a dedicated icemaker. These self-contained systems are usually installed in a cockpit or main cabin cabinet. On the *Kaycy,* we built an entire cockpit wet bar from teak plywood around our icemaker.

Marine icemakers are sturdy, dependable units that are much tougher than their landside counterparts. Some have vinyl exteriors while the better models come with a stainless steel finish. Either variety is quite expensive, usually $450 or more when purchased through a marine discounter. Add to that price another $150 or so for installation, and you can quickly conclude that this is not an inexpensive accessory.

TV Antennas

Even at dockside, boats will move back and forth a bit. This motion is even more apparent when swinging on the hook. Conventional television antennas, particularly "rabbit ears," cannot cope with this motion. It is maddening to watch your favorite show, and have it fade out when the boat swings one way, and fade back in when it swings back.

Many marinas now offer "Cablevision" type connections, but if your home port does not offer this useful service, take heart. There is another solution.

Marine television antennas.

Fading signals can often be overcome by the use of omnidirectional marine television antennas. These units are housed in a round plastic dome and are permanently mounted on the flybridge or cabin roof. A coaxial cable is then run to the television in the cabin, and, poof, your reception is now immune from fading difficulties.

Some of the best antennas come complete with their own signal boosters that operate alternately from 12- or 120-volt power sources. The power booster can be a considerable advantage when pulling in distant, weak stations.

Purchase price is about $100. Most new owners can install the antennas themselves. The only tricky part is routing the antenna cable to the cabin. There is often a conduit pipe from the flybridge to the bilge through which the upper station electrical wiring and steering controls are routed. If this passage is not already too full, you can sometimes snake the cable below decks through this pipe. Failing everything else, you can always crack a window, pull the wire through and make the television connection. Of course, with this arrangement, you will probably want to disconnect the cable while underway. Cruising with an open window is a good invitation to a wet cabin.

VCR and DVD

My mate and I keep a VCR (and DVD—see below) aboard our boat at all times. It's great to relax with a good movie minus all the usual commercial interruptions. We usually take a good selection of tapes and DVD disks with us on a long cruise. It's also a great idea to become affiliated with a video rental store in your home port. When you are aboard for a weekend, or just a few days, a quick trip down to the video shop may yield that movie you've been wanting to see for months.

I do not know of any "marine" grade VCRs currently available. Certainly, VHS format, four-head systems are to be preferred in any environment. Digital effects and stereo sound are up to individual tastes and budgets.

A new alternative in the home/marine movie industry is the DVD (Digital Video Disk) player. This unit uses a disk (which looks almost exactly like a conventional CD) to store its visual content in digital form. This format has several advantages. First, because the media is digital, the resulting television picture has the most clearly defined colors and the sharpest focus that this writer has ever seen. Secondly, the only thing that ever touches the surface of the DVD is a beam of light, so it can theoretically last forever. Anyone who has a video tape collection will quickly tell you how diametrically opposed this long enduring condition of DVDs is to the relatively short life of conventional VHS tape.

Unfortunately, only a limited number of movies are now available on DVD, though the ranks are growing daily. DVD disks are also usually a bit costlier than their VHS tape counterparts, though DVD players are in about the same price range as high quality VCRs.

Speaking purely for our own personal tastes, we now cruise with both a VCR and DVD aboard. If a movie we like is available in DVD, we choose that format every time.

Stereo Systems

Several excellent marine stereo systems are now available through any number of nautical equipment suppliers. These units are usually more compact than typical home systems. More importantly, their internal parts have been protected with polymers to resist the corrosive effects of salt air. This sort of protection is particularly important for tape players. While perhaps not as spectacular as the finest of home stereos, marine sound systems are durable, compact, and relatively easy to install. Most include an amplifier, tape player, and FM

On-board stereo sound system.

tuner in one integrated box. Speakers are extra, but they too have been constructed with the marine environment in mind.

A good addition to a marine stereo system might be a CD (compact disk) player. A CD's stable playing system is far more appropriate for an often rocky boat than a traditional phonographic turntable (record player).

Installation of marine stereos is a simple matter of hooking the system to any 12-volt power source. Captains with the most rudimentary electrical experience should be able to do the job without undue difficulty. If you don't want to tackle the task yourself, a marine electrician can probably finish the installation in less than two hours.

SHORESIDE STORAGE

No matter how much storage you have aboard your boat, take my word for it, there are always going to be large, seldom-used items of nautical gear that are better kept ashore. For this reason, many boat owners build or purchase a "boat box" and place it at the end of their slip. These boxes are invaluable for storing such items as automatic oil changers, extra rope, and a variety of polishing and cleaning products that are only used once or twice a year.

Some boat owners skilled in carpentry build their own boat box. This is a much cheaper alternative than purchasing a ready-made unit. I myself have used such a homemade box for almost ten years without a problem. If you should choose to go the self-made route, be careful to caulk all seams thoroughly and coat the interior with epoxy resin. The exterior should be primed and finished with the most durable outdoor paint that you can find.

Pre-made fiberglass boat boxes are also a good shoreside storage alternative. They are long-lasting and require only an occasional polish and wax to maintain their attractive appearance. Homemade boxes, on the other hand, require periodic repainting. Unfortunately, fiberglass storage boxes are quite expensive. Typical purchase prices run to four and five hundred dollars. If you can fit this sort of figure in your boating budget, then so much the better. If not, it's time to haul out the old power saw.

A LAST WORD

Let me reiterate that the listing of boat accessories in this chapter is by no means exhaustive. Pick up any marine catalog, and you will see scores of items that I have omitted from this account. However, the first-time power boater can confidently use this discussion as a basis for considering which accessories should come first. I find accessorizing my craft to be one of the most enjoyable of boating pastimes. Just remember to keep within your budget, and you too can have a great time purchasing practical, "neat" gear for your new vessel.

CHAPTER 5

Maintenance in All Its Forms

THERE IS AN OLD MAXIM in the boating game that runs something like this: if you don't enjoy working on a boat, then you had better be very wealthy or not own one in the first place. Make no mistake about it, pleasure craft *do* require a great deal of maintenance to preserve their appearance and keep the power plants (and other mechanical equipment) in good working order. There always seems to be something else yet to be done. If you are the sort of person who doesn't enjoy polishing fiberglass till it shines, replacing a fouled spark plug, or ferreting out an electrical short, then owning a boat could be a long and frustrating experience.

Of the many tasks necessary to keep a boat looking like new (known as "Bristol" in nautical jargon), most can be performed by the owner and/or his mate. In fact, in many ports it is often difficult to find paid workers who are willing to perform the more mundane chores. Of course, there will always be repairs and services that should be carried out by boating professionals. Engine tune-ups and bottom painting are two examples of spring outfitting jobs best left to seasoned pros.

In this chapter we will explore together the many maintenance jobs that you, even as a new boat owner, can accomplish. These tasks will be grouped into "Spring Outfitting," "In-Season Maintenance," and "Winterizing." With this account in hand, you will have a good overview of what needs to be done to keep your boat in Bristol condition. However, be warned—there always seems to be something new to learn in boating maintenance. That's another way of saying that different sorts of problems always seem to be popping up just to

Boat hauled out on marine railway.

keep boat ownership interesting. It would, therefore, be erroneous to conclude that the listing below represents *all* the chores that will ever be necessary to keep your craft in top-notch shape!

Finally, I suggest that you approach boat maintenance not as a set of "must do" activities, but rather as a fun challenge. Some of my most rewarding times aboard the *Kaycy* have come in identifying a problem and fixing it myself. Similarly, when you have polished and waxed your craft for a day or two, standing back and looking at the gleaming gel-coat and stainless steel can impart the feeling of a job well done, which is sometimes all too lacking in our modern world. So, approach your tasks with good cheer and, above all, remember to "have fun with it."

SPRING OUTFITTING

Ah, the sounds of spring in a coastal marina. There is the deep rumble of the travel-lift engine as it raises another boat for a bottom job, the whine of an electric polisher, and, it must be said, the curses of some boater who can't free a rusted nut or a captain who is losing his religion over an engine that refuses to start. After sitting for the long, cold winter, your boat needs extensive cleaning and attention. Spring outfitting is the most important, time-consuming period in boat maintenance. You should set aside several days for all the necessary tasks. All the jobs need not be accomplished in one fell swoop. Several weekends strung together should do the trick. Just be sure to follow through on *everything* your boat requires. An omission in the spring is likely to come back to haunt a boater in the summer,

Bottom Painting

Anyone who has ever visited a coastal dock and observed all the barnacle and oyster-encrusted pilings can readily understand the need to coat your boat's bottom with anti-fouling paint. Those barnacles you see on the pilings will grow just as happily on the hull, props, and rudders of an unprotected boat. Even a light coating of marine growth on your propellers can cause a remarkable loss in power and fuel efficiency.

Most anti-fouling paint formulations now contain copper as their principal active agent. In years past, a tin compound known as TBT was also employed, but this paint was outlawed due to toxic effects on the aquatic environment. Barnacles, underwater weeds, and other sorts of marine life are repelled by the copper content of anti-fouling paint. A *good quality* coating can repel barnacle growth on a fiberglass hull for an entire season.

Modern anti-fouling paint is available in a variety of types and brands. There are soft and hard finishes, vinyl- and epoxy-based paints, each with varying quantities of copper. Power craft will want to choose a hard-finish bottom paint. Personally, I have never been impressed with vinyl-based paints. Most of the boat owners I know choose an epoxy-based coating. As for copper content, obviously the more copper, the better the protection. Unfortunately, the price of the paint increases in direct portion to the amount of copper. A gallon of 67 percent copper paint recently listed for $85 while a 43 percent paint sold for $65. For my money there is no comparison. Doesn't it make sense to spend the extra $25 to $40 dollars to be sure that your hull remains free of barnacles for the entire season? If you use a cheaper paint and it fails during the boating season, the only alternative is to have your craft hauled out of the water again and repeat the entire process. Suddenly that extra $40 a gallon looks quite small in comparison.

Some types of anti-fouling paints are more effective in waters with certain fouling conditions. For instance, one company produces northern, tropical, and offshore formulations. I suggest you consult the professionals at the boatyard of your choice for their recommendations. Just remember, if you must choose between a better or a lesser expensive grade of paint, take the premium product every time.

Props, rudders, and shafts have their own protection problems. Anti-fouling paints that cling quite effectively to fiberglass hulls can slough off these metal parts during your first spring cruise. Some boatyards coat the underwater hardware with paints that have been developed for this purpose while others employ a special "prop wax" that is formulated to repel marine growth. Either variety cannot be depended upon to last an entire season. As the summer progresses, I often have to don the old diving mask and putty knife in order to scrape a few barnacles from the underwater hardware. However, compared to the marine growth that would be experienced with unprotected shafts, props, and rudders, this is a minor problem indeed.

While a few "do it yourself" boatyards allow *experienced* captains to apply their own bottom paint, the vast majority of boat owners will want to employ a professional marine painter to do the job *right.* Most boatyards can handle this chore. In fact, bottom painting is the principal activity in most yards. After hauling your boat out of the water with a travel-lift, marine railway, or (less frequently) a crane, the yard will first clean the bottom, possibly using a "power wash" device. Then they will replace all your underwater zincs and finally apply several coats of the anti-fouling paints. It's a long, messy job, and without the best equipment, this task can take forever. Consequently, I most heartily suggest allowing your boatyard to handle the entire process.

Before leaving our discussion of bottom painting, let me briefly mention the importance of "zincs." Saltwater sets up a so-called galvanic (electrical) action with any metal. Even the hardest stainless steel can become brittle and break if this process continues unabated. So, all boats come equipped with underwater zincs. For some reason known only to the scientists, saltwater would rather make electric current with zinc than harder metals. By having various pieces of zinc on the bottom of your boat, this metal will slowly be eaten away through the course of a season, instead of your shafts, props, and rudders. It's very inexpensive to replace these "sacrificial" metals every season, and certainly more desirable than investing in new underwater hardware. Almost any yard should automatically install new zincs whenever a boat is hauled out for bottom painting. However, it never hurts to check and make *sure* this most important task has indeed been accomplished!

Cleaning and Waxing the Fiberglass

Now that you have the bottom painted (or even before), it's time to begin your own spring outfitting chores. While you might prefer to sneak up on it by accomplishing some smaller jobs first, the cleaning, polishing, and waxing of all the smooth gel-coated surfaces above the rub rail is one of the most formidable but cosmetically important spring outfitting tasks. Of course, the hull from the waterline to the rub rail also needs care, but many boaters let their boatyard polish and wax this area while the boat is hauled out for bottom painting. If you should choose to do this portion of the job yourself, a dinghy and a lot of elbow grease will be required.

Gel-coat, as mentioned in Chapter 1, is subject to oxidation. A neglected fiberglass finish appears dull and chalky. Left untreated, it will soon become necessary to recoat the topsides with Awlgrip, Imron, polyurethane, or some other fiberglass paint. This is a costly operation!

So, come spring it's time to haul out the polish and wax. First, give the boat a good wash with detergent and fresh water. The next step in restoring your gel-coat to a like-new condition is to remove all the oxidation from the fiberglass surface. In times past, polishing com pounds were used for this purpose. These paste-like mixtures contain micro-bits of grit. When rubbed across an oxidized surface, in theory, the dull layer of gel-coat is polished away, revealing a bright, shiny surface below. While some boaters still swear by polishing compounds, and they are still readily available, the new "color restorers" have largely supplanted the older polishes. Color restorers also contain some polishing grit, but this substance is supplemented by oils that bring out the original gel-coat color. While both polishing compounds and color restorers will eventually remove the oxidized gel-coat, it requires considerably less elbow grease to accomplish the same result with the latter material.

If you happen to purchase a used boat that has a neglected gel-coat, it may be necessary to first go over the surface with a polishing compound, followed by a color restorer. This double work can be avoided in the future by taking care of your boat's finish *regularly*. It requires two, three, or four times as much effort to make up for past lapses of proper care, than to simply keep up with the task seasonally.

Color restorer or polishing compound is usually applied with a cloth and rubbed vigorously over a small area. Then, using a clean cloth, quickly remove the residue. *Don't try to polish too large an area at one time!* If the compound (or color restorer) stays on the gel-coat for too long a period of time, particularly in direct sunlight, it can require a cold chisel to remove the surface residue.

Some boaters apply and then polish off rubbing compounds, color restorers, and wax with an electric polisher. While this would seem to be a great work saver, electric polishers, unfortunately, need to be used on a flat surface to be really effective. You will undoubtedly see many boatyards successfully using electric polishers on boat hulls. The large expanse of flat area on a hull makes this an ideal area to use such a system. However, topside fiberglass usually has so few flat places, many boaters forgo using an electric polisher entirely when working above the rub rail. When polishing and waxing gel-coat above the rub rail, I suggest a compromise. Keep an electric polisher at hand to use when possible, knowing all the while that good old elbow grease will be necessary for most topside work.

Whether by hand or electric polisher, removing the oxidation from the gel-coat is just the first step in your fiberglass maintenance. Now that the surface is bright and clean, it must be protected from the damaging effects of sun and saltwater, or its chalky appearance will soon return. Marine wax has been the traditional material of choice for this protection. As you might have guessed, there are literally hundreds of brands, each promising the best protections from the elements. You will most certainly want to experiment for yourself. Sometimes it takes years to find the brand that suits your needs.

Be sure to use *boat,* not automobile, wax. Manufacturers have specifically formulated nautical-type wax to handle the marine environment. Nautical formulations, quite simply, last much longer in a saltwater climate than their landlubber counterparts. One spring I found this out the hard way. Thinking that there really wasn't much of a difference in waxes, I used an auto brand that had given me superior service in the past on our cars. Thirty days later when chalking began to reappear, you could have found me at our slip busily reapplying "boat wax" to all the topside gel-coat.

Like polishes and color restorers, wax should be rubbed vigorously onto a *small* area and then quickly polished off. Change to a clean buffing cloth frequently to avoid streaking the surface. Be warned—gel-coat is far more porous than automobile finishes. Wax that is allowed to stay on gel-coat for too long a time before being buffed off sticks like glue. Even though you can often wax one whole side of your car before polishing off the residue, this practice on a boat will result in catastrophe. I suggest working in sections of one or two square feet, carefully overlapping your work.

Owners of thirty-plus-foot power craft might as well expect to occupy two full days of their time with polishing and waxing. Bring along a good supply of cleaning cloths. You'll need them. If you happen to have any "friends" who owe you favors, this might be a good time to call in your markers.

The news is not all bad though. Once you are finished, your boat will look *great!* Stand back and admire your work. It's a wonderful feeling to see your boat gleaming in the sunlight, reflecting the ripples from the water. At times like this, it really does seem worth the effort!

Teflon Alternative

A newer alternative for maintaining gel-coat is professionally applied teflon coatings. First, a rigorous cleaning of the fiberglass is performed with both a rubbing compound and color restorer. Then, the teflon compound is carefully applied to the gel-coat using a special electric buffer/applicator. The result, when applied correctly, is a beautiful protective finish that will last for a full year even when open to the weather. In a covered slip, our teflon coating has endured for better than two years.

Teflon application is a tricky process that is most definitely not recommended for amateurs. It is also quite expensive. A full cleaning and application to our thirty-one-foot craft's hull and topsides once set us back $950. However, for long-term enhancement of your gel-coat, teflon simply can't be beat.

Oiling the Teak

Ask three boaters what they think of exterior teak trim and two will tell you that it lends a warm, nautical look to fiberglass boats, while the third will swear loudly and proclaim teak to be the bane of modern pleasure boating. Both would be right.

A teak bow pulpit, swim platform, step pads, flybridge ladder, and trim look great when they are cleaned and oiled. In fact, if you ever see one of the modern power craft that completely lacks any exterior teak, you may agree that the boat has a truly plastic, artificial look. Some unkind captains have been known to call such craft, "Chlorox bottles." *However,* the task of preserving the teak's warm, golden appearance is one of the most demanding cosmetic jobs in boating.

Teak is used for nautical purposes because the wood is naturally filled with oil. This renders teak almost impervious to rot. Unfortunately, the internal oils also mean that it is difficult to coat the wood with hard varnishes as would be practical with mahogany, for instance.

Just to make matters worse, when teak is allowed to weather in the natural elements without protection, it assumes an ugly, gray appearance that seems to scream, "Clean me!" The worse the appearance, the harder it is to clean. So, if your craft is indeed garnished with some exterior teak, you can confidently look forward to the two-step clean and oil process *at least* twice a season. Don't worry overmuch. Allow me to impart some of the collective wisdom that I've garnered from cleaning and oiling my teak dozens and dozens of times.

First, you have to remove all the dirt and aging that gives the weathered teak its gray appearance. Be sure to wear waterproof gloves when cleaning teak. The scouring agents are caustic and quite strong. If the wood has been cleaned and oiled within the past year, you can use one of the single solution teak cleaners that are available from any marine supplier. Mix the cleaner by following the instructions provided. Pour a small quantity of cleaner on the teak and scrub a square-foot patch of the surface vigorously with a nylon (not wire) brush. Then rinse the area, including the surrounding fiberglass, thoroughly with a freshwater hose. Repeat the process until you have cleaned the entire surface.

If the teak in question has not been cleaned and oiled for some time, you may need to employ a stronger, two-part teak cleaner. You should use two-part teak cleaners *only* when the single-solution variety will not suffice. Two-part teak cleaners consist of a strong, acidic cleaner and a neutralizer. Unlike most one-part solution cleaners, two-part solutions can be harmful to gel-coat. Be careful to avoid contact with the surrounding fiberglass as much as possible. Sometimes it's wise to use masking tape. In any case, keep the freshwater hose close at hand to quickly wash away any spills or splatters.

To use two-part teak cleaners, first wet the wood thoroughly with fresh water. Then pour a small quantity of solution A (the cleaner) on the teak. Again, confine your efforts to a one-square-foot area. Scrub the surface vigorously with a nylon brush. You will see the cleaner lift off a motley collection of dirt and grime. It will soon look like you have a dollop of molasses atop the teak. After a good scrubbing, rinse the area quickly with fresh water. Then apply a liberal quantity of solution B (neutralizer). This solution will dissolve the surface gunk, and the light, natural character of the teak should appear.

After letting the teak dry thoroughly, it's time to apply a protective coating of oil. Pick any coastal marina, and every year you will find someone who claims to have finally found "the" teak oil that will last through an entire season. To this assertion, I would politely reply, "Bull!" After trying more brands and formulations than I care to recall, I have yet to find a product that does not require at least periodic brush-ups through the boating season.

Teak oils can be divided into two distinct camps. The most popular type of oil is a penetrating finish that resides within the grain of the wood. On the other hand, there are solutions that seem to be a cross between a varnish and an oil. This latter variety of teak oil partially penetrates the wood, while a portion of the finish dries on the surface. Unfortunately, while these two types of oil are very different, it's not always easy to decide which is which at the time of purchase.

I have very strong opinions about teak oils. Several years ago we applied the most popular brand of the varnish-oil finish to our exterior teak. At first, we were elated. The finish lasted longer than anything we had tried before. *However,* when it finally came time to recoat, we discovered that no teak cleaner, not even the two-part variety, would budge the old finish. In the end, it was necessary to painstakingly remove the worn out coating with a marine paint stripper. This was a difficult and tedious chore.

Consequently, I recommend the "soak in" or regular variety of teak oil only! One good tip for purchasing this variety of coating is to read the manufacturer's directions and determine if a drying time is recommended between coats of oil. If the instructions call for applying coat after coat, "wet on wet," chances are you have a varnish-oil. Now, check further to see whether you are instructed to wipe off any "excess" oil after applying. If so, you *may* be dealing with a varnish-style teak oil. Unfortunately, this instruction sometimes appears on normal teak oils as well. If after performing both these tests, you are still unsure, ask for help before making your purchase. If the clerk doesn't seem to understand the term "varnish-oil," tell him that you *don't* want a "Deks Olje"-type teak oil. Hopefully, that should get through.

I wish you good luck in selecting a teak oil. Several trials will probably be necessary before you discover a brand that seems to fill the bill. Oh yes, if you do happen to discover an oil that lasts through the whole season, please let me know.

Anyway, when you finally do select a teak oil, I recommend applying at least three coats. Some boaters use a rag to spread teak oil, but I have always preferred a brush. Be liberal with your application of the oil, but don't leave large quantities of the finish lying on top of the wood. As always, read the manufacturer's recommendations. Every oil is a little different, and the directions are your best first clue for a successful application. Don't be surprised, however, to eventually discover that a slightly different application method seems to work better on your particular boat. You can wait as little as twelve hours between the first and second applications, but it is best to wait a full day or two before applying the final coat. If you have the time, a fourth application a few days later would be ideal.

Polishing the Stainless

Have you ever had a salesman tell you that stainless steel is immune from rust? After all, even its name seem to imply this protection. Well, maybe in a non-saltwater environment that might be true, but boats docked at the seashore can suffer extensive rust on their stainless. A good polish is the best cure and protection from this problem.

Even if your stainless-steel bow rail and deck hardware was not subject to rust, you would probably want to polish it anyway. There's just something about a boat that pulls into a marina with the sun winking off its stainless that speaks of superior care by its owner.

Until just a few years ago, I would always polish my stainless with a heavy-duty cleaner, and then go over all the surfaces again with a coat of wax for long-term protection. Now, several polishes have been introduced that effectively combine a polishing agent with a protective wax. The Boat/US generic stainless polish is my personal choice.

If your stainless is especially rusty, it might still be necessary to use a heavy-duty cleaner, and follow this application with a separate coat of wax. The single part wax/cleaners are great, but they can't boast the same scrubbing power as a dedicated cleaning agent.

Stainless polish is applied much like fiberglass wax. Be sure to have a good supply of rags on hand. You'll be surprised how quickly they will become loaded with black residue.

Apply a liberal amount of polish to your cleaning cloth and rub the metal vigorously. You should be able to visually judge when the polish has succeeded in removing all the tarnish and rust. Polish as much stainless as you like before buffing off the residual cleaner with a clean, dry rag. Unlike gel-coat, polishes and wax can easily be removed from stainless steel surfaces.

Cleaning the Vinyl

Vinyl seats (including flybridge seats) and other vinyl-covered surfaces require periodic cleaning and dressing to insure a long, useful life. A good scrub doesn't do any harm for the material's appearance either.

Various vinyl care products are available to help you accomplish this task. For really first-rate care, you should purchase a separate vinyl shampoo (cleaner) and dresser. Coupled with a stiff nylon brush, vinyl shampoo can take on even the dirtiest jobs. A quick coating of vinyl dressing (or wax) afterwards seals the vinyl and helps to protect against future soiling and fading from UVL (sunlight) exposure.

For lighter-duty jobs, a combination vinyl cleaner/dressing is appropriate. I often use this solution to clean my shorepower cables every spring. As long as the vinyl surface in question is not too heavily soiled, a combination solution can be used with confidence.

Spray vinyl shampoo or combination cleaner-wax directly onto the dirty surface. Scrub briskly with a nylon brush and then wipe off the residue with a clean rag. Sometimes, when cleaning a large, especially dirty vinyl surface, such as a bimini top, it is a good idea to first wash it with fresh water and a laundry detergent. By removing a portion of the dirt with this preliminary step, you will save more than a few cleaning rags.

Vinyl dressing is simply sprayed on and them wiped off. This is one product that is difficult to overuse.

Hatch and Glass Cleaning

Modern power cruisers have quite a collection of cabin windows and deck hatches. During spring outfitting you should consider cleaning and coating the glass with a rain-resistant solution. Some boaters first clean their glass meticulously with Windex glass cleaner, or a similar product. Then, they apply a solution know as "Rain-X." This compound coats the glass with a slick surface to which raindrops cannot cling. When underway, rain seems to just fly off the windshield. Often, you don't even need to use the windshield wiper to see from the lower helm station.

Recently, some combination glass cleaner/coatings have appeared on the market. Inquire at your local auto store as to the availability of this product in your area.

Deck hatches require additional attention. While standing or sitting on deck, open the hatches and clean the underside edge thoroughly. Then use a spray-type lubricant such as CR6-66 and coat the sliding support and set screw. These parts are particularly subject to corrosion as they are frequently open to salt air and spray. Open and close the hatch and set screw several times to work in the lubricant. Then, use a cloth sprayed with "Armor All" or a similar product to coat the rubber gasket on the underside of the hatch's top edge. This wise practice will help to preserve the rubber seal for many years to come. Finally, you might want to consider coating the bottom of the hatch's main (clear) section with an anti-condensation compound. During humid conditions, this amazing product actually prevents the formation of water droplets. In such damp times, boats need all the drying help they can get. Anti-condensation solutions are available at most marine supply stores and catalog centers.

Check the Electronics

One spring outfitting task that is often overlooked by many boaters is a quick check of all the onboard electronics. Take a few minutes to hook up the VHF, depth sounder, GPS, fuel totalizer, and whatever other electronic gizmos you may have chosen for your boat. Take enough time to be sure they are all operating properly. Don't forget a test call on the VHF. Remember, though, radio checks are now forbidden on channel 16.

If any of the units are not operating properly, this is the time to take them to the electronics repair shop. Then, they'll be up and ready for your first cruise.

Bilge Tasks

As a new boat owner, no one expects you to tackle a full engine tune-up as part of your first (or even second or third) spring outfitting. This is a job for a professional mechanic. As a matter of fact, I highly recommend that you spend the extra funds to have your power plant tuned and inspected by a qualified mechanic at the beginning of every boating season. Don't forget to ask the technician to check the water pump impeller while he's there. This spongy rubber, wheel-like object is located inside the water pump and is solely responsible for pulling in the engine's necessary cooling water. Sand, foreign matter, or simple age can destroy an impeller. I replace both my impellers every two or three seasons, even if an inspection shows them to be intact.

There are many other maintenance tasks in the bilge that you can manage. Indeed, you will have a difficult time finding a mechanic who is willing to undertake these simple duties.

As mentioned in Chapter 1, most boats have filters in their saltwater cooling lines to remove any sand or weeds that might be drawn into the intakes. These units should be cleaned every spring. You will find the filters somewhere between the intake valve and the water pump. Once you have located it, *cut the intake valve off before proceeding!* Otherwise, you might have a rather wet experience.

Sometimes, it's easiest to remove the whole cooling line and disassemble the filter on the dock. With other installations, it's better to remove the hose clamps on either side of the filter and take the unit out of the line. In either case, once you have the filter on the dock, disassemble the unit and flush it thoroughly with fresh water. You will be surprised what a collection of weeds, small shells, and sand your cleansing will most likely remove. Before reassembling the filter, spray all the rubber gaskets with CR6-66 or some similar spray-type lubricant. Be sure all the gaskets are in place before screwing the filter back together. Then, simply reinstall the assembly (or entire hose), open the intake valve, start the engine to check for leaks, and the task is done.

Next up, if your boat has gasoline engines, you can clean the flame arrestors. These combination air filters/safety devices sit atop the carburetors. They inevitably become clogged with carbon and should be cleaned at least once a season. Diesel engines, of course, do not have carburetors or flame arrestors.

After donning rubber gloves, I usually plunge my flame arrestors into about a quart of lacquer thinner, poured into a shallow plastic tray. Then, using a small nylon brush, you can easily scrub all the gunk out of the filters. This procedure should be performed on the dock or ashore. It is most decidedly unsafe to allow lacquer thinner fumes to accumulate in a boat's bilge.

The engine oil should be changed in the spring if this task was not accomplished when the boat was winterized. Those captains who purchase a used boat should play it safe and change the oil just to be sure. Many skippers pay a professional mechanic to change their engine oil. It's really a bit silly to fork out $35 or more per hour for a job that can be performed so easily. Why not give it a try yourself? You may find that the job is not very difficult, and the savings can pay for another cruise.

Most boats will need an engine oil pump (as described in Chapter 4) to suck the lubricant out of the dipstick passage. I prefer the self-contained variety, but, as noted earlier, this is the most expensive approach. In any case, before changing the oil, run the engine long enough to attain its operating temperature (usually about five to ten minutes). This warmup period will allow the oil to circulate and collect the pollutants and combustion byproducts in the engine. Changing engine oil while the power plant is still cold negates many of the process's benefits.

Once the engine is warmed up, remove the dipstick, carefully wiping it clean to prevent any oil spillage in the bilge. Then, feed the small tube of the oil pump down the dipstick passage until you feel it hit the bottom of the oil pan. Before activating the pump, be sure the exhaust hose is situated in a bucket or other appropriate container. Of course, if you have a self-contained oil pump, this would not be a consideration.

Activate the pump and hopefully the old, blackened oil will soon begin collecting in your container. Sometimes, oil pumps can be a bit of a pill to prime. If the old lubricant does not begin to flow within thirty seconds, try moving the dipstick hose up and down a bit. Usually, you can hear a change in the pump's sound when it begins to suck up the oil.

Once the old oil is removed, you must next change the filter. Be sure you have an oil filter wrench on hand before beginning this job. This inexpensive tool is available at any auto parts store.

To begin, first prepare the new filter for installation by removing it from its box, and lightly coating the rubber gasket on the bottom of the unit with oil. Consult your engine owner's manual for the type and size filter that your power plants require. Use the wrench to loosen the old filter *slightly*. Then, using one hand, hold a small tray under the filter, while screwing the unit off the engine with the other hand. If the filter is hot, be sure to use a cloth to avoid burning your hand.

As the filter is removed, some oil will begin leaking from its base. The tray held underneath the assembly will keep this old lubricant from soiling your bilge. When the filter finally comes free, pull it up slowly off the base, keeping the tray underneath all the time. Drop the old filter quickly into the tray and continue holding it under the filter mount area. Have the new filter at hand, ready for installation. Sometimes, after removing the old filter, a small stream of oil will continue to leak from the filter base. By keeping the tray in place until the new filter is installed, you can prevent any spillage into the bilge.

Tighten the new filter with your hand until it is snug. Then remove the oil tray and old filter to some secure location. Using the oil wrench, tighten the new unit one turn *only*. Overtightening can cause leaks!

After wiping up any errant leaks, refill the engine with new oil. Consult your engine owner's manual for the best oil type and your engine's capacity. Surprisingly, marine engines usually require more oil than an automobile motor of the same size. Finally, start the engine and check for leaks. If all seems well, cut the engine off and check the dipstick to make sure the oil registers the proper level.

That's it. Now you should have a real feeling of accomplishment. Not only have you performed a necessary chore for your boat, but the savings are substantial!

If you know the engine oil was changed the preceding fall, then it is only necessary to check the level. Most boaters, even new ones, know how to read an oil dipstick. Simply remove the unit, wipe it clean with an old cloth and then reinsert the stick back into its hole. Pull it out again and look at the oil level on the bottom scale. If the stick reads as much as one quart low, you should add oil to make up the difference. *Be sure* to use the same brand and weight of oil. If you are unsure of these vital statistics, it would be better to change the oil and filter completely. Always use the same brand and grade thereafter.

After changing or checking the engine oil, you should also check the transmission fluid level, if your engine is so equipped. It may be necessary to search a bit for the transmission fluid dipstick. If you have "V-drives" you will probably find the measurer just in front (toward the bow) of the engines. If you have straight drive transmissions, the dipstick will be found on the opposite side of the motor.

If your check reveals the transmission fluid to be low, call in a professional mechanic. Theoretically, transmission fluid levels should remain constant unless there is a leak in the system.

Next check the water level in the batteries. If it appears low, *don't* just dump in more water. It is quite possible to overfill batteries. Purchase one of the inexpensive, battery water filling cans available at any auto parts store. These handy devices are designed to fill your batteries to the proper level and then stop.

While you are checking around the batteries, it's a good idea to spray their terminals with CR6-66 or a similar lubricant. Battery terminals are particularly subject to rust and corrosion around saltwater, and this simple preventative action can save a lot of trouble in the future.

Now, start the engines and let them run for about ten minutes or so. Watch the oil pressure and temperature gauges. Check the stern to make sure you have water coming out of all the exhaust ports. If anything appears to be operating incorrectly, shut down and call a mechanic.

While the engines are running during this check-out period, take a few moments to observe the various belts attached to the motor. If any seem to have excessive vibration, it's a good bet they are loose. New power boaters should probably ask one of the technicians around their marina to at least be on hand for advice when tightening the belts for the first time. Once you know where the various bolts are located, this will be a simple task in the future.

As you gain experience with your boat and its engines over several seasons, you may eventually want to take on additional spring outfitting tasks in the bilge. For instance, many seasoned boaters with gasoline-powered craft change their own spark plugs and set the engine's timing. These tasks involve setting the spark plug gap and using a timing gun (plus RPM meter). This can be a bit daunting at first, but, to repeat myself for the *n*th time, I suggest watching a professional mechanic as he goes about his various jobs on your boat and, without being too obtrusive, ask questions about anything you don't understand. Before too long, you may find yourself able to perform all sorts of mechanical jobs yourself!

Finally, before leaving the bilge, take a few moments to inspect all thru-hull valves for rust and corrosion. Gate valve-type fittings are much more subject to these sorts of problems than bronze seacocks. Horror stories are occasionally heard around the marina about a rusty gate valve breaking off when turned, followed by a very prodigious stream of water. If any of your thru-hulls exhibit rust or seem to be coated with excessive corrosion, consult with the service technicians at your marina or boatyard. If, in their opinion, the valve needs replacement, I suggest authorizing the necessary service work without delay.

It's also a good idea to cruise with a collection of softwood plugs (tapered sticks) that could be driven into a thru-hull that fails while underway to quickly staunch incoming water. Ask around most boatyards and you should be able to find someone who can provide the appropriate materials.

Freshwater System

Marine freshwater systems are notorious for delivering plastic-tasting water, occasionally tinged with a bit of green algae. Spring outfitting is the perfect time to clean your system and change the charcoal filter (if so equipped). You can then enjoy fresher tasting drinking water for the rest of the season.

Recently, several effective freshwater system cleaners have been introduced on the nautical equipment market. To use any of these products, first consult the directions for the gallons per batch concentration. In our case, we have a forty-gallon onboard freshwater tank. The particular product we use treats twenty gallons per bottle. Therefore, we used two bottles.

Dissolve the cleaner in about a quart of hot water, and, using a funnel, pour the solution in your freshwater tank. Then, cut on the internal water pressure pump. Go to *each* water outlet aboard and run enough water so that the cleaning solution reaches the faucet. You can usually tell when the cleaning solution arrives by the strong smell of chlorine coming from the outlet.

Allow your freshwater system to sit idle for two hours. After that time has passed, open all water outlets and empty the freshwater tank. Then refill the tank with untreated fresh water and flush the entire contents through all the water faucets again. I usually repeat this freshwater flush a second time to make sure all the chlorine has been expunged from the system.

Now, take a few moments to change the charcoal freshwater filter if your boat is so equipped. If you don't have one of these useful (and inexpensive) devices installed yet, this would be a great time to make the addition.

Interior Cleanup

Every spring I attack my boat's interior with Fantastik, a vacuum cleaner, Soft-Scrub, and furniture polish (for interior woodwork). It is surprising just how grungy a vessel can become after sitting idle for the winter season. Our homes seldom get this dirty, and it's a real feeling of accomplishment to restore your craft's interior to Bristol fashion.

You don't need me to explain how to use cleaning cloths and a vacuum. Just remember to be thorough! However, allow me to impart one piece of advice gleaned from years of experience with spring outfitting. To really do the job right, consider removing all the gear from every locker and cabinet. Vacuum and wipe out each storage compartment thoroughly. Then, as you return the equipment to its appropriate resting place, take this opportunity to check each item for needed repairs or replacement, clean the gear where appropriate, and reorganize the storage arrangement. Take my word for it, your boating season will be happier for the effort.

Don't overlook a thorough check of your boat's interior equipment. Be sure to inspect the stove, head, and pressurized water system operation. If anything malfunctions, you must either track down the cause or call in a qualified technician.

A Look Back at Spring Outfitting

As important as in-season and winterizing maintenance jobs are, spring outfitting is "the" most important and demanding service time for almost any pleasure craft. We have discussed many of the basic tasks associated with this annual period in your boat's life, but don't be surprised to find additional duties necessary to keep your craft "spritely and Bristol." Try not to envision all these necessary chores as simply drudge work. Everything done aboard a boat should be as fun as possible, *including maintenance!* I suggest looking on spring outfitting as a fun, fulfilling time. With this attitude, you can't go wrong!

IN-SEASON MAINTENANCE

Taking proper care of your vessel during the boating season is perhaps almost as important as a good spring outfitting or winterizing. Indeed, just a few additional moments spent on maintenance during and after a cruise will preserve all the hard work that has gone before. New boat owners should make every effort to set up a regular routine based on the tasks described below. As the years go by, your boating enjoyment will be the rich beneficiary of this extra effort.

Washdown

After a long day of cruising, your boat will become encrusted with salt left over from the evaporation of saltwater splashed on the hull and superstructure. By the time you dock, your craft will be the nautical equivalent of a marguerita glass. If often surprises me just how much salt can accumulate, even on surfaces where there didn't seem to be any water. Just take my word for it, you can barely leave the marina before salt water finds a way to begin its insidious work.

To say the least, salt is a corrosive agent that can quickly rust stainless steel, dull gel-coat, and eat away teak oil. Some boating authorities claim that salt left on stainless steel can begin its destructive work within hours. To alleviate these less than desirable results, you must wash away the salt with fresh water as soon as possible!

After tying up for the night, break out the freshwater hose first thing, and give the entire boat a thorough washdown. Don't overlook the hull and the stainless steel. If you miss a single spot, the salt will begin its destructive work at that point. It's much better to use plenty of water than to be conservative. Try to avoid wetting the deck chairs. Then, after the washdown is over, you can relax with your own marguerita in hand.

Soap Wash

Nightly washdowns are fine for removing the daily accumulation of salt from your vessel. However, after returning to your home marina, responsible captains should give their boats a really good washing with soap and water. This preventative action will help to further alleviate the destructive effects of the saltwater environment.

There are many so-called boat soaps on the marine market. After experimenting with any number of these products, I have concluded that ³⁄₄ cup of Tide laundry detergent dissolved in a two-gallon bucket is the best washdown soap you can use. Boats protected with Teflon are a major exception to this rule. Harsh detergents can injure the protective coating of these fortunate craft. You should only use mild soap to clean Teflon treated gel-coat. Many firms provide the boat owner with an appropriate detergent at the time of installation.

Various mops and brushes are available to help in your washing chores. One particularly noteworthy model consists of an aluminum handle with removable tips. Thus, with a single handle, you can have a mop and several different sized brushes ready at hand. For many areas though, I have found a large synthetic sponge, used by hand, to be the most effective cleaning tool. Sometimes the good old manual approach just can't be beat.

Engine Fogging

Many boaters, including some veteran captains, don't realize the mechanically destructive effects of letting their *gasoline* engines sit idle for weeks or even months. Within a surprisingly short period of time, rust can begin to form on cylinder walls and valves. While the engine may start the next time, the loss of metal due to internal corrosion will eventually result in decreased compression and possibly a stuck valve. Valve and ring jobs must then be performed to correct the problem. These major mechanical operations are expensive!

To preserve gasoline engines, boaters should "fog" their intakes when leaving their boats for a week or more. This simple, inexpensive practice can save literally thousands of dollars further down the road. Boats equipped with diesel engines do not suffer as readily from these internal corrosion problems. Also, lacking any carburetor, diesel engines cannot be fogged as described below. If you plan to leave a diesel-powered boat idle for several weeks or longer, arrange for your marina to periodically start the engines, thereby circulating the internal lubricants.

All you need for engine fogging is a quart of "Marvel Mystery Oil," readily available from any auto parts dealer or supply company. While some other non-detergent, lightweight oils are also acceptable, "MMO" is the best and should be used whenever possible.

Fogging your engine(s) is best accomplished with your first mate at the ignition key while you reside in the bilge. The first step in the process need be performed only once. Locate the fuel shutoff valve to your engine(s). Start the motor, allow it to warm up normally, and then shut off the fuel valve. Carefully time the interval before the engine stalls due to lack of fuel. Now, turn the fuel back on and restart the engine. This may require some extra cranking to replenish the fuel supply in the fuel pump and carburetor.

If you have two engines, be sure to conduct the timing test separately on both motors. It is sometimes surprising how different the times can be for two identical power plants in the same boat.

Once you have determined the fuel stall interval, record this information in a safe place for future use. I always scratch the times on the tops of my flame arrestors with a sharp nail or tack.

Now it is time to begin the actual fogging operation. *After* starting the engine, remove the flame arrestor from the top of the carburetor. Be sure to put the securing wing nut aside where it can be easily located. Now, have your first mate bump up the throttle until the engine is running about 1,500 RPMs. Then, shut off the fuel valve. Start timing immediately. About one minute before the engine is scheduled to stall (determined by your earlier stall time test), pour ⅓ cup of MMO down into the carburetor. Be sure to cover all the various barrels (compartments) of the carburetor.

At first the engine will almost stall out, and you may see a puff of white smoke from the exhaust. Don't worry about the smoke. It's normal and harmless. Sometimes if you pour a little too much oil in the carburetor, the engine will completely stall out. Don't worry. Just start it again and continue the process. Be warned, the engine may be a little slow in starting, but just keep trying and it should catch soon.

Let the engine return to normal idle speed, then repeat the process in another twenty seconds or so. Finally, when you hear that the engine is just about to stop from lack of fuel, pour one last shot of MMO into the carburetor. Then, allow the last of the gas to run out of the carburetor.

This "fogging" process accomplishes two objectives. First, it removes the residual gasoline from your carburetor where it might deteriorate over a period of time, and it coats the carburetor, valves, and cylinder walls with a thin film of protective oil. You can scarcely do anything better for your engine. If you have gasoline power plants in your boat, I would suggest performing a fog operation whenever leaving the boat idle for longer than a week or two. Soon, it will become a quick routine that requires very little effort!

Fog the Generator

If your boat is equipped with a gasoline generator, it is subject to the same risk of internal corrosion as the main engines. To protect the generator during long periods of non-use, employ the fogging procedure outlined above for the primary power plants. Again, if you have a diesel-powered generator, arrange for the marina to run the unit periodically.

One difference you may note between the generator and the main engines is the amount of time necessary for the former device to stall out after the fuel valve has been shut off. In many cases, it can seem to take forever. If your patience is a bit short like mine, and you don't intend to leave the generator idle for more than a month or two, consider the following variation in the fogging procedure. Pour the MMO into the carburetor twice (at twenty-second intervals) and allow the motor to reattain its usual speed. Then pour in a larger than usual amount of MMO and choke the generator out completely. This procedure can be used confidently through the boating season, but for longer storage (such as through the winter), you should evacuate all the fuel from the carburetor and fuel line, as described in the previous section.

Check the Bilge

After every cruise it's a good practice to check the bilge carefully. Look for anything that might have gone wrong while underway. In particular, check the bilge floor for oil leaks. A little bit of leaking oil is, unfortunately, the norm. However, if you spot as much as a cup or two of old oil, it's time to call your friendly, professional mechanic and discover which seals have failed.

Treat the Head

Finally, before leaving your craft after a weekend (or longer) cruise, take a few moments to treat the head (toilet) and holding tank (if so equipped) with a marine odor-fighting chemical. Even those of you with an onboard waste treatment system (such as Lectra-San) can benefit by dumping a small quantity of the solution into the toilet bowl. Your next arrival will be a sweeter-smelling event for the effort.

WINTERIZING YOUR BOAT

Proper winterizing maintenance makes all the difference as to whether your boat comes through the cold months fit as the proverbial fiddle or demands major repairs in the spring. Engine and generator blocks can be cracked due to icing. Valves and pistons can freeze. Hot water tanks can burst. In short, a lot can go wrong on a boat during cold weather. However, with a day or two's preventative action, your craft should come through the winter without any of these unfortunate (and expensive) mishaps.

The first time you set out to winterize your boat, set aside some extra time for the job. I well remember our first experience. We had journeyed down to Morehead City, New Year's Day, 1980. After bringing a bevy of heavy coats and long underwear, we rejoiced in a seventy-degree day. However, our joy was not to last. Beginning at 10:00 A.M., we worked to 7:00 P.M. that evening to accomplish all that was necessary. We now typically winterize the boat in about three hours. Practice, as they say, makes perfect.

Change the Oil

Over the course of a boating season, motor oil accumulates acids and other destructive pollutants. If allowed to sit in an idle engine through the winter, vital parts can be weakened, eventually leading to a major overhaul. Consequently, you should *always* change the engine *and* generator oil when winterizing your boat, even if the craft in question has only seen limited use throughout the spring and summer. Refer to the "Spring Outfitting" section for tips on changing the vital lubricant.

Fog the Engines and Fill with Anti-freeze

As you can readily imagine, two of the most important winterizing tasks are to fog gasoline engines with MMO (as described earlier) and fill with anti-freeze the blocks and manifolds (on raw water-cooled engines) or the heat exchanger and exhaust system (on boats equipped with freshwater cooling). Both of these tasks can (and probably should) be done together after changing the oil.

Before launching into a discussion of this vital seasonal chore, let's spend a few minutes discussing a different option. Some boaters drain their blocks, manifolds, and/or heat exchangers of all water during the winter season. Indeed, drain plugs are provided by the manufacturer for just this purpose. However, I strictly advise against this procedure. In an empty engine, air can easily reach all the metal parts. This encourages internal rust on a large scale. It is far better to fill your motors with anti-freeze rather than risk the long-term damage of draining.

The procedure described above applies to gasoline engines only. For diesel power plants run at least two gallons of the anti-freeze-freshwater mixture through each engine. *Don't* attempt to fog the power plant or turn off the fuel supply valve.

Purchase at least two gallons of good quality anti-freeze for each engine, plus another for the generator and a final container for the head. You will also need a two-gallon plastic bucket.

Be sure to perform the timing test described under the "Engine Fogging" section presented earlier in this chapter before beginning the engine winterization process. This vital statistic can save you a lot of expensive anti-freeze.

Start the engine and cut off the in-line fuel valve. Begin timing immediately, and run the motor to within *30 to 40 seconds* of its stall time. Then, have your mate cut the ignition.

Mix one gallon of anti-freeze with one gallon of fresh water in the plastic bucket. Then, *cut off the raw water intake valve,* loosen the hose clamp, and remove the hose from the thru-hull fitting. Put the hose end into the plastic bucket and secure the container in a stable position. This procedure can require more than a little creative imagination in some boats.

Next, remove the flame arrestor and open the can of MMO. Now, have your mate start the engine and push the speed up to 1,500 RPMs. While keeping one eye on the anti-freeze bucket, begin the fogging procedure described earlier.

Usually, it will require more than one two-gallon bucket of the anti-freeze mixture to evacuate all the gas. Just keep pouring in the MMO as you go along. Finally, when the engine stalls, have your mate immediately cut the ignition.

Now reinstall the cooling water hose onto the thru-hull fitting, being sure to screw the hose clamp down tightly. I suggest leaving the thru-hull valves closed during the winter season. If you do follow this advice, be sure to inform the marina staff of this procedure. If it should become necessary to move your boat during the winter months, this little tidbit of info will avoid a ruined engine.

Repeat the process for the second engine and generator, if your boat is so equipped. Once you have completed these additional chores, the most vital and time-consuming part of the winterizing process is complete!

Manual Cylinder Lubrication

For maximum protection against rust, some boaters manually lubricate each cylinder with a small quantity of MMO. To accomplish this objective, you must remove each spark plug one by one and, using an oil can, deposit one or two squirts of MMO into each cylinder. Then, after disconnecting the hot wire from the coil to the distributor cap, the engine should be cranked over several times. Finally, the spark plugs must be reinstalled, being very careful to attach the proper wire to the correct spark plug. This process coats the walls of each cylinder and the tops of the pistons with an additional protective film of oil.

If a boat owner is mechanically adept enough to understand the above-described procedure, I would encourage him to manually lubricate the cylinders if time allows. I have sometimes followed this wise practice, while my schedule during other years has not allowed me to do so. While I have never had a piston to freeze to the cylinder wall one way or the other, this practice certainly comes under the "better safe than sorry" category.

Close All Thru-hulls

Before leaving the bilge, I suggest closing all thru-hull valves. Generators, marine air conditioners, and toilets usually have one or more water inlets or outlets associated with their operation. By closing all these valves, you can remove the threat of a burst hose during cold weather. This sad event can quickly sink your boat before the marina personnel have a chance to react.

Winterizing the Head

The water in your head, holding tank, and/or waste treatment system can also freeze during the winter months and leave a nasty cleanup job in the spring. Consequently, the entire waste system must also be treated with anti-freeze.

First, if you have a holding tank, have it pumped out just before winterizing. Yes, I know what a pill it can be to find a pump-out station, but remember that *dumping untreated waste overboard carries a $10,000 fine!*

If, on the other hand, your boat is equipped with an onboard waste treatment system, I suggest running several cycles, flushing with clean saltwater in between each treatment. Both of these will help to minimize any odor problem from the head winter storage.

After flushing the head, slowly pour about half a gallon of antifreeze into the toilet bowl. Then, flush the head just until the anti-freeze disappears into the holding tank or waste treatment system. Pour the remaining half gallon of anti-freeze into the bowl and repeat the process.

As a last step, I usually add a cup of marine toilet chemical to the head's bowl and allow this solution to sit during the winter months. The procedure seems to lend further help with odor problems.

Freshwater System

Obviously, you must protect your freshwater system with some sort of anti-freeze agent. Lacking even the meager defense afforded by the dissolved salt in your engine's cooling water, a freshwater network can freeze and crack before any other system on your boat.

Several non-toxic anti-freeze products are now available for winterizing your freshwater system. However, all of them are more expensive than my own choice of winterizing agent. Late every fall I journey down to my local liquor store and purchase four gallons of the cheapest vodka available.

Sounds crazy, but it works. As a rule of thumb, I suggest one gallon of vodka for each ten gallons of freshwater tank capacity. We have a forty-gallon tank, hence we purchase four gallons of "anti-freeze." Dump the vodka into an empty freshwater tank along with an appropriate supply of fresh water. Run the solution through the system to each cold water outlet. If you cannot drain your hot water heater (discussed below), add some more vodka and repeat the procedure with the hot water faucets as well. One might conclude that you will be leaving a very "happy" boat behind. It takes only a quick flush with one new tank of fresh water next spring to remove the vodka, and there is no residual taste.

If you can access the hot water heater drain plug, it might be a good idea to completely drain the contents rather than trust the "anti-freeze" system outlined above. While most of your freshwater system is composed of flexible pipe and plastic tanks, which can put up with some mild freezing, the hot water heater can be quickly cracked by ice. On some boats, however, the hot water drain plug just can't be reached. In this circumstance, my best advice is to add another gallon or two of vodka.

Should you decide to drain your hot water tank, *be sure to cut off all power to the unit before beginning the drain procedure.* Also, it is very important to refill the tank next spring before turning the power back on. Failure to follow either of these procedures will result in an immediate burn-out of the internal heating element, necessitating professional repairs.

Marine travelift.

Check the Batteries and Charger

It is very important to check the condition of your batteries and automatic charger (if your boat is so equipped) as part of your winterizing routine. During the winter months, your batteries will be called upon repeatedly to power the automatic bilge pump as it throws off any water that collects in the bilge as a result of rain or minor leaks. If the battery fails, it could lead to major problems.

Check the battery water level and inspect the terminals for rust or corrosion. Refill with water and scrape (and spray) the terminals as needed. If you have noticed any hesitancy or slow engine cranking, this is the time to have the battery checked by a professional. Using either a float check or a battery meter, a mechanic can quickly ascertain the condition of your 12-volt power sources.

Many boaters overlook this essential winterizing chore. Don't join the ranks of those unfortunate captains who arrive next spring only to find a waterlogged vessel.

Wax the Gel-Coat?

Some boaters follow the wise practice of waxing their exterior fiberglass finish as part of their winterizing routine. During the cold season this extra coat of protection will ward off chalking and weathering of the gel-coat. Then, next spring, it is considerably easier to restore your fiberglass to a shiny, like-new appearance.

While the wisdom of this winterizing chore is undeniable, I have yet to find the time to fit it into my fall routine. Perhaps you will be more fortunate. If you can indeed find the time, a good late fall waxing is certainly recommended.

Remove all Gear

It is a good idea to remove all clothes and portable equipment from your boat during the winter season. Mildew is still a possibility, even during cold weather, and a thief in your marina can't make off with the VHF if it's in your closet at home. Some captains even go so far as to take down their cabin curtains and truck them home for a good winter cleaning. Then, next spring you can rehang the cleaned fabric.

Haul-out?

Boaters on the East Coast of the United States, north of Norfolk, Virginia, will have to consider the possibility of dry storage for the winter season. The further north you travel, the greater the risk of ice damage. Marinas and boatyards in these cold weather climes usually haul boats out of the water and deposit them on ready made "cradles" where the craft rest until the spring thaw. To say the least, this is a complicated job better left to your marina personnel. If you live in an area where dry storage is called for, make arrangements well ahead of time with your marina or local boatyard. It just doesn't do to be caught with an imminent freeze in the forecast and no open cradle for your "pride and joy."

A FINAL WORD OF ADVICE

Whether your boat rests in its slip through the winter, or is stored on a landside cradle, be sure your marina checks the craft on a regular basis. While a thorough winterizing vastly reduces the chances of anything going wrong, you never know when a thru-hull fitting might give way, or the odd thief might pay your vessel a call. Periodic inspections by the marina staff are your best security insurance!

Dinghy dock with anchorage in background.

CHAPTER 6

It's Time to Go "A-Cruising"

AT LAST, THE TIME has come. Your new craft sits waiting in her slip, seemingly straining at her lines, ready to begin your first long-distance cruise. All the necessary equipment as well as a few accessories are aboard, and you have a good idea how to maintain your boat while underway and upon returning to home base.

I won't keep you waiting much longer, but please allow me to impart a few lessons learned from planning and undertaking many a cruise. Doubtlessly, you will discover certain cruising truths for yourself after you have undertaken several watery sojourns. This is only as it should be. Every boat is different and every captain's desires are not the same as those of his fellow cruisers. However, there are certain good cruising practices that seem to be universal. Let's spend a few minutes exploring some of these maxims together.

PLAN THE TRIP

When I first began cruising aboard my own vessel, good fortune led me to the local library where I discovered a fine nautical book entitled *Practical Boating* by W. S. Kals. The sage words of Captain Kals have stuck with me ever since. He advocates always having an "alternate plan." If something goes wrong while underway, or even if you simply don't make it as far on a particular day as had been planned, doesn't it make sense to already have a plan in mind for just such a contingency? Suppose unexpected engine repairs become necessary. The situation is suddenly simpler if you already have the location of a marina offering mechanical services noted on your chart. How about bad weather? If a storm appears over the horizon, do you have the necessary chart on board to make a quick run for the nearest harbor, even if you never intended to visit that refuge on this particular trip? All of these contingencies and many more like them have to do with *planning*. Whether it is a master cruising plan or an alternate agenda for unexpected events, there is no substitute for this pre-cruising activity. The captain who takes the time and effort to cover all the bases *before beginning his trip* is most likely the one who will have the most fun and come through with the least trouble.

Start Small

I suggest scheduling a three- or four-day cruise as your first undertaking. Lessons learned from these short hops will make your first week-long (or longer) trip a safer, more rewarding experience. Pick a destination within one day's cruising range of your home port. It wouldn't hurt to choose a port of call with interesting sights ashore and good marina facilities as well. Then, if the weather cooperates, you can relax and explore the local sights and return home on the third day in plenty of time for a good washdown.

Longer trips of four or five days are good first-time possibilities as well. Just remember to take it slowly until your store of cruising experience begins to accumulate. Undertaking a too ambitious project too soon can discourage captain and crew from boating in general. Working up to a major effort is a far smarter strategy!

The Planning Process

It has often been said that anticipation is half the fun of any outdoor activity. That old saw holds true in the cruising game as well. The challenge of putting together a good, workable cruising plan that takes the unexpected into account is an experience thoroughly enjoyed by all true cruising skippers and their first mates.

To begin the process, gather together all the charts that cover the waters through which you will be passing. Don't confine yourself to a single chart that details only the immediate area. Remember, circumstances may force you to change course in mid-cruise. It is far wiser to carry along enough charts to safely cruise the waters adjacent to your intended track as well.

You should also purchase the most detailed guide available for your cruising waters. If your intended trip strays into waters covered

Fixed bridge crossing busy waterway.

by a separate guide, buy both! It is far better to have two detailed books rather than a "broad and shallow" guide that attempts to cover both shorelines.

Now, starting at your home port, lay out the chart that covers the initial portion of your passage. Consult the cruising guide and make note of *all* the marinas and anchorages both on and near your intended course. Mark the various locations neatly on your chart with a *waterproof* felt-tip pen. As a further refinement, put a small *F* next to the facilities that offer gasoline and diesel fuel, and an *R* next to the marinas with repair services. Continue this process with all the charts, detailing the waters between home base and your intended port of call.

Consult the cruising guide and evaluate anchorages along the way with a critical eye. If the entrance passage is tricky, or the swinging room seems skimpy for your size craft, it might be better to forgo marking this questionable haven on your chart. Access the anchorage's shelter from bad weather if possible. As you might imagine, the more protection the better. As a new cruiser, it's best to stick with roomy, easily entered anchorages with plenty of protection. Sometimes actual on-the-water conditions don't allow you to be so choosy, but it pays to pick out only the best spots while ensconced in the safety of the chart table.

Lift-type bridge in Jacksonville, Florida—watch for restricted opening schedule.

As you study the charts and cruising guide(s), make careful note of any bridges with restricted opening schedules. Consult the chart for the closed vertical clearances of these regulated spans. If your craft cannot clear one of the restricted bridges when closed, be sure to take the span's opening schedule into account. While there is always a bit of "guess-timation" in this sort of process, try to time your arrival to coincide with a scheduled opening. There are few more boring boating activities than sitting idly by, cruising aimlessly back and forth, waiting for a bridge to open.

Next, it's time to plot the various courses between your home base and destination. Plotting compass courses while on the water is a very difficult proposition. Keeping the chart steady, drawing a straight line, and positioning the course finder can be a study in frustration on a bouncing boat. Sometimes, unexpected situations force boaters into this sort of activity. I remember once having to plot a twenty-mile course in eight-foot waves on North Carolina's Pamilco Sound. However, when pre-planning your cruise, boaters should take advantage of their stable chart table environment and plot *all* the courses they might need.

New cruisers often wonder what courses should be plotted and which can be safely left to eyeball navigation. As a rule of thumb, if

Power yacht passing under bascule bridge (Fort Lauderdale, Florida). This can be a busy and confusing time.

you are following a well-marked track with aids to navigation *less* than one nautical mile apart, compass courses are not usually necessary. However, if the channel in question is quite narrow, it might be a good idea to set down the courses anyway. Runs of more than one nautical mile between landmarks or aids to navigation should be carefully plotted. I always mark my courses neatly on the appropriate chart with a waterproof felt-tip pen. Some captains prefer a separate course log. Experiment and decide for yourself which approach fits your cruising style.

Don't stop with the courses needed to reach your intended port of call. Remember, "have an alternate plan!" As you work your way through the charts, have an eye for nearby harbors of refuge and marinas. Go ahead and plot any necessary courses for these alternate destinations. If bad weather suddenly descends on you, or one engine fails, it's a great feeling to know that a quick study of the chart will guide you to safety and shelter.

These days there is also an electronic equivalent to the above described procedure. This approach calls for calculating the latitude and longitude of any point along the way that might prove beneficial. This "point" could be something as elementary as the genesis of the entrance channel leading to an anchorage or marina, or it might be a navigationally crucial point where the channel takes an unexpected turn. Once you record the various "Lat-Lons" (which you should learn how to do in any good study of coastal navigation), you can then feed this information into your GPS and set up what are known as "waypoints." When you are on the water, you need simply tell your GPS that you want to go to a particular waypoint, and this marvelous machine will give you the compass course, how far it is to the waypoint, and even an estimated time of arrival based on your craft's average speed. Most GPS units also offer the option of stringing your various waypoints together into what is called a route. Sophisticated users can lay out their entire cruise, with the GPS pointing the way every inch of your trip.

While this procedure is most definitely of inestimable value, may I be allowed to insert one word of caution. *What if the GPS fails along the way?* Cruisers who don't have compass courses plotted out by the good old tried-and-true Dead Reckoning method could be up the proverbial creek without a paddle. So, while setting up waypoints and even routes with your GPS ahead of time is a worthwhile enterprise, I still suggest manually calculating compass courses and noting them down in black and white on your chart before taking to the water.

Now, try to calculate how far you can reasonably expect to travel on a particular day. Don't overestimate your daily mileage. Eight hours of cruising makes a long day on the water, and a six- to seven-hour stretch is better. Even if your craft has a brisk cruising speed of twenty knots, many on-the-water delays will slow your progress. For instance, it always amazes me how much time is lost waiting for the various bridges along the way to open. On well-traveled waterways, there are always "No Wake-Idle Speed" zones to slow your progress further. Couple these delays with lunch and fuel stops, and you can begin to understand why it is better to err on the conservative when estimating daily on-the-water mileage.

After calculating the day's run, use your cruising guide to pick out a good marina or anchorage that can be easily reached before sunset. If you decide to dine ashore, a nearby restaurant of good reputation is also a prime consideration. As a new boat owner, I suggest that you break into the power cruising life by staying at marinas. After a trip or two, try anchoring off. As discussed later in this chapter, cutting the dockside umbilical cord can be one of the most rewarding cruising experiences.

Allow me to impart one word of warning about cruising guides. The vast majority of these publications can be used with confidence.

However, a few employ the unfortunate practice of sending out questionnaires to the various marinas covered in their guide and never bother to visit the facilities in question. While most marinas are honest, there is the odd exception.

Several years ago, two friends, Robert and Susan, were bringing their new sailcraft home from Edenton, North Carolina, to Morehead City. The initial portion of their passage tracked across Albemarle Sound. The Albemarle has the deserved reputation of being the roughest body of water on the entire Atlantic Intracoastal Waterway. In planning the cruise, Robert asked my opinion of the sound. I sagely predicted rough conditions and plenty of wind for sailing.

In actuality, the sound resembled nothing so much as a mill pond during the couple's entire cruise. Having planned to sail most of the way, our friend's onboard fuel supply soon began to reach the critical point. Robert hauled out the only available cruising guide then covering the North Carolina coast and discovered a port of call that appeared to have everything they needed. The listing of services included dockage, gasoline, and grocery supplies. After traversing a dredged channel for many miles, our intrepid cruisers finally arrived at the tiny village of Stumpy Point, only to discover a single commercial fishing dock without any facilities for pleasure craft. Fortunately, a friendly native gave them a ride to a service station *several miles* down the road where they were able to replenish their fuel supply. However, as Susan commented, "When those fishermen saw our sailboat coming into Stumpy Point, they looked at us like we were crazy!"

Let this story be a word to the wise. Read the small print of a cruising guide before purchasing the volume. Be sure the author(s) has personally visited all the various ports of call detailed in the guide. Of course, you should understand that things change. The first-rate marina this year may be out of business the next. So, buy the best book available, lay out the optimum plan, but expect the unexpected anyway. With care, however, perhaps you won't have to face another "Stumpy Point."

Don't overlook a plan covering your shoreside activities as well. Knowing where to go and what to see ashore is an integral part of cruising fun. I have always believed that for any boater to enjoy his cruise as he should, some knowledge of the heritage of the land and the waters through which he is traveling is required. Read everything you can about your intended port of call. Maybe there's an interesting historic site within walking distance of the docks; perhaps there is even an old house with a ghost story connected with

"When those fishermen saw our boat...they looked at us like we were crazy!"

its past. Some seaside communities present outdoor plays that are always worthwhile. How about natural history museums, displays, or weekend celebrations? Then, of course, there are the more modern considerations such as where to find the best food or the liveliest nighttime entertainment. In short, to enjoy your cruise fully, you should take the time and effort to learn as much as possible about your intended port of call. A good cruising guide should help you with a portion of this information. However, it would be ideal to find one or more books dealing specifically with the area to be visited. However you manage it, knowing something about where to go, what to see, and where to dine ashore is an integral part of any cruise planning.

A Case in Point

Before going on to discuss cruising supplies and techniques, a real-life example may better illustrate how the just-discussed cruise planning process works. In the winter of 1979 the "first-rate, first mate" and I began to plan our first week-long cruise aboard our new power craft, the *Kaycy*. We decided to journey from our home port of Morehead City to Washington, D.C. During the course of the cold weather months, I spent many hours pouring over the charts and cruising guides planning every step of our journey.

The first jump was to have been from Morehead to the tiny village of Coinjock on a canal connecting two open portions of the Intracoastal Waterway. This daily run would traverse the feared Albemarle Sound, but the mileage seemed well within our reach. The second night we planned to drop the hook in what one cruising guide described as an "idyllic" anchorage on the Great Wicimico River, just off Chesapeake Bay. The next morning should find us entering the mighty Potomac River early in the day, and arriving at Washington by mid-afternoon.

By making use of several excellent cruising guides, I noted the charted locations of every marina and anchorage, both on and near our planned track. We carefully designated which facilities offered overnight dockage, gasoline, and/or mechanical repairs. As the cruise unfolded, this extra work was to pay big dividends.

Then, it was on to plotting the various compass courses for long runs between aids to navigation. On the wide open Chesapeake, it was necessary to lay out courses between practically every marker. Trying to think of every contingency, I even plotted a nighttime passage between lighted buoys.

As our planning progressed, we purchased a first-rate guide for the D.C. area. Besides learning something about our capital's history, the book allowed us to plan which museums and governmental centers we would visit during our stay. A restaurant evaluation section even let us make advanced plans for our evening dining arrangements.

Finally we made overnight dockage reservations with the chosen marinas along our route and in Washington itself. Good fortune smiled on us, and we were able to secure a berth at the Capital Yacht Club within a stone's throw of Jefferson Memorial.

Everything seemed to be set. North Carolina had been enjoying a warm, dry spring. There was no hint of a major change in the weather. The beautiful spring days only served to whet our appetite anew for a great cruise. As you can imagine, we couldn't wait for the departure date to arrive.

After a quick journey down to the boat, we awoke the next morning to overcast skies and cool temperatures. The weather forecast was inconclusive, so, trusting in luck, we cast off the lines and headed for Coinjock. After a scant four and a half hours of cruising, a dark, ominous cloud appeared on the southwest horizon and quickly began to overtake our speeding craft.

A hasty study of the chart revealed that we were near Belhaven, a tiny village boasting excellent marine facilities. Within five minutes of securing the lines at the first marina on the town waterfront, a violent thunderstorm burst upon us. We could not see the bow of our boat from the main cabin windshield in the driving rain.

The storm lasted some thirty to forty minutes. Then, like someone had flipped a switch, the sun appeared and we were left to contemplate the changeable nature of Carolina spring weather.

With all the time we had lost in docking and waiting out the storm, it was now too late in the day to continue our journey. Again, our cruising plans were consulted, only to learn of a famous dining spot just a short walk from our dock. In fact, the marina we had chosen was an adjunct of this noteworthy establishment. River Forest Manor was (and is) famous all up and down the Intracoastal Waterway (ICW for short) for its nightly smorgasbord buffet with a minimum of 88 items to choose from. To say the least, we dined in style that evening.

The next morning dawned reluctantly, swathed in thick fog. After waiting until 10:00 A.M. to see if the mist would lift, we finally decided that it was high time to get underway. The *Kaycy* crept along the waterway, following compass courses between the various markers. Our earlier chart work was paying large dividends.

Within one mile of the Belhaven harbor entrance, we ran out of the fog and had clear sailing up the waterway. It only goes to show, you never really know what cruising conditions are like just down the road.

By the time we approached Albemarle Sound, the southwest wind had freshened considerably. At the sound's entrance we met up with two other larger craft, and, after a conference on the VHF, we all headed across together. That was one of the roughest coastal crossings we've ever faced. Spray constantly cascaded high over our bow, sometimes drenching us on the flybridge. Again, we were following pre-plotted compass courses between the daybeacons on the sound. In the less than ideal weather, it was impossible to spot the beacons by eye. It wasn't easy to maintain our heading, but with the use of our binoculars and compass, we were eventually able to spot all the aids to navigation.

Soon, the two larger boats left us behind, wallowing in the eight-foot waves. By the time we sighted the North River entrance on the sound's northern shore, the sun had disappeared and a cold, steady rain had begun. It did not require too much thought to choose an early stop at Coinjock, our first day's intended location. Fortunately, a quick check on the VHF revealed that berths were still available.

Again, our early planning paid off. The Coinjock Marina had been written up in several guides as having an excellent restaurant. After our hair-raising adventures earlier in the day, no one felt like galley duty. Knowing that there was a well-thought-of dining spot at hand made all the difference.

The next morning we awoke refreshed and ready to make some time at last. A light morning fog did not impede us as much as the forty-degree temperatures. With socks on our hands to serve as gloves, we at last made our way into Virginia. The sun came out, the temperature warmed into the sixties, and captain and crew could perhaps have been excused for thinking their troubles were over.

Soon after entering Norfolk harbor, we came face to face with a low-level swing bridge that was supposed to open on demand. However, repair work was in progress on the span. The construction workers kept us cooling our heels for two hours before they deigned to open the bridge for the peon boaters waiting to go through.

While being held up, a study of the chart revealed a large marina nearby. We were able to spend some of our time profitably by topping off the fuel tanks and replenishing a few food supplies.

Finally, the bridge opened, and we were soon skimming up the Chesapeake Bay's mirror-like surface. In spite of the delay, we were able to reach our designated anchorage, Horn Harbor, before sunset. The setting was all the guidebook promised. Beautiful, natural shores, lush in tall hardwood trees were set amidst an almost landlocked harbor with more than adequate depths. That evening has, ever since, remained one of our fondest cruising memories.

The fourth day of our little jaunt saw us picking our way up the mighty Potomac River marker by marker. Again, a light fog impeded our vision and we followed pre-plotted compass courses.

About ten o'clock I made a quick trip down from the flybridge to see if all was well below. There was no reason to suspect that anything was amiss. I was simply following the wise cruising practice of checking the engine compartment while underway from time to time. Upon opening the bilge hatch, I was shocked to see several quarts of black oil sloshing around in the bilge. A careful study of the engines revealed a steady stream of oil leaking from the port motor. We were in trouble!

Fate was kind to us on this occasion. A quick study of the Potomac River chart revealed that the port of Colonial Beach was only a few miles away. Even more encouraging was the noted location of several marinas and boatyards labeled with a small *R*, indicating mechanical repair capabilities.

Lock filling with water—have your largest fenders ready.

We cruised into Colonial Beach and stopped at the first facility. A thoughtful dockhand informed us that his mechanic was off that day, but another yard just up the way could probably handle our problem. A quick cruise further up the channel did indeed bring us to a yard that immediately gave us their attention. After an inspection, the mechanic revealed that the bolt holding the port oil filter in place was loose. A simple tightening solved our problems. With my previous visions of a major repair, that was welcome news indeed.

It was only a matter of some thirty minutes to pump as much of the old oil out of the bilge as possible, bring the engine oil level up to normal, and then be on our way. We have always been grateful to that boatyard for their honesty and efficiency. It would have been all too easy to indicate that major repairs were necessary, and we would never have known the difference.

Again, our pre-planning had come to our rescue, just when it seemed as if our goal was in sight. Later that afternoon we were tucked snugly into our reserved slip at the Capital Yacht Club. I might add that the *Kaycy* occupied the last transient berth available. If arrangements had not been made ahead of time, there would probably have been no room at the inn. Now, it was time to relax from our travels, take in the sights, and even spend a few minutes contemplating our cruising lessons and adventures.

CRUISING SUPPLIES

When you leave home port for a weekend or longer, there are certain supplies that must be taken aboard that would not normally be required for a day-long trip. Some of these items will already be at hand, while others, such as food and drink, require careful selection and consideration. In either case, thoughtful cruisers should take the few extra moments necessary to see that everything is on board and stowed securely *before* untying the dock lines. Replacements further down the waterway are always an expensive proposition.

Power Cords, Water Hoses, and Docklines

When most cruisers head out for a day swinging at the hook in a popular anchorage, it's a simple matter to untie the docklines, unhook the power cables and water hoses, and be on the way. It's different when you plan to cruise further from your home port over the course of several days. This dockside gear must accompany you in order to berth at other ports.

Shorepower cables should be disconnected from the dockside electrical boxes and stowed as neatly as possible. I don't recommend just coiling the cables in the cockpit. They inevitably get in the way of some other activity. One idea is to coil them neatly in a locker below decks. On the other hand, I have seen several boats on which the captain has secured two life ring hooks under the gunwales in the cockpit. The shorepower cable(s) is then wrapped between the two hooks.

Water hoses should also be stowed neatly out of the way. Some boaters opt for a flat nylon hose while cruising. These handy units come with their own reel storage assembly. As an added bonus, any water left in the hose is automatically squeezed out as the flexible tube is reeled into its container. Unfortunately, this sort of unit is easily crimped, but many cruisers deem this disadvantage as inconsequential when stacked up against a nylon hose's convenience.

Docklines should be coiled and left ready at hand. You never know when you might need a rope. A convenient line can be readily pitched to any crew member who falls overboard. Sometimes a line heaved to a drifting, disabled vessel can make all the difference. Let this be a lesson to the wise. Keep your lines ready for instant use!

For maximum convenience, some cruisers purchase a second complete set of docklines. These fortunate captains can simply cast off when leaving for an extended cruise with the comforting knowledge that their familiar docklines will still be in place upon their return to home port.

Towels

When we first began cruising, one of our biggest surprises was the quick accumulation of damp towels while on a long cruise. In the often humid, saltwater environment, towels do not dry quickly. More and more clean, dry cloths are inevitably hauled out at wash-up time, eventually resulting in a cabin littered with semi-dry towels.

To help manage this cruising problem, I suggest installing a large number of towel racks at convenient locations, preferably out of sight. While cruising, used towels should be spread out on a rack immediately for quick drying.

Some boaters string a temporary clothesline across the bow or cockpit to facilitate towel drying. This arrangement is certainly useful, though it can eventually lead to salty towels. Don't forget to remove any cloths hung on the line before getting underway. We once saw a high-speed motor yacht gaily cruising down the waterway, unaware that the towels hung across its cockpit were gaily blowing away one by one.

Bring an extra supply of clean towels aboard for an extended cruise. Take my word for it, you'll need them. If you are voyaging with another couple, an even larger supply will be necessary.

Even with additional cloths and imaginative drying arrangements, you may as well know that damp towels are a fact of cruising life. If anyone out there ever finds a complete cure for this problem, short of installing an onboard clothes dryer, please let me know.

Ice Chest

Most power boats are equipped with an onboard refrigerator. Captains and their mates usually transport food to their boat via an ice cooler, transfer the perishables to the fridge, and then store the emptied chest in their car. While this arrangement is fine for a weekend at the marina, it has one serious drawback while on an extended cruise. Unless your craft is equipped with a separate icemaker, the supply of ice produced by the few trays in your refrigerator will soon be exhausted. The simple answer to this problem is to keep the ice chest aboard. Every day or two you can purchase a bag of ice at a convenient marina. Then there will always be plenty of cold drinks for a hot, thirsty crew.

Food and Drink

There are two mistakes often made by first-time power cruisers when stocking their boats for an extended cruise. Some boaters bring so much food that the onboard storage compartments are overwhelmed. The result is likely to be a loaf of bread stowed in the towel locker. To say the least, this is a less than ideal cruising arrangement.

Other captains and their mates decide to bring only a limited quantity of food and drink aboard with the intention of purchasing supplies as they travel. Cruising couples of this ilk often find themselves paying premium, convenience store prices for their foodstuffs at the various marina stores along the way.

The best plan is to fall somewhere between these two extremes. Bring as much food aboard as you can conveniently stow without excessive fear of spoilage. Try to plan for all three daily meals as well as between-time snacks. You should also remember that there has never been a cruising cache that contained too many cold drinks. When you do need to purchase additional supplies while cruising, take the extra time and effort to visit a nearby supermarket rather than the convenient marina store. Your cruising budget will be the great beneficiary of this approach.

Then, there is the question of what food supplies to bring and how to prepare them once aboard. Years ago, I had the good fortune to make the acquaintance of Corinne Kanter, author of *The Galley K.I.S.S. Cookbook.* Before anyone derives a romantic notion from the title, let me hasten to add that KISS is an acronym for "Keep It Simple Sailor." Corinne's philosophy is to prepare tasty, appetizing meals aboard with the simplest equipment and the fewest possible ingredients. This is good advice for power boaters as well as sailors. Every recipe in her book can be prepared with a single-burner stove, a skillet, saucepan, and/or a pressure cooker. With an oven aboard, the process becomes even simpler. *The Galley K.I.S.S. Cookbook* is highly recommended by this writer.

Unless you are lucky enough to cruise aboard a fifty-five-foot motor yacht with a full-size kitchen, a ship's galley is no place to prepare a dish that requires three individual mixtures formulated separately with a multitude of ingredients. Keep your cruising menus simple! Once, I myself did not follow this wise advice. I decided to prepare pepper steak in a wine sauce, broiled squash casserole,

Tied up for lunch at a restaurant with its own dock—a great way to break up your day on the water.

stuffed potatoes, spinach salad, and Bavarian Creme for dessert. Everything turned out fine, but it was 10:00 P.M. before we finally sat down to dinner. I don't even want to mention the time when I finished cleaning up!

Power boaters have one great advantage over their sailing brethren when it comes to food preparation. Most sailcraft have only an icebox for cold food storage while the vast majority of power craft are equipped with a refrigerator and *freezer.* This handy piece of equipment allows power boaters to prepare dishes ahead of time, transport them to the boat still frozen, and pop them in the freezer. When dinner time rolls around, it's a very simple matter to unthaw the dish followed by a quick warm-up. After a long day fighting wind and waves, a tasty, precooked dish can make the difference between a memorable hot meal and cold cuts. Spaghetti sauce and small meat casseroles are good entrees for this purpose.

Unless your freezer is quite large, it will not be possible to take enough frozen dishes for your entire cruise. Consider stopping at a likely-looking seafood dock along the way and purchasing fresh fish, shrimp, scallops, etc. There's *absolutely nothing* like the taste of fresh seafood cooked in your own galley after a day spent on the water. Just writing about it makes my mouth water! Again, I refer the reader to *The Galley K.I.S.S. Cookbook* for some wonderful fresh seafood concoctions.

Broiled steaks coupled with mashed potatoes and a green veggie are another great cruising combination. Some captains purchase a nautical charcoal grill with just such a meal in mind. These clever units are mounted on a stern rail or separate stanchion. They swing out over the water for safety while cooking and then swivel inboard when turning the meat and serving the steaks. The finest grills are made from stainless steel, but, be warned, they can be expensive.

Few cruisers will wish to stop long enough to have a hot lunch. I suggest a good selection of quality cold cuts and cheeses with fresh bread. Chips and dip are a welcome sidebar.

Cruisers seem to have differing tastes for breakfast. Some captains and their mates settle for a quick piece of toast while others start every cruising day with country ham, hash browns, and scrambled eggs. Suit your own tastes, but, remember, if you do have an elaborate breakfast, you must take the time to clean up before getting underway. It's a truly bad idea to leave port with dirty pans rattling around in the sink.

Whatever recipes you choose, good food and drink is an integral part of any fun cruise. Be sure to take the time and extra effort to plan your menus carefully and select the freshest ingredients. If possible, prepare at least one or two dinners ahead of time and keep them frozen until needed. Don't miss the opportunity to purchase local specialties (such as *fresh* seafood) along the way. With a little practice, you'll be cooking like a galley chef professional in no time at all.

MEETING THE OTHER GUY

When studying the "rules of the road" as a part of coastal navigation, you will discover certain strictures that apply to meeting, passing, and overtaking another vessel. These guidelines should be carefully memorized and observed whenever you are underway.

It is an unfortunate fact of modern pleasure boating that numerous boat owners do not take the time to commit these very important rules to memory. Some captains seem to feel they always have the "right of way," and everyone else should stay clear. Beware of these "waterway hogs!" Always be alert for the actions of your fellow boaters, and do not assume that they will follow the conventional guidelines.

Unfortunately, the rules of the road, even when followed strictly by all parties, do not solve what has become one of the most strained on-the-water relationships. Pick up almost any boating magazine and you will probably find some sailor railing at power boaters for their insensitivity to the problems caused by their wake. Similarly, you are just as likely to discover an article taking sailors to task for clogging up the waterways and refusing to yield the right of way to faster vessels. This stressful situation has been caused by a mutual misunderstanding of the needs and problems of the two ilks of pleasure boaters.

Sailors certainly have a legitimate gripe about the heavy wake generated by many power craft, particularly those with planing hulls. Sailcraft are very vulnerable to large stern waves, particularly when cruising under auxiliary power in confined waterways. I have seen sailboats almost capsized by the prodigious wakes thrown by large sportfishermen.

On the other hand, sailors often don't realize that power boaters have a genuine problem with frequent starting and stopping. It is not at all uncommon for a power boat to overtake numerous sailing vessels in a day's cruising on protected intracoastal waterways. If power captains slowed down for every single sailboat, their progress would be considerably impeded and the increased fuel expenditure (particularly with planing hulls) necessary to regain cruising speed after slowing down would be quite significant. Additionally, power craft captains often expend a considerable amount of time and effort fiddling with the trim tabs and engine synchronizer to adjust their boat to an ideal cruising condition. This process must be repeated every time after slowing for a sailcraft.

So, what's the answer? How can we reconcile the very different needs of power boaters and sailors? Perhaps a little common sense will solve the problem. If you are cruising in a narrow channel and must pass a sailcraft at close quarters, common sense and minimal courtesy require slowing down. Maintain just enough speed to pass the sailboat. On the other hand, if you are traversing a wide channel where the sailcraft in question can be passed by some thirty to fifty yards to one side or another, I do not think it necessary for you to slow from cruising speed. Some sailors might disagree, but only if they do not understand a power boater's needs.

For every three clear-cut, slow down or maintain-speed situations, there will be one that requires a judgment call. Can you really leave enough space between your boat and the sailcraft, or should you bite the bullet and slow your speed? Experience will help you decide these matters, but there will always be situations where you will wonder if you did the right thing.

BERTHING AT A STRANGE MARINA

Most boaters untie and moor their boats at their home port numerous times before venturing out on a longer cruise. It is understandable that many first-time power cruisers come to think of their particular slip or dock as the typical mooring situation at every marina. Believe me, this notion is far from the truth. When visiting a strange marina, you will almost certainly be called upon to perform maneuvers and formulate tie-down plans very different from those used in your home slip. While, as always, experience will be your best teacher, the tips presented below should get you started on the right track.

Maneuvering (or "Everyone Hits the Dock Sometime")

Every boat handles differently and it would be impossible for me to describe in words how best to maneuver your particular craft. Experience is truly the *only* real teacher in this situation, so you should be sure to acquire at least some expertise before visiting a new marina. Be sure to practice docking and undocking at your home port in a variety of conditions before beginning your first long cruise. Then, you can approach any new situation with confidence in your ability to handle the craft.

As mentioned earlier, twin-screw power boats are much more maneuverable than single engine craft. Boats with only a single engine are particularly hard to maneuver when backing up. Former owners of outboard or I/O-driven craft will be surprised how little force a rudder exerts on inboard boats when powering astern. After you think about it for a moment, the reason for this condition is obvious. Rudders depend on the force of water to turn their craft. Either the boat must have sufficient speed through the water for the rudder to do its job, or the force of the water pushed back from the propeller (known as "backwash") must suffice. When going in reverse, both of these necessary conditions are absent. Usually, the boat is going so slowly while backing, there is very little water pressure brought to bear on the rudder from the boat's speed through the water. Also, since the propeller's rotation is reversed, the wash from the prop is now *heading toward the bow and away from the rudder.* Now you can readily understand why skippers of single-screw boats must take great care when docking, particularly stern first.

Twin engine boats, on the other hand, have vastly superior maneuvering ability. Remember that twin propellers are offset to one side or the other of the boat's hull. Thus, if you want the boat to turn slowly to port, put the starboard engine in forward and the port in neutral.

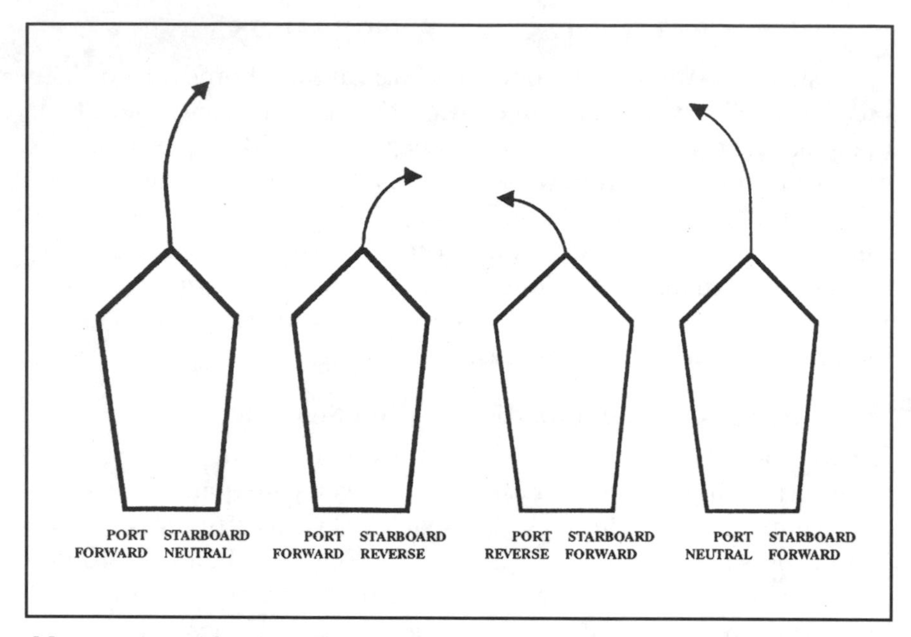

Maneuvering with twin engines.

The power of the starboard propeller without the compensating of the port screw will begin to turn the boat to port. If you really want to turn to port on a dime, put the starboard engine in forward and the port in reverse. Now the force of the starboard prop is pushing the boat to port, while the reverse action of the port screw is pulling the boat to port. This may sound complicated when explained verbally, but, trust me, a little on-the-water experience will clear up all the hocus-pocus.

I suggest that captains of single-screw boats attempt to dock stern first only in the absence of strong tidal currents and stiff winds. Even twin-engined boats might do better to go into a slip bow first in the face of particularly strong blows or swift currents.

Even after practicing, and gaining experience, there will always be some occasions when you hit the dock while trying to berth at a strange marina. It seems to be a fact of boating life that there is always a crowd around when you make a mistake while nary a soul is in sight during a perfect landing. Once, after many years of cruising on the *Kaycy,* we pulled into a large marina in Wrightsville Beach, North Carolina, for the evening. The winds were calm and the water movement seemed to be nil. Wrong! Unknown to us, there was a strong tidal current flowing. As I leisurely maneuvered toward the dock, the water flow pushed our craft broadside into a houseboat. Fortunately, the "first-rate, first mate" quickly threw a large fender between our boat and the other craft just before the collision occurred. Her quick action prevented any damage to either craft. Nevertheless, there was a large crowd watching my wonderful piloting ability from the adjacent pier. Talk about feeling embarrassed; well, I can only advise you to do what I did then—grin and bear it. Remember, absolutely *everyone* hits the dock sometime.

The story presented just above brings home another moral. Legs and hands are no match for the force of a boat caught by wind and current. All hands should use extreme caution when fending off from a dock or another boat. Many serious accidents resulting in crushed limbs have occurred when a too-zealous crew member attempted to physically push a boat one way or another. While everyone uses hands and feet sometimes to fend off, never put your limbs in a position where they could be caught and trapped. If in doubt, let the boat hit the dock. As one professional captain put it to me years ago, "That's what the pilings are there for!"

Mooring

Most docking situations call for one of three tie-down situations. You can generally depend upon mooring either at a slip with pilings far out in front and behind your craft, a slip with the tie-offs at nearly right angles to the bow and stern, or at a face dock with no pilings on the opposite side (from the dock). Each of these situations requires its own special tie-down plan that must be customized to each particular dock's configuration.

Before moving on to review the three moorings described above, let's take a moment to discuss the variable of floating docks. In waters with a large tidal range, floating piers and docks are often used to compensate for the wide variation in water levels. As discussed earlier, floating docks rise and fall with the water level, so you need not leave any play in your docking lines to allow for the changing tide. When mooring to fixed slips or piers, on the other hand, enough slack must be left in the lines so the ropes will not come under too much strain at low water, and yet not be too loose at high tide. Ask the dockmaster at any fixed pier marina you might visit for advice about the play that should be left in your lines.

Mooring in a slip with pilings well fore and aft is perhaps the easiest of all the various mooring situations discussed in this account. While most boaters use one spring line for added safety, the angle of

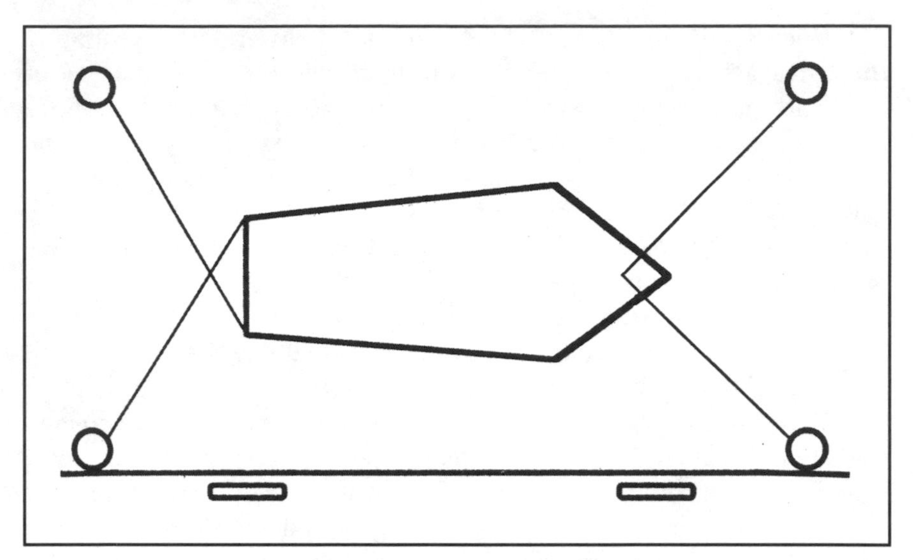

Tie-off plan for slip with pilings well fore and aft.

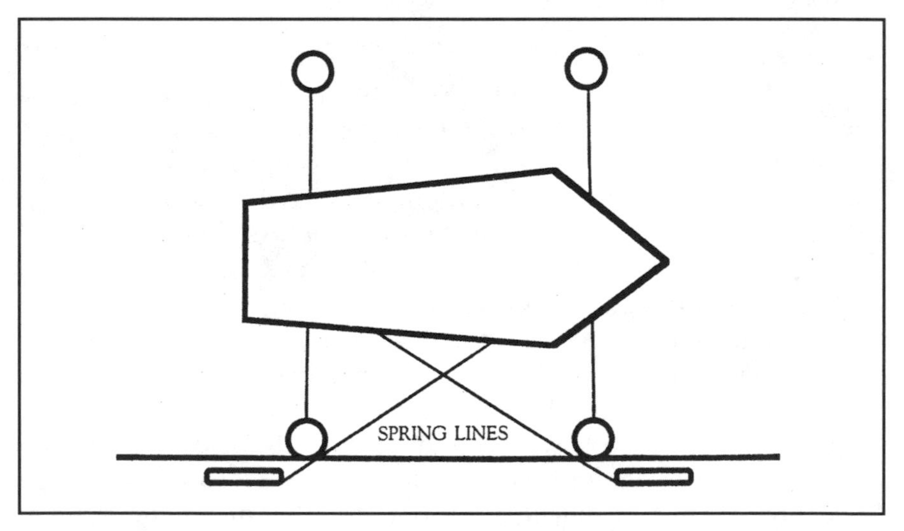

Tie-off plan for slip with pilings at right angles.

the four primary lines constrains the boat from moving too far forward or backward. Similarly, the four corner docking lines should be adjusted to keep your craft from hitting either the port or starboard side pilings. In order to facilitate stepping ashore and returning to your craft, most captains offset the four principal lines so the boat will lie closer to the access pier. In other words, if the dock is configured

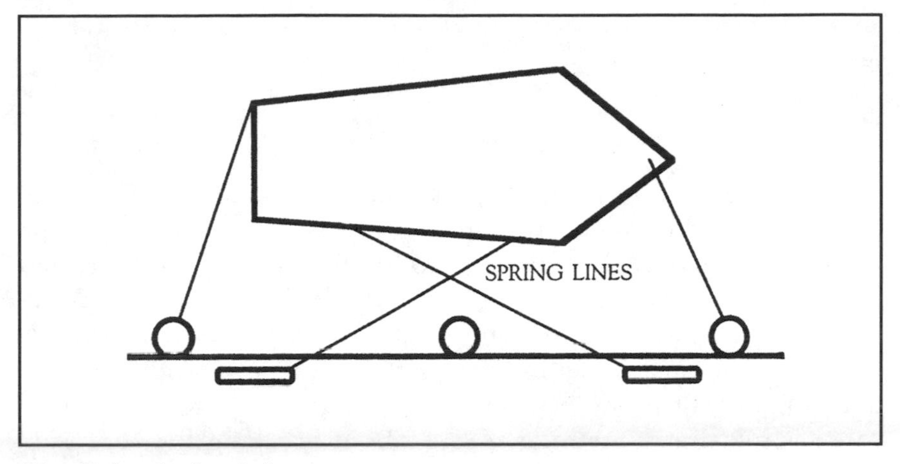

Tie-off plan for face deck.

so that you step off your boat on the starboard side of the vessel, lengthen the port side lines a bit and shorten the starboard ropes accordingly. Be sure to keep enough strain in the port lines to prevent the boat from hitting the pier.

Mooring at a slip with the pilings at nearly right angles to the bows and stern differs from the first tie-down plan, discussed above, in one significant detail. The two lines from each corner of the stern and the two from the bow leading to the port and starboard pilings cannot be depended upon to prevent the boat from sliding too far forward or backward in the slip. Therefore, two spring lines must be used to prevent this action.

Tying to a face pier differs from mooring in a slip in that there is no mechanism to prevent the boat from rubbing against the dock. To prevent damage to the boat, use your fenders. It is best to affix the fenders to the boat rather than the dock pilings. By using this approach, the fender will stay with the boat as the tidal level changes. Once in South Carolina, where the tidal range is almost eight feet, I awoke one morning and spotted a boat in the Charleston Municipal Marina with its fenders affixed to the pilings at least six feet above the level of the deck. Obviously, the night before when the boat arrived, the tide was high. The owner apparently tied his fenders to the pilings at what was then the proper place and turned in. I'm sure he was a little surprised and embarrassed when he awoke to his mistake.

Twin spring lines should also be used when mooring to a face dock to prevent excess backward and forward motion. This requirement is similar to the situation encountered when docking in a slip with right angle tie-offs.

ANCHORING OFF

On several occasions during the course of this book, I've mentioned the joys of anchoring off in an isolated cove far from the remote vestiges of civilization. This wonderful aspect of modern cruising should not be underestimated. Indeed, many captains make anchoring off a habit, and only berth at marinas when resupply becomes necessary. Sometimes, isolated anchorages are not available, and you must drop the hook on heavily developed waters. Even so, there is still that something special about breaking the shoreside umbilical cord. Perhaps it is a sense of independence that is all too rare in our modern, well-planned world. Whatever this indefinable quality may be, it is part and parcel of the joy of cruising.

Assessing the Anchorage

Along with the pleasures of anchoring off come added responsibilities for the power boat captain. While your pre-planning, including the use of a good, reliable cruising guide, should point out the safe havens along your route, there is no substitution for "on-the-water" evaluation of a potential anchorage.

As you approach a new anchorage, there are several questions that must be answered from personal observation:

1. Is there enough swinging room for my size boat?—In other words, can your boat swing back and forth at anchor without encroaching on the shoreline or shallow water.

2. Do I need to set a Bahamian moor to limit swinging room?—Bahamian moorings are discussed later in this chapter. For now, we need only note that this procedure allows boats to safely drop the hook in anchorages that otherwise might not have sufficient swinging room.

3. Is there sufficient protection for the expected weather?—With a forecast of light winds and fair weather, captains need not be too concerned about the protection afforded by a particular anchorage. However, if there is even the mention of foul weather on the NOAA weather forecast, you need to access the protection of your potential anchorage with a critical eye. High, well-wooded shores render the best shelter from strong winds, while low marsh banks afford minimal sanctuary. Usually, an anchorage is open to winds from at least one quarter. If an incoming blow is forecast to blast in from this particular direction, it would certainly be better to drop the hook elsewhere.

4. What is the aesthetic value of the anchorage?—Are the shores undeveloped or are they lined with unsightly development? Every captain must evaluate an anchorage's natural beauty (or lack of it) based upon his or her personal tastes. If a particular haven does not seem to fill the bill, consult your cruising guide for another nearby anchorage. Often, by traveling just a bit further, you can find a spot with just the qualities you are looking for.

Setting the Hook

Before beginning to set the anchor, you must first determine how much anchor line is necessary for a secure hold on the bottom. The ratio of water depth to length of anchor line is known as "scope." Most experts agree that a 6 to 1 or, better yet, a 7 to 1 anchor scope is required to maintain a stable anchorage. For example, if the water depth is 10 feet, then you should use 60 feet of anchor line for a 6 to 1 scope or 70 feet of line for a 7 to 1 scope.

Scope and anchor line length obviously affect swinging room. If you must pay out 150 feet of anchor line for a safe scope, your craft will clearly need more room to swing to and fro upon the line than if you need only use 60 feet of anchor rode. Thus, you must take anchor scope into account when assessing a potential anchorage's swinging room.

One of the most unfortunate nautical catch phrases ever developed is "throw out the anchor." Anchors should *never* be thrown. It is all too easy for an anchor to foul its rode (rope) when pitched out in this haphazard fashion. Rather, the hook should be carefully lowered in the water with a critical eye to preventing the rode from becoming entangled around the anchor.

Before lowering the anchor, take a moment to determine the direction in which the prevailing tide and wind will attempt to push your boat. If in doubt, simply put your engines in neutral for a bit and see which way the boat drifts. Now, have your mate carefully lower the hook and play out the anchor rode while you use the engines (in reverse) to back the boat away from the anchor *in the direction of the wind and tide.* Be sure, however, to disengage the engines before snubbing against the anchor.

After carefully lowering the anchor and letting out the proper amount of rode, take several minutes before going below to see if the anchor is holding properly. Once your boat has snubbed against the anchor line, pick out a fixed object ashore and watch to see if it is staying even with you. I suggest spending at least ten minutes in evaluating your anchor's set before going below. Sometimes, it can seem as if an anchor is holding at first, only to discover that your boat is slowly moving with the prevailing current and wind. Continue to check your position at regular intervals before turning in. While, in fair weather, a dragging anchor is a somewhat rare occurrence, it is an event that must be guarded against constantly.

Bahamian Moors

As mentioned earlier, a Bahamian moor is an anchoring procedure often used to limit a boat's swinging room. This plan is particularly useful in crowded anchorages or otherwise desirable coves and creeks that are a bit skimpy for your particular craft.

There is nothing magic about a Bahamian moor. To accomplish this anchoring plan, a second anchor is set at a 180-degree angle to the first hook. See the diagram.

As you can see from the drawing, a Bahamian moor limits a boat's swinging room by providing two alternate supports. For instance, if

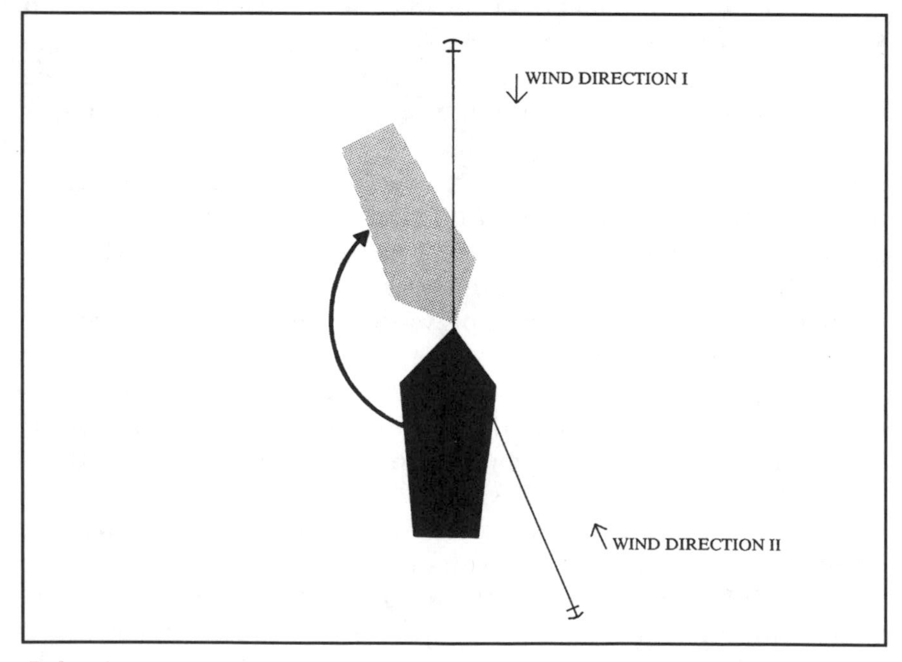

Bahamian moor.

the wind and tide are initially running from the north, your boat will lay to the south. Suppose, however, that the wind shifts during the night to a southerly direction. With a normal anchor set, your craft would drift through a change in position equal to the length of anchor rode. With a Bahamian moor, however, the boat would simply begin to bear on the opposite anchor, and would only move a very small distance from its original position.

The really big pill in setting a Bahamian moor is getting the second hook placed properly without fouling your prop. I've read any number of exotic procedures outlined in other boating books that supposedly allow you to accomplish this procedure using engine power. I've tried them all, and it's always been a white-knuckle experience. I suggest setting the first anchor, then break out the dinghy and row the second hook out. This procedure vastly simplifies the process, and there is very little chance of fouling an anchor carefully dropped from a dinghy.

Heavy Weather Procedures

Anchoring in high winds, or with the threat of heavy weather in the forecast calls for extra caution. Most boats usually make a run for a protected marina when the skies begin to turn nasty. However, if you cannot reach a sheltered harbor, special precautions come into play.

Be sure to pick the most sheltered anchorage possible before the weather really closes in. Choose a haven with good protection from the prevailing winds. Consult the forecast for expected wind direction.

Increase your anchor scope to at least 8 to 1. In a really heavy blow, consider a 10 to 1 scope. If the wind is not yet so high and the waters so rough to make it hazardous, set a second anchor at a 45-degree angle to the first hook with the dinghy. Try to let out exactly the same length of anchor rode. This procedure will allow the boat to pull against both hooks at the same time.

Finally, set an anchor watch. Crew members should take turns watching the boat for an hour or two while everyone else tries to get some sleep. The primary concern is, of course, a dragging anchor(s). If the watch person observes the vessel changing positions, that's the signal for all hands to don foul weather gear, start the engines and reset the hook(s).

Most boaters will go a lifetime without ever encountering these worrisome conditions. However, the possibility is always there, so every boater had best be ready!

A FINAL WORD

If I can leave the new boat owner with one last piece of advice, it would simply be to have fun with his new vessel. After all, pleasure boating, as its name implies is meant for relaxation. Leaving all the troubles of the land and one's job behind and exchanging these cares for the simple relationship between man, his boat, and the water can be one of the most renewing experiences you will ever enjoy.

One of my themes throughout this book has been to simply take your time. With adequate prior preparation, your chances of having good old fun on the water are vastly increased. So, take whatever time is necessary to carefully select, outfit, accessorize, and maintain your boat, as well as plan your cruise. I can promise you that some of the most beautiful and memorable experiences of your life are waiting just down the waterway, if you follow these simple procedures.

There are few feelings to match the pride and excitement when the new boat owner first sees his boat floating tranquilly at the slip. Something in the craft's lines just seems to say, "Let's go!" If, with this book, I can help the reader to maintain that wonderful feeling throughout his time on the water, then I will be happy indeed.

Fair winds to you all. Good luck and good cruising!

Glossary

Aft—Heading toward the stern section of the boat.
Anchor chocks—Metal devices attached to the deck, usually by screws, which allow an anchor to be securely stowed without fear of moving about in rough seas.
Anti-fouling paint—A special paint formulation that reduces the growth of marine life on a boat's hull and underwater hardware.
Automatic float switch—A floating mercury switch that senses when water levels in the bilge have become too high and turns on the bilge pump. After water has dropped to a safe level, the switch deactivates the bilge pump.
Bahamian moor—A special anchoring procedure that minimizes the swinging room of a vessel in changing winds and tides. This technique uses two anchors set at almost 180-degree angles from each other.
Ballast—Weight placed in the lowest section of the hull to minimize rolling from side to side and the possibility of capsizing.
Bilge—The lower, below-decks portion of a boat.
Bilge pump—A high output pump located in the bilge with an overboard discharge. This pump is responsible for evacuating any water that accumulates in the bilge, whether by rain, spray, or hull leaks.
Binding post—An upright post of metal or wood with a small cross member at a right angle to the main post. This device is usually found on the bow and is used to attach lines to that section of the boat.
Bow—The front of a boat or other vessel.

Bow pulpit—A tongue support, usually made from teak wood or fiberglass, that extends out from the bow. Crew members can conveniently perch atop this support while anchoring or docking.
Breakwater—An artificial barrier, composed of wood or concrete, which shelters a harbor from the more destructive effects of wind and rough seas.
Brokerage—A dealership in used boats.
Carburetor—A complicated device found on gasoline engines that mixes the fuel with fresh air to form the proper mixture for ignition in the cylinders.
Chocks—A device with two hornlike metal appendages curving inward through which rope is passed. The chock helps to determine which direction the rope will lay in.
Circulating pump—A water pump found on the interior of an engine block that circulates water throughout the block for cooling purposes. Do not confuse this device with a raw water pump, which is mounted to the exterior portion of an engine.
Cleat—A piece of wood or metal with projecting ends to which one can safely secure rope and line.
Cockpit—An open area found at the stern of some boats. Cockpits are ideal for fishing from.
Cradle—A device, usually made of wood, on which a boat's hull can rest securely during out of the water storage.
Deck pipe—A metal, through-deck fitting, attached to the deck on the bow, through which anchor rope or rode is passed for ready storage below decks. The pipe is usually fitted with a cap to protect against water entry.
Depth sounder—A device used for accurately measuring the depth of water under a boat's keel.
Dockmaster—The individual in charge of all non-repair operations at a marina.
Draft—The depth of water necessary to keep a boat off the bottom. For instance, a boat with a 4-foot draft must be in a minimum of 4 feet of water to stay off the bottom.
Engine block—The main portion of an engine in which resides the pistons and cylinders.
Exhaust port—A thru-hull fitting attached to the stern of a boat through which exhaust gases and heated cooling water is expunged from the onboard power plants.

Face dock—A dock that lacks any pilings of tie-offs on its opposite side.
Flame arrestor—A device that resembles an automobile air filter. On gasoline engines the flame arrestor sits atop the carburetor and prevents any flames caused by backfires from entering the bilge.
Following sea—When you are traveling in the same direction as the prevailing waves or chop, you are said to be in a following sea.
Forward—Heading toward the bow section of a boat.
Freshwater pump—A small electric pump that provides pressure for the onboard freshwater system.
Galley—Nautical term for the kitchen area on a boat.
Gate valve—A valve that uses a round turning handle attached to an internal, threaded valve. This type of valve aboard a saltwater vessel is more subject to corrosion and failure than a seacock-type valve.
Gel-coat—The smooth, final coat finish found on most fiberglass boats. Gel-coat is an epoxy compound that is usually sprayed on the interior portion of a mold as the first step in building a boat's hull.
Generator—A mechanical device powered by either a gasoline or diesel engine and that produces a 120-volt electric current.
Head—Nautical term for the toilet and bathroom area on a boat. This term can also refer to a marine toilet only.
Hook—Synonymous with anchor in nautical jargon.
Intake—A general term describing any source from which seawater can be pumped or drawn into the boat.
Keel—The central portion of the underwater section of the hull. A keel is sometimes referred to as the "spine" of a boat. The keel is responsible for the structural integrity of the hull and must be strong and adequately supported.
Lock—A large enclosure used for lowering or raising vessels to different water levels. A lock usually has waterproof doors on either end. After the doors are closed, water is pumped in or out to adjust the level.
Manifold—A cast-iron device attached to each side of an engine block. The manifold is surrounded by a cooling water jacket. Hot exhaust gases are pumped into the central section of a manifold, thereby partially cooling them before being exhausted overboard.
Oil dipstick—A metal rod that feeds into an engine block down to the oil pan below. By withdrawing the rod it is possible to check the oil level in the engine.

Pressurized water system—An onboard system consisting of a self-contained water supply and pump that can deliver a steady flow of fresh water, often hot or cold, to a faucet or other outlet.
Raw water pump—An impellor-type pump that is bolted onto an engine block. This pump draws in seawater for the purpose of engine cooling.
Rear cabin—A cabin located near the stern, under the superstructure decking. This design usually eliminates a cockpit and calls for a high stern.
Rub rail—A metal or wooden strip attached to the very top of the hull, just below deck level. At dockside, without adequate tie-offs or fenders, this is the area of the boat that will "rub" against the pilings.
Seacock—The preferred type of marine thru-hull valve. This device is sometimes called a "cock valve." When the lever is moved to the cut-off position, the entire central structure of the valve moves to restrict the liquid flow.
Slip—A dockage arrangement in which the vessel is tied between two sets of pilings on either side of the craft.
Spring line—A small gauge line that is used to prevent a docked vessel from drifting too far forward or backward. Spring lines are also occasionally used to "spring" a boat alongside a dock.
Stanchion—A vertical support often used for bow and stern railings.
Step pads—Rectangular pieces of teak wood attached to the fiberglass superstructure, designed as a stepping surface for those coming aboard or leaving the vessel.
Stern—The rear portion of a boat.
Struts—Metal rods or bars that support the propeller shafts on the exterior portion of the hull.
Stuffing box—Packing material through which the propeller shafts pass between the inner and outer portion of a boat's hull. This stuffing or packing minimizes the water that attempts to leak around the shaft into the bilge.
Teak—An oil-filled wood native to India that is very resistant to rot.
Thru-hull—A general term for any valve and its associated hardware that penetrates the hull.
Transom—The stern portion of a boat's hull.
VHF radio—An FM band radio that has become the standard means for ship-to-ship and ship-to-shore communications in American coastal waters.

Index

A

B

C

M

N

O

P

R

S

T

U

V

W

Z